D0010110

THE GALÁPAGOS ISLANDS

Pierre Constant

Nothing gets lost,
nothing is created,
everything transforms
—Lavoisier

ODYSSEY BOOKS & MAPS

Odyssey Books & Maps is a division of Airphoto International Ltd.
1401 Chung Ying Building, 20–20A Connaught Road West, Sheung Wan, Hong Kong
Tel: (852) 2856 3896; Fax: (852) 3012 1825
E-mail: magnus@odysseypublications.com; www.odysseypublications.com
Follow us on Twitter—www.twitter.com/odysseyguides

Distribution in the USA by W.W. Norton & Company, Inc. 500 Fifth Avenue, New York, NY 10110, USA. Tel: 800-233-4830; Fax: 800-458-6515; www.wwnorton.com

Distribution in the UK and Europe by Cordee Ltd., 11 Jacknell Road, Dodwells Bridge Industrial Estate, Hinckley, Leicestershire LE10 3BS, UK. Tel: 01455 611185; info@cordee.co.uk; www.cordee.co.uk

Distribution in Australia by Woodslane Pty Ltd. Unit 7/5 Vuko Place, Warriewood, NSW 2012, Australia. Tel: (2) 9970-5111; Fax: (2) 9970-5002; www.woodslane.com.au

***Galápagos—A Natural History Guide*, Seventh Edition Revised**
ISBN: 978-962-217-766-6
Library of Congress Catalog Card Number has been requested.
Copyright © 2014, 2013, 2010, 2007, 2006, 2004, 2002 Airphoto International Ltd.
Copyright © 2000, 1999, 1997, 1995 Odyssey Publications Ltd.
(Original edition first published in 1994 in French by Calao Life Experience, under the title *Archipel des Galápagos*)

All rights reserved. No part of this book may be translated, reproduced or transmitted in any form or by any means, electronic, mechanical, photocopying or otherwise, without the prior permission of the publisher, except for brief passages for inclusion in critical articles or reviews.

Although the publisher and author of this book have made every effort to ensure that all information was correct at the time of going to press, the publisher and author do not assume and hereby disclaim any liability to any party for any loss, including loss of life, or damage caused by errors, omissions or misleading information.

Managing Editor: Helen Northey
Cover designer: Au Yeung Chui Kwai
Photography/illustrations by Pierre Constant

Production by Twin Age Limited, Hong Kong
E-mail: twinage@netvigator.com
Manufactured in China

Reading the safety information on these websites is advisable before travelling overseas:
US Department of State: www.travel.state.gov/travel/
UK Foreign and Commonwealth Office: www.fco.gov.uk/travel
Canadian Department of Foreign Affairs & International Trade:
www.voyage.gc.ca/dest/sos/warnings-en.asp
Australian Department of Foreign Affairs & Trade: www.dfat.gov.au/travel/http://www.sos.travel

(Front cover) *Land iguana under* Opuntia *cactus, South Plaza 2002;* (Back cover) (top) *Nazca booby;* (middle) *Flightless cormorant, Punta Moreno, Isabela Island;* (bottom) *Marine iguana on the beach, Isla Lobos*

CONTENTS

FOREWORD 7

PART ONE — SCIENTIFIC AND HISTORICAL DATA

Chapter One — General setting of the islands; Geology and origin of the Galápagos; Volcanism; Glacial ages 12

Chapter Two — Ocean currents; Seasons and climate; Temperatures; The 'El Niño'–'La Niña' phenomenon 27

Chapter Three — The Human history of the Galápagos Islands; Island names; Darwin and the Galápagos 33

Chapter Four — Arrival and establishment of the flora and fauna 40

Chapter Five — The theory of evolution and the Galápagos 44

Chapter Six — Flora and vegetation zones 66

PART TWO — FAUNA OF THE GALÁPAGOS

Chapter One — Reptiles: geckos, snakes, lizards, marine and land iguanas, marine turtles, giant tortoises 74

Chapter Two — Sea birds; Shore and lagoon birds 102

Chapter Three — Land birds; Darwin's finches 137

Chapter Four — Mammals: bats, rats, sea lions 146

Chapter Five — Marine life: fish, whales, dolphins; List of the 492 species of fish and marine organisms 150

Chapter Six — The Galápagos Marine Reserve; La Pesca Artesanal; Lobsters and black coral; Illegal fishing and the 'Pepinos' affair 189

PART THREE — DESCRIPTION OF THE ISLANDS

Chapter One — The Central islands: Baltra, North Seymour, Santa Cruz, South Plaza, Santa Fé, Daphné, Rábida, Pinzón 201
Puerto Ayora 204

Chapter Two — The Southern islands: Floreana, Española, San Cristóbal 225
Puerto Baquerizo Moreno 231

Chapter Three — The Northern islands: Genovesa, Marchena, Pinta, Darwin and Wolf 238

Chapter Four The Western islands: Santiago, Bartolomé, Sombrero Chino, Isabela, Fernandina, Puerto Villamil 242
Chapter Five The Landings 261
Chapter Six Scuba diving 263
Diving sites 265

PART FOUR THE GALÁPAGOS NATIONAL PARK
Chapter One Administration and history 269
Chapter Two Introduced animals; Rules of preservation for the visitor; The role of the guide 276
Chapter Three The Charles Darwin Research Station 283

PRACTICAL INFORMATION 284

CHRONOLOGY OF EVENTS 288

LEXICON OF THE FAUNA OF THE GALÁPAGOS 300

APPENDICES
Appendix 1: Oceanographic research and 'hot spots' in the Galápagos 302
Appendix 2: Distribution of land birds according to vegetation zones 304
Appendix 3: Human population of the Galápagos 305

GLOSSARY 306

RECOMMENDED READING 307

ABOUT THE AUTHOR 308

TABLE OF MAPS AND ILLUSTRATIONS 309

INDEX 1—GENERAL 310

INDEX 2—ANIMALS AND PLANTS 313

FOREWORD

One morning in June 2009, I was sitting at the cafeteria in Baltra airport, passing time watching four planes landing and taking off, one after the other. Struck by the reality that the Galápagos airport had become a beehive of activity, I thought to myself, "Gee, do you remember the days when there was only one flight a day?" Yes, now 30 years later the United Nations World Heritage Council has listed the Galápagos as a 'World Heritage Site in Danger'. Yet to many overseas visitors, the Galápagos islands remain the image of paradise; a mythical place—so symbolic per se—like a child's dream that beckons beyond imagination; an oasis of life in the middle of the vast expanse of the east Pacific ocean; a magical speck of land inhabited by fabulous animals, survivors of another place and time, which live in harmony with nature; a place so far away from civilization, that it must have been chosen by the Gods to be a haven of peace and beauty. In short, the perfect postcard Eden.

To me, however, these islands evoke feelings both sweet and sour. Time plus 27 years' experience in the Galápagos, have given me a deeper perspective about events and a seasoned approach to the challenges facing this unique land. Believe me, from my window, the outlook is not pretty any longer and I have a bitter taste in my mouth. The evidence is convincing. The presence of men is not compatible with paradise. Man has become a greedy, merciless predator, a destroyer and a powerful master key to what Darwin once called 'evolution'. Man prefers to call it progress, but what sort of improvement is it, if it is detrimental to mother nature? Money has become the new 'blood' of the Galápagos environment.

Tourism brings riches to some, and envy to others. Conservation, protection and scientific research bring large amounts of money to the Galápagos, through the Darwin Foundation, but these activities trigger jealousy and anger from the fishermen, locally referred to as the 'fishing sector'. In turn, the confrontation brings enormous pressure upon the Galápagos National Park administration (PNG), which has currently lost credibility for being so politically oriented. Corruption has infiltrated on all fronts. Unlike the first settlers who came to the islands in the early days, looking for a quality of life in tune with nature, nowadays everybody just wants to make money.

Once regarded as the 'pariahs' of the Galápagos, the fishermen want to make money too. Regardless of the PNG and without any respect for the Marine Reserve, they pitch their anger at the PNG, which wants to control the game. All in all, here is the vision: the Galápagos or the hidden face of Eden. You may come as a dreamer but, the jolt of reality could hit hard.

Yet the fact remains that the Galápagos have a strong magnetic aura. Somehow, the islands always find a way to be in the limelight. The media love it, every happening, every scandal, every disaster is a good excuse to analyse, criticise, condemn; in short, to write and talk about the islands. Everybody complains and as a result, tourism is booming; almost 185,000 visitors will have discovered the archipelago in the year 2009, an alltime record!

The oil spill of the tanker *Jessica* that affected the islands dramatically in January 2001 is already history, proving only one thing: the Galápagos can never be protected enough from human catastrophes. Who could have predicted such a drama? Luckily, every technical and human resource was used to allay disaster. Nature helped wonderfully in dispersing the spill with the South Equatorial Current. It was as if divine providence protected the Galápagos, reassuring the people who really do care.

I shall never forget the vision of the stone arch, emerging slowly above the surface of the Pacific Ocean at first light, after a long night on a sailing boat in Galápagos waters. This monumental arch, made of volcanic tuff—a haven for snow-white Nazca boobies—is the Great Arch of Darwin Island, at the extreme northwest of the archipelago. Swept by surf and foam, and looking like an oceanic Arc de Triomphe, Darwin Arch, oriented east–west, is the symbol of the 'Gate'. As a silent witness of time forgotten, the arch shows the direction from which the first unsuspecting discoverers of history came: an archbishop from Panama, drifting with the currents, lost on an ocean in the middle of the 16th century.

The first name given to the islands, Las Islas Encantadas or 'the Enchanted Isles', evokes the magical aura that has always surrounded the Galápagos. Since I first came to the archipelago in 1980—as a young trainee of an Ecuadorian tourism company but soon to become a naturalist guide for the Galápagos National Park—the islands have changed tremendously. The population has increased fourfold in 15 years, and has doubled in the last five years. Today, the population is estimated at 25,000 people, scattered on four main islands. Tourism has been booming on this chain of volcanic isles, and the number of visitors, (about 17,500 people in 1980, though limited to 25,000 visitors by the 'Master Plan' of 1981) eventually passed the 70,000 persons mark by the end of 2000. Souvenir shops multiply in Puerto Ayora, and hotels are sprouting like mushrooms after the rain (of dollars).

The fire on the slope of the Sierra Negra volcano in 1985 not only devastated hundreds of hectares of vegetation but, following a worldwide advertising campaign, provoked a blaze of tourism, which saw a dramatic boom in 1986. The same year, a second airport was inaugurated on San Cristóbal Island, and the Reserve of Marine Resources was created by presidential decree. Since then, a lot of ink has been spilt; this includes my book, *Marine Life of the Galápagos (1992)*. An updated new edition, *Marine Life of the Galápagos—The Diver's guide to fishes, whales, dolphins and marine invertebrates* with 288 photos, was published in 2006. Even though this trend stimulated the development of scuba diving, it also invited all sorts of abuse. Among these are the intensive plundering of the submarine riches and schools of sharks by Japanese commercial fishing boats, which first became interested in shark fins, then in *pepinos*, or sea cucumbers. Scandal broke in 1992, despite laws passed by the Ecuadorian government for the protection of sharks and *pepinos*, but illegal fishing continues.

The economic stake for Galápagos fishermen is enormous. The number of tourism boats, which was limited in the Galápagos to avoid a 'tidal wave', was soon exceeded. Nowadays, about 100 boats operate in the archipelago. Will the hen that lays the golden eggs be exploited to the point of exhaustion? There are profits to be made, but the economic pressures that they bring are so unavoidable that one may fear that the Galápagos have already lost their sacred aura, their image of a lost, unviolated natural paradise. Ultimately UNESCO became concerned in 1995–96, and made the Ecuadorian government change the situation. The special law for the Marine Reserve—already a 'Whale Sanctuary' and a 'Biological Reserve' by INEFAN (Instituto Ecuatoriano Forestal, de Areas Naturales y de Vida Silvestre) since November 1996—was enacted in 1998.

Meanwhile, the Darwin Station goes on with its research programme as if everything were fine, and the Galápagos National Park continues with programmes of protection, conservation, environmental education and the breeding of giant tortoises. Curiously, the PNG is now in the hands of politicians, triggering an unprecedented instability in the last five years. Not to mention the training of multilingual naturalist guides, who are, to some extent, the 'arrowhead' of integrity in the Galápagos National Park. It is pleasant to imagine the Galápagos as a kind of Noah's ark in the middle of the deluge.

I do not wish to darken the picture more than I should. The magic and the spell of the Enchanted Isles really do exist. They are found in the inquisitive look of the blue-footed boobies; in the sweetness and frolicking of the sea lions on land or in the water; in the peaceful and detached somnolence of marine iguanas flat on the rocks under the equatorial sun; in the enigmatic smiles of the land iguanas under the *opuntia* cacti; in the eternal immobility of the giant tortoises in their centenarian shells, overlooking the world from the rim of the volcanoes; in the mystical contemplation of the pelican standing on its rock, facing the glowing ocean at sunset; in the grace and innocence of the flightless cormorant during its courtship display; in the comical duel of the albatrosses fencing with their beaks in the mating season; in the joyful gamboling of the bottlenose dolphins, for which each boat is a pretext to play; in the wave that crashes against the Great Arch and turns into one thousand drops of iridescent light...

For all that, I pay my respects to these islands. Despite the thunder and lightning, the Galápagos must be safeguarded as the innocence of the world. For the sun rises east on Noah's ark or on the arch of Darwin, and glows west on the great blue yonder of the Pacific. The magic of 'Las Encantadas' may one day disappear under the surface of the ocean, but by then, humans will have gone long before.

Pierre Constant, October, 2009.

If a person asked my advice, before undertaking a long voyage, my answer would depend upon his possessing a decided taste for some branch of knowledge, which could by this means be advanced. No doubt it is a high satisfaction to behold various countries and the many races of mankind, but the pleasures gained at the time do not counterbalance the evils. It is necessary to look forward to a harvest, however distant that may be, when some fruit will be reaped, some good effected.

...If, as poets say, life is a dream, I am sure in a voyage these are the visions which best serve to pass away the long night... The short space of sixty years has made an astonishing difference in the facility of distant navigation. Even in the time of Cook, a man who left his fireside for such expeditions underwent severe privations. A yacht now, with every luxury of life, can circumnavigate the globe... If a person suffer much from sea-sickness, let him weigh it heavily in the balance. I speak from experience: it is no trifling evil, cured in a week.

In conclusion it appears to me that nothing can be more improving to a young naturalist, than a journey in distant countries. It both sharpens, and partly allays that want and craving, which... a man experiences although every corporeal sense be fully satisfied... The effect ought to be to teach him good-humoured patience, fre edom from selfishness, the habit of acting for himself, and of making the best of every occurrence. In short, he ought to partake of the characteristic qualities of most sailors. Travelling ought also to teach him distrust; but at the same time he will discover how many truly kind-hearted people there are, with whom he never before had, or ever again will have any further communication, who yet are ready to offer him the most disinterested assistance.

Charles Darwin, A Naturalist's Voyage *(1845)*

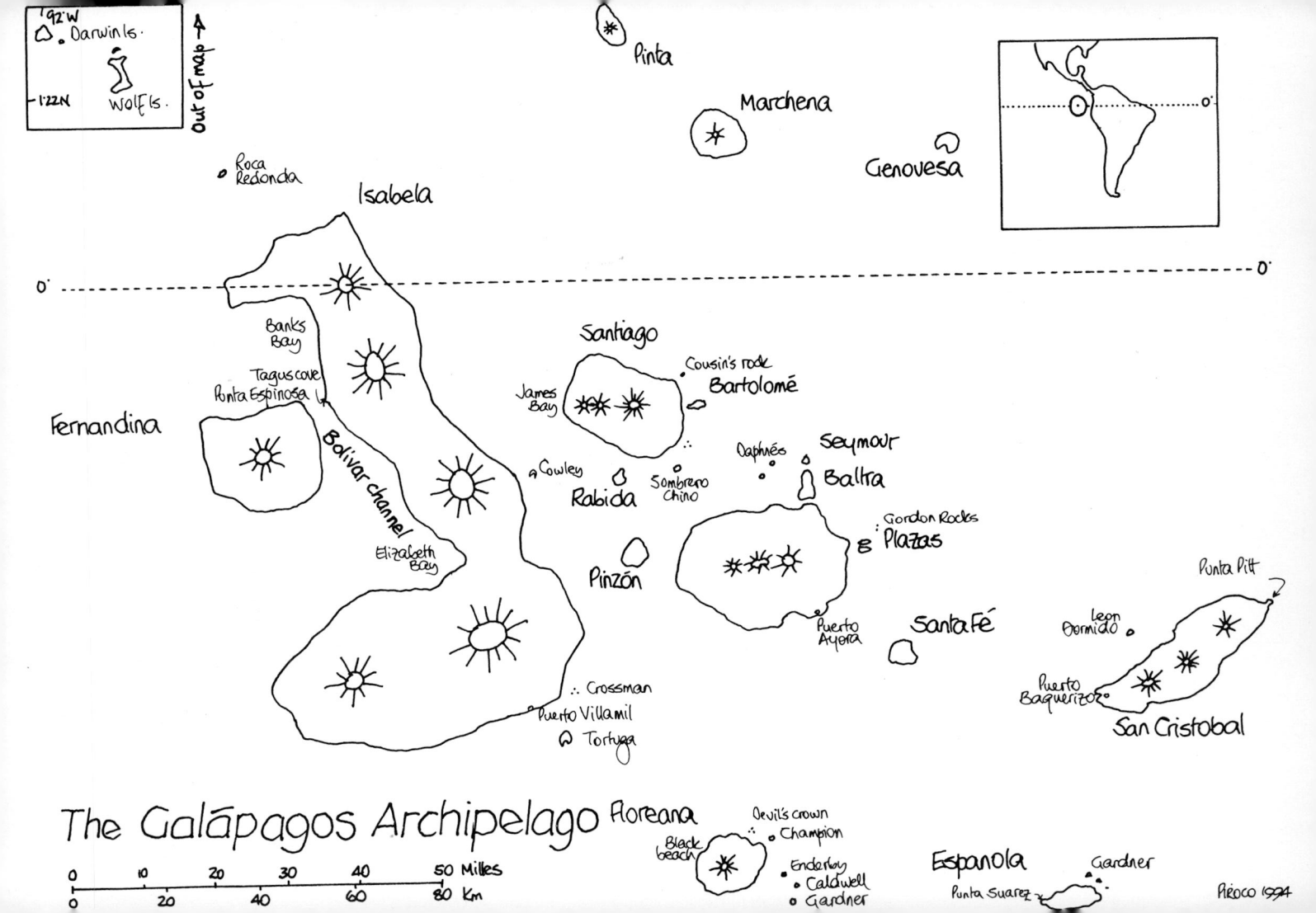
92°W
Darwin Is.
1°22N
Wolf Is.
Out of map
Pinta
Marchena
Genovesa
Roca Redonda
Isabela
0°
0°
Banks Bay
Tagus cove
Punta Espinosa
Fernandina
Bolivar channel
Elizabeth Bay
Santiago
Cousin's rock
Bartolomé
James Bay
Cowley
Rabida
Sombrero Chino
Daphnés
Seymour
Baltra
Gordon Rocks
Plazas
Pinzón
Puerto Ayora
Santa Fé
Crossman
Puerto Villamil
Tortuga
Punta Pitt
Leon Dormido
Puerto Baquerizo
San Cristobal
The Galápagos Archipelago
Floreana
Devil's crown
Champion
Black beach
Enderby
Caldwell
Gardner
Espanola
Gardner
Punta Suarez
0 10 20 30 40 50 Miles
0 20 40 60 80 Km
Pérez 1994

PART ONE

SCIENTIFIC AND HISTORICAL DATA

CHAPTER ONE

General Setting of the Islands; Geology and Origin of the Galápagos; Volcanism; Glacial Ages

The Galápagos Islands stretch over a 320-kilometre (174-mile) axis from east to west, and the equator passes precisely across the crater of Wolf volcano in the north of Isabela Island. The archipelago is made up of 19 islands and 42 islets or surfacing rocks. San Cristóbal, the easternmost island of the Galápagos group, lies about 1,100 kilometres (600 miles) west of the mother country, Ecuador, on the South American mainland.

The total land surface of the archipelago is just over 8,000 square kilometres. Isabela, the largest island, has an area of 4,588 square kilometres; Santa Cruz, the second in size and the most central, is only 986 square kilometres; Santiago is 585 square kilometres; San Cristóbal is 558 square kilometres; Floreana is 173 square kilometres. Among the tiniest islands, with a land surface between one and five square kilometres, are Rábida, Seymour, Wolf, Bartolomé, Tortuga and Darwin. Forty-two islets have a landmass smaller than one square kilometre, and 26 emerging rocks are numbered.

Oceanic Islands

The islands are purely oceanic, which means that they have never been connected to the mainland by any sort of land bridge. In the past, it was assumed that the Cocos and Carnegie ridges, underwater mountain ranges rising up to 2,000 metres above the sea floor, once connected the islands to the mainland of either Central America or South America, but this has been disproved, because of the sheer drop of the Peru-Chile trench. The conspicuous absence of land mammals in the Galápagos also helps to confirm the oceanic island theory.

The islands rise on the Galápagos Platform, a basaltic submarine plateau located between 200 and 500 fathoms (ie, between 360 and 900 metres, 1 fathom being equal to 1.82 metres) under the surface of the ocean. The archipelago is entirely volcanic, and Isabela Island alone is made up of six volcanoes side by side. Five of them are typical shield volcanos, the craters of which are huge 'calderas'.

Calderas

Caldera means 'cauldron' in Spanish. This geological name is used to define the aging of a shield volcano. This huge craterlike depression is formed by the subsidence of the upper part of the volcano when the inner walls of the central crater fall in, widening the cross section of the crater over time.

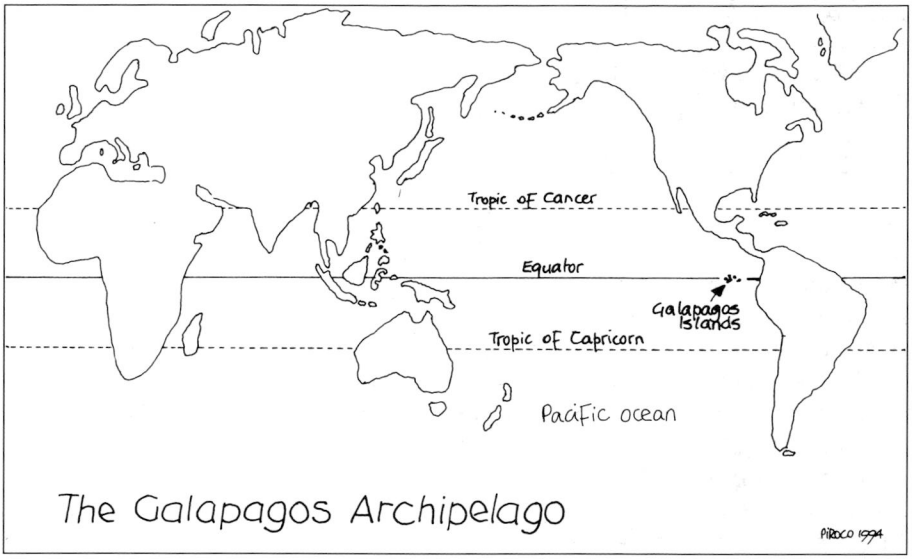

Following repeated eruptions and regular volcanic activity, the magma chamber gets larger and swells up each time the magma rises. As magma creates pressure on the roof of the magma chamber, circumferential fissures form around the crater. Sometimes the lava spreads out through the cracks and creates parasitic cones on the slopes of the volcano. When the eruption comes to an end, the level of the magma subsides. The roof of the magma chamber is no longer supported and it collapses. Through successive collapses of the crater, the caldera is formed.

The most recent example was the collapse of the Fernandina volcano in 1968. The crater floor—800 metres deep at first—collapsed another 350 metres after a violent explosion. Ashes were launched 25 kilometres high into the sky and spread over an area of a few hundred square kilometres. Fernandina is the youngest caldera in the Galápagos, with a diameter of 6.5 kilometres. Sierra Negra, the oldest caldera of Isabela Island, measures 10 kilometres across. Santa Cruz and the southern part of San Cristóbal are also large shield volcanoes, whose summits have been eroded.

Geological Zoning

A deep oceanic trench, 3,000 metres under the ocean surface, separates the small northern islands of Darwin, Wolf, Marchena, Pinta and Genovesa from the rest of the archipelago to the south. MacBirney and Aoki (1966) show that the Galápagos are divided in three zones, comprising islands of like structure and of similar petrography.

The first zone to the southeast is made of Fernandina, Isabela and Floreana Islands. The second zone is made up of the northern islands mentioned above, adding Cerro Pitt, the northeastern tip of San Cristóbal Island. The third zone is made of the central islands of Santiago, Rábida, Santa Cruz, Pinzón, Baltra, Santa Fé, Española and the south of San Cristóbal.

Plate Tectonics

According to the theory of plate tectonics, the Galápagos archipelago is located in the north of the Nazca Plate, just under the Cocos Plate, and east of the South East Pacific mid-oceanic ridge, also called the East Pacific Rise (see map of Tectonic Plates, page 15). The islands are connected by two submarine ridges: the Carnegie Ridge to the east and the Cocos Ridge to the northeast.

The SEP mid-oceanic ridge (SEPMOR) stretches roughly north-south from California (San Andreas fault) to Easter Island and farther west into the southwestern Pacific. It spreads magma on the ocean floor, westward and eastward, pushing the oceanic Nazca Plate east, towards South America. At the same time, we have an extension of the SEPMOR from west to east, called the Galápagos Fracture Zone (GFZ) or Galápagos Rift, which eventually evolves in a transformation fault* between the Carnegie and Cocos ridges. The GFZ also expands magma on the ocean floor, northward and southward, thus pushing the Nazca Plate southward.

We understand now that the Galápagos are located on an oceanic plate that receives pressure from the west (SEPMOR) and from the north (GFZ). What happens next? Well, think of a window pane on which you exert pressure from two adjacent sides. Crack!

Hot Spot

The archipelago is a 'hot spot', an area of high thermic flux* and intense seismic and volcanic activity, subject to almost annual eruptions. A hot spot is related to a weakness of the oceanic crust, a zone of remarkable fragility in the tectonic plate, which leads to fissures on the ocean floor. In the Galápagos there is a system of parallel and orthogonal fractures*, which resemble a checkerboard. Under the Nazca Plate, the hot magma is always in motion due to convection currents. The hot spot, being a more sensitive area, creates a magmatic plume which pierces the oceanic crust in a weak part of the plate. The magma rises upward into the ocean (see figure Hot Spot, page 15). Upon contact with the cold ocean water, the lava cools off rapidly, builds a platform and keeps rising. It eventually creates a volcanic cone, which in a few years reaches the surface of the ocean. The base of the volcanic construction of the Galápagos could be 10 to 15 million years old. The hot spot is now responsible for the making of an archipelago, ie, a chain of volcanic islands more or less aligned. Hawaii is a classic example which is much older than the Galápagos, with an age of about 20 million years.

* See Glossary, page 305

Yellowstone
North America
Hawaï
Acores
Cape Verde
Africa
Ascension
South America
Galápagos
Easter Is.
Tuamotu
Marshall Gilbert
Mac Donald
Australia
Rio Grande
Bouvet

Hot Spots and Mid-oceanic ridges

⊙ Hot Spot ⊢ Transform Faults / Mid-oceanic ridge

Tectonic situation of the Galápagos

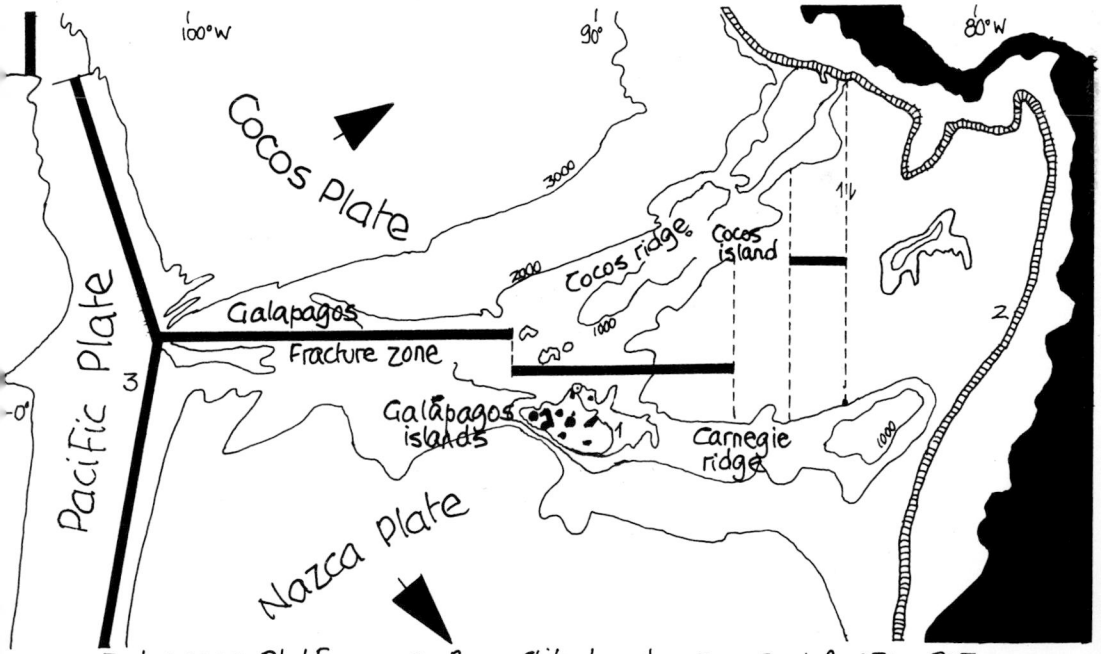

1- Galapagos Platform 2- Peru-Chile trench 3 - East Pacific Rift

The magma rising up from the SEPMOR creates the expansion of the oceanic floor and the migration of the Nazca Plate to the southeast at a rate of five centimetres per year. The Nazca Plate will be forced under the continental plate of South America. The point of contact between the two plates (continental and oceanic) forms a trench, which is called the subduction zone. The Nazca Plate will then be in subduction under South America, and the Cocos Plate will migrate northeast and dive in the subduction zone of Central America (see Appendix 1).

If the hot spot does not move, the tectonic plate will shift. An island is created, then the oceanic plate moves east. A second island will be made later on, when the plume pierces the oceanic crust again, which in turn will migrate eastward with the plate. And so on, forming a chain of islands, that is to say, an archipelago. The Galápagos hotspot has been active for at least 20 million years and maybe as long as 90 million years. In 1990, it was found that the Galápagos hotspot had a bent plume model, with an eastward direction (see sketch of the 'Galápagos Plumology' after Karen Harpp and Dennis Geist).

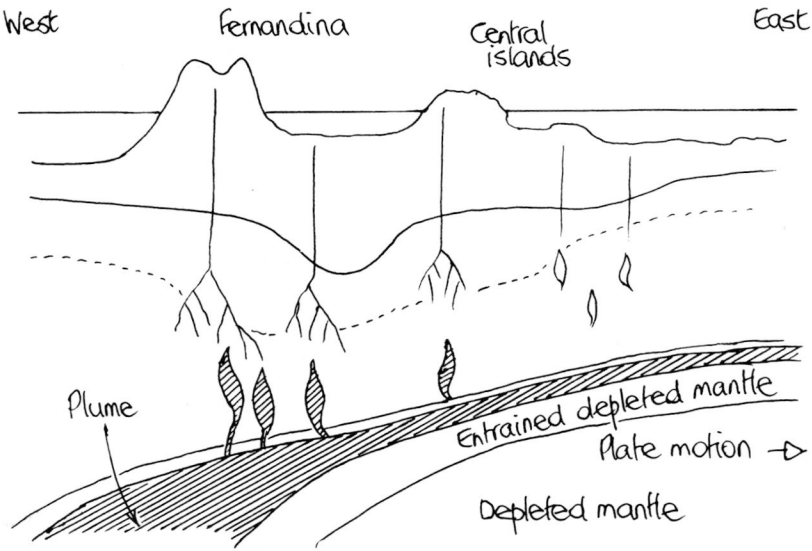

Galápagos Plumology
cross section of the plume - progressive eastward dilution of the bent plume as it entrains depleted mantle
[after Karen Harpp, Lawrence University, Appleton, Wi + Dennis Geist, University of Idaho, Moscow, Id. April 1998].

The Age of the Galápagos

The consequence of this phenomenon is that, logically, the eldest islands will lie to the east and the youngest to the west. That is where the volcanic activity is resumed nowadays in the archipelago, mainly on Isabela and Fernandina islands. This brings us to determining the age of the Galápagos.

Various methods, including potassium-argon (P.A.) and paleomagnetism, have been used to date the age of volcanic rocks, essentially basalts. The first dating technique, P.A., shows that the Galápagos have a maximum age of three million years. The oldest basalts analyzed, using the radioactivity of the elements, gave the following results: 3.2 million years (+/- 0.2) on Española; 2.7 million years (+/- 0.1) on Santa Fé; 4.2 million years (+/- 1.8) on South Plaza.

Many of the analyzed rocks come from submarine lava like Santa Cruz (1 million years), basalts of Wolf volcano (0.72 million years) and San Cristóbal (0.66 million years). Isabela Island was dated at about 700,000 years, and so are the islands of Fernandina, Santiago, Genovesa, Marchena and Darwin (Culpepper).

Wolf, Santa Cruz, Baltra, Rábida, Pinzón and Floreana are between 0.7 and 1.5 million years old, while the age of San Cristóbal is between 2.4 million years (Cox) and about 4 million years (Paul Colinvaux). Geist et al. (1985) adjusted the age range of the Galápagos from 1 to 5.6 million years.

Former studies on magnetism also proved the young age of the islands. Most samples analyzed were dated in the period of Bruhnes (between 0 and 0.7 million years) and the period of Matuyama (0.7 to 2.4 million years). The age of the archipelago stands of course for the aerial part of the islands, ie, the date when the volcanoes surfaced above sea level. The islands' submerged bases could be of Miocene geological times, about 15 million years.

The Galápagos archipelago is one of the largest and most active groups of oceanic volcanoes in the world. The islands, never connected to the mainland, were built on a large but shallow platform 2,000 kilometres east of the SEPMOR. The localization of the main volcanoes seems to have been controlled by two systems of quite orthogonal fractures: one has a north–northwest direction; the other is rather east–west.

Uplifts

Numerous examples of island uplift have been observed on Santa Fé, Española and Santa Cruz. Cerro Colorado, facing Plazas Islands, is a rocky hill east of Santa Cruz Island which was uplifted in the past, bringing up tuff formations bearing fossils of Miocene times. Most recently, in Urvina Bay, on the west coast of Isabela Island, a tectonic uplift in 1954 brought coral heads and marine life five metres above sea level. It was followed a few months later by an eruption on the slope of Alcedo volcano.

Bathymetry of the Galapagos
(after "Bureau of Commercial Fisheries", 1962) - Soundings in metres - Dotted line < 360 m.

The submerged islands
(source: "Nature" magazine and New York Times News s.)

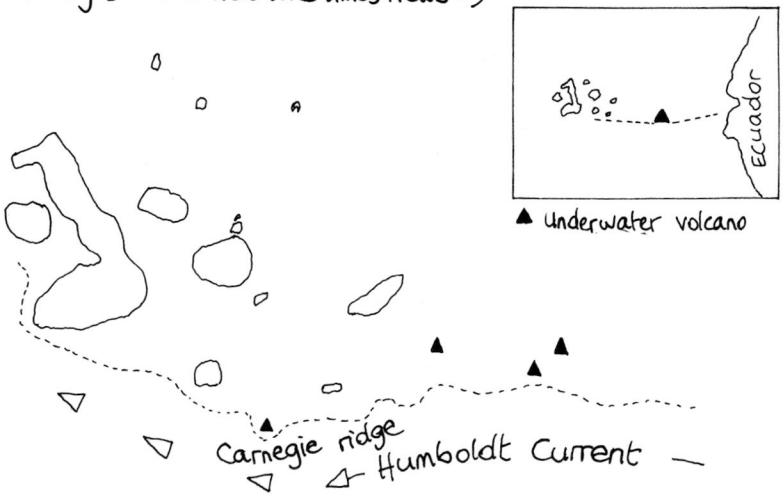

▲ Supposed sites of the submerged islands.

The Sunken Islands

In the beginning of 1992, in an issue of the English magazine *Nature,* American scientists from Oregon, California, Cornell University and the NOAA (National Oceanic and Atmospheric Administration) on a 26-day expedition discovered submarine mountains along the Carnegie Ridge, to the south and southeast of the Galápagos, in the direction of South America. David Christie and his colleagues gathered samples of volcanic cobblestones (typical of the shoreline) resulting from aerial and marine erosion. This demonstrated the existence of a chain of islands that were once above sea level and which were later submerged. The submarine mountain closest to the continent, only 590 kilometres away, had an estimated age of nine million years. Obviously, there should be even older sunken islands of the Galápagos group, which, according to the latest thinking, could now be as old as 90 million years (see drawing, page 18).

Petrology

Chemically speaking, the petrology of the Galápagos is different from Hawaii's, for the magma of our archipelago is typical of the southeast Pacific ridge. The plutonic rocks and the effusive tholeïtes (subalkaline basalts, ie those rich in silicon) follow similar modes of differentiation, being enriched in iron and magnesium, in alkaline products and with an excess of silicon.

The islands are composed of basaltic lava, rich in iron and magnesium. Black at first, the lava becomes gradually brown, then brick red after alteration when iron becomes oxidized over time. This erosion process is typical of the 'basic' kind of lava; in the 'acid' kind, it is totally different.

Volcanism of the Galápagos Islands

If the Galápagos Islands are well known for their extraordinary fauna, let us not forget that their appearance depends first on volcanic phenomena. A few elements of vocabulary will be essential for the proper understanding of the volcanic activity. Let us consider, first of all, volcanic activity in general, then the volcanic materials or volcanic products and, finally, where the magma comes from.

Volcanic Activity

It is divided into aerial and the submarine activities. The aerial eruption depends on two factors: the viscosity of the magma and the quantity of liberated gases. Four major types of eruption are usually distinguished:

- the explosive or Vulcanian type: where the gas phase is predominant.
- the extrusive or Domean type: where the magma is viscous and acid.
- the effusive or Hawaiian type: where the magma is fluid and basic. This is precisely the case of the Galápagos.
- the mixed or Strombolian type: the eruption is rich in gases, liquids and solid products.

This can be represented in a triangular diagram, where the three poles would be gases, fluid magma and acid viscous magma.

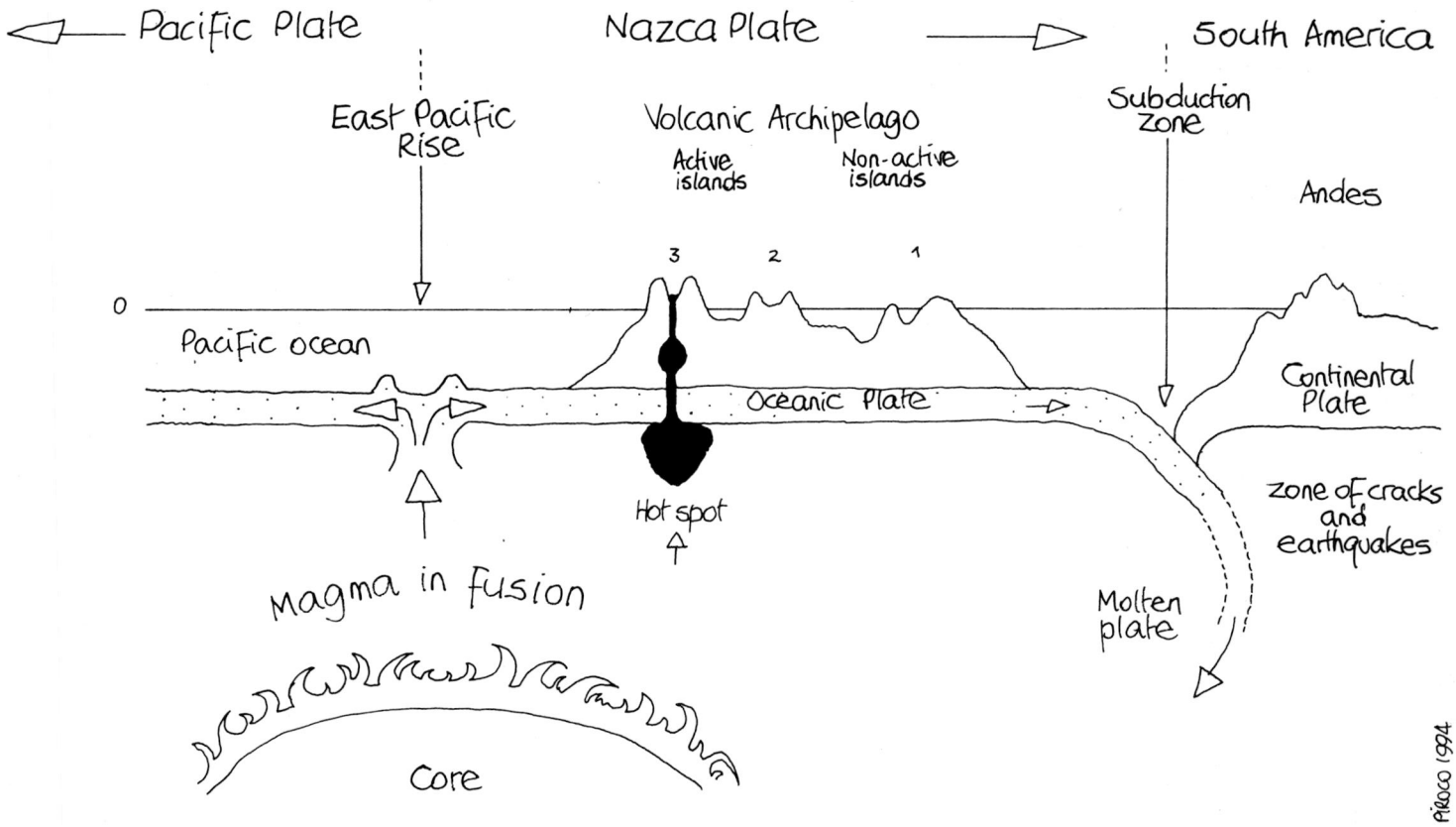

Hot spot and tectonic plates ~ south east Pacific

In submarine activity, the magma coming out of the ocean floor explodes violently when it contacts the cool water. Pieces of lava are torn apart and pulverized. Vitreous fragments spread over the ocean floor, cement and form submarine volcanic tuffs or 'hyaloclastites' (a Greek word meaning 'broken pieces of glass'), which can build real mountains. The submarine tuff cones thus formed are called 'guyots'. Their summit is flat, for the crater is soon to be filled by marine sediments.

The submarine lava flows come from aerial flows which have reached the shore. Steaming at the point of penetration, these flows once underwater are known as a 'giant's highway', for their surface is made of blocks (resembling tiles) with a polygonal structure. This is true when the slope is mild. When the slope is steep at the point of entry, however, the flow gives way to 'pillow lava', or lava cushions, which roll downhill and pile up at the bottom of the ocean.

VOLCANIC ERUPTIONS IN THE GALÁPAGOS ISLANDS (13 in the last 100 years)

1801	Alcedo or Darwin	from James Bay, seen by US captain Amasa Delano
1813	Isabela and Fernandina	seen by *USS Essex*, David Porter
1825	Fernandina	(lava flows into the sea), seen by captain Benjamin Morell on *Tartar* from Banks Bay.
1890	Santiago, southeast	lava flows of Sullivan Bay?
1954	Urvina Bay, Isabela	uplift of coral reef
1968	Fernandina	collapse of caldera: 900 metres
1972	Fernandina	within caldera
1977	Fernandina	
1978	Fernandina	
1979	Cerro Azul and Sierra Negra (Volcan Chico), Isabela	
1982	Wolf, Isabela (August–September)	
1984	Fernandina (April)	
1988	Fernandina (September)	lava flows inside the caldera, displacement of crater lake, fumaroles on outer slope.
1991	Alcedo (March 21)	earthquakes
	Fernandina (April)	
	Marchena (September)	
1995	Fernandina (February-March)	lava flows to Cape Hammond
1998	Cerro Azul	(one and a half months)
2005	Fernandina (May 11–13)	two lava flows to the south; plume of ash at 1,800 metres, extends 130 kilometres west
	Sierra Negra, Isabela (Oct. 22)	lava flow towards Elizabeth Bay in the north
2008	Cerro Azul, Isabela	check Smithsonian Institute (www.volcano.si.edu/world)
2009	Fernandina (April 11–30)	lava fountain rising 30 metres, radial fracture 250 metres wide, lava flow to Cape Hammond

VOLCANIC MATERIALS

FUMAROLES

Gas emanations are called fumaroles. These are seen on the slope of the crater and within the crater itself. Gases are important, as they help the magma to come out, pushing upward and acting on the viscosity of the lava. The two main components of fumaroles are water and carbon dioxide (CO2). Nevertheless, their classification is based on chemical composition and temperature, which can rise up to 500° C. Thus we may distinguish chlorated, chlorhydrated, ammoniacal, sulphurhydrated, 'mofettes' (CO2), thermomineral waters, geysers (H2O) and 'soffionis' (sprays of steaming water). Sulphurhydrated fumaroles can be seen on Isabela Island, in the craters of Alcedo and Sierra Negra volcanoes.

LAVAS

Lavas are molten materials which pour out of the crater. The movement of a flow depends on the viscosity, the push-up action of the magma in the chimney of the volcano, and the substratum. The speed of the flow, a few kilometres per hour at the exit of the vent, can be reduced to a few metres per hour at the bottom of the slope. The cooling action is quick at the surface of the lava flow, in which two types are distinguished:

- the 'aa' type: (Hawaiian word, meaning 'to hurt'), where the chaotic aspect of the surface of the flow is due to the gas explosions, having torn apart the external crust. We have there a fluid lava, rich in gas. This can be seen when climbing volcan Alcedo.

- the 'pahoehoe' type: or ropey lava (after the Hawaiian word meaning 'ropey'). Here the surface is smooth, and shows 'ripple marks', 'intestinal figures', waves in the directions of the flow, and 'ropes'. The lava progresses by tongues; it is not as fluid and has lost its gas (eg on Sullivan Bay, Santiago Island). The hardening of the basalts is generally quick under the crust. The cooling process often generates prismatic figures in columns. These are the organ pipe basalts, with four, five or six faces.

LAVA TUBES

These tunnels are frequent in the Galápagos. When lava spreads out of the crater, the surface of the flow cools off rapidly, while the inner flow rushes downhill quickly. When no more lava comes out of the crater, an empty tube is often left behind, surrounded by a solid outside crust. These natural tunnels, usually five to six metres wide and up to ten metres in height, can be seen at Puerto Ayora and Bellavista, on Santa Cruz Island.

Tephras

Also called 'pyroclastites' or broken fire pieces (from the Greek), tephras are volcanic projectiles, mainly bombs, shapeless fragments or ashes. In the shapeless fragments, we have 'pumice', pieces of acid magma, viscous and grey-white in colour. These are ejected following violent explosions (eg Alcedo volcano, Isabela Island).

The 'scoriae', pieces of fluid magma with no set shape, are the most common volcanic projectiles. The red-purple colour is due to iron oxidation. Cinder cones are frequent in the Galápagos. Among 'bombs', we may distinguish 'spindle bombs' (rotated in flight), or 'spatter bombs', formed by the ejection of fluid magma. Spatter cones are seen on Bartolomé Island. Ashes appear because of violent volcanic projections up in the air. These consist of pieces of crystal or glass. The white colour of the ashes persists in acid lava, but in basic lava, the black ash may turn to red or orange-brown with time.

'Lapilli' and volcanic sands are scoriae fragments, which vary in size from 2 to 20 millimetres in 'lapilli' and from 0.2 to 2 millimetres in sands. Little bombs, drops of glass, are part of the same family, and may form hardened layers of crystals.

'Volcanic tuffs' (0.2 to 20 millimetres) are lapilli and sands cemented by ashes. 'Cinerites', or hardened ashes, form distinct, stratified layers.

Parasitic Cones

Frequent in the Galápagos (James Bay, Santiago Island, or Bartolomé Island), tuff cones are always found near the coast or on the shoreline, for they are created in shallow sea water. Magma is blown up in small grains and ashes, which cement later on. Spatter cones are formed on firm land by projections of fluid magma patches, lava fountains (Bartolomé Island). Cinder cones are made of light small volcanic bombs cooling off in the air, after a dry explosion.

Where Does Magma Come From?

If we consider the chemical composition of magma, we could simply say that they differentiate into two main groups: the acid and the basic.

The 'Basic Group' (basalts, gabbros)

Also called basaltic magma, it is black in colour, poor in silica (SiO_2) and alumina (Al_2O_3), with mean contents of 60-70 per cent, but rich in iron (Fe), magnesium (Mg), calcium (Ca), sodium (Na) and potassium (K). Thus, when the content in 'bases' is superior to the amount of silicon, we talk about 'basic' rocks.

The 'Acid group' (rhyolites, granites)

Comes from the granitic magma, rich in silica and alumina (80 to 90 per cent of the contents) and poor in bases: Na, K, Fe, Ca, Mg. When the silicon content is greater than the base content, the term used is 'acid' rocks.

SUMMARY OF MAGMAS

CHEMISTRY	BASALTIC	ANDESITIC	GRANITIC
	Basic	Calco-alkaline	Acid
Depth of Formation	35-100 km	10 to 35 km (mantle)	less than 20 km (crust)
Temperature of Formation	1200-1500° C	1200-1300° C	550-750° C
Effusive Products	Frequent	Frequent	Rare
Petrography	(+) Basalts (-) Gabbros	(+) Andesites Diorites (-) Basalts	(+) Granites (-) Rhyolites

(+)= more of (-)= less of

Basalts and rhyolites are eruptive rocks (surface); granites and gabbros are plutonic rocks (deep).

Theory of Bimagmatism (last century)

According to this theory, there are two sources from which magma comes. In the crust is the acid magma (SiAl), at a depth of less than 20 kilometres. In the mantle is the basic magma (SiMg), at a depth between 35 kilometres and 100 kilometres.

The MOHO or 'Mohorovic discontinuity line' separates the crust and the mantle at a depth of 15 to 35 kilometres. The theory of bigmagmatism explains simply where the magma comes from, be it in the crust: SiAl (silicon-aluminum) or SiMa in the mantle (silicon-magnesium).

Later on, as the process became better understood, it was theorized that there is a common origin for the magma ('monomagmatism'). Furthermore, a more recent theory was posited by Yoder and Tilley (1962), based on the differentiation of the basalts.

Glacial Ages in the Galápagos

It has been proved that the age of the Galápagos is between three and five million years. For the last two million years, glaciations have been important on earth and have contributed to modifying the geography of the continents. Today, ice covers 10 per cent of the planet's surface. Twenty thousand years ago, in Pleistocene times, that ice surface was three times as extensive as it is now. Ice comes from the ocean. If the ice of the poles should melt today, the sea level would rise up as much as 65 metres. In the Pleistocene, the ice cover had a volume of 77 million cubic kilometres, which means that the sea level then was at least 120 metres below its present level. Many islands in the Galápagos would have been joined together then.

The glacial ages of the Galápagos have been studied by Paul Colinvaux (1984) and measured by the study of sediments in ancient lakes. The Galápagos appeared to be more arid in glacial times. Four lagoons were investigated:

- Darwin Lake, in Tagus Cove (Isabela Island), had a bottom of salt and lava. No sediment, so quite young in age.
- Beagle Lake (Isabela Island) possesses a 15-centimetres deep sandy bottom. The age is not significant.
- Arcturus Lake (Genovesa Island), 30 metres of salt water cover a muddy sediment five metres in depth. The age was estimated to be 4,000 to 6,000 years.
- El Junco (San Cristóbal Island) was the most interesting. With a diameter of 273 metres, this fresh-water lake, only six metres in depth, had a sediment depth of 16 metres, which was aged 40,000 years. A red clay sediment was also found which had a core more than 48,000 years old. This lake seems to have existed for at least 100,000 years. It was protected from evaporation by the cloud layer and the annual March rains.

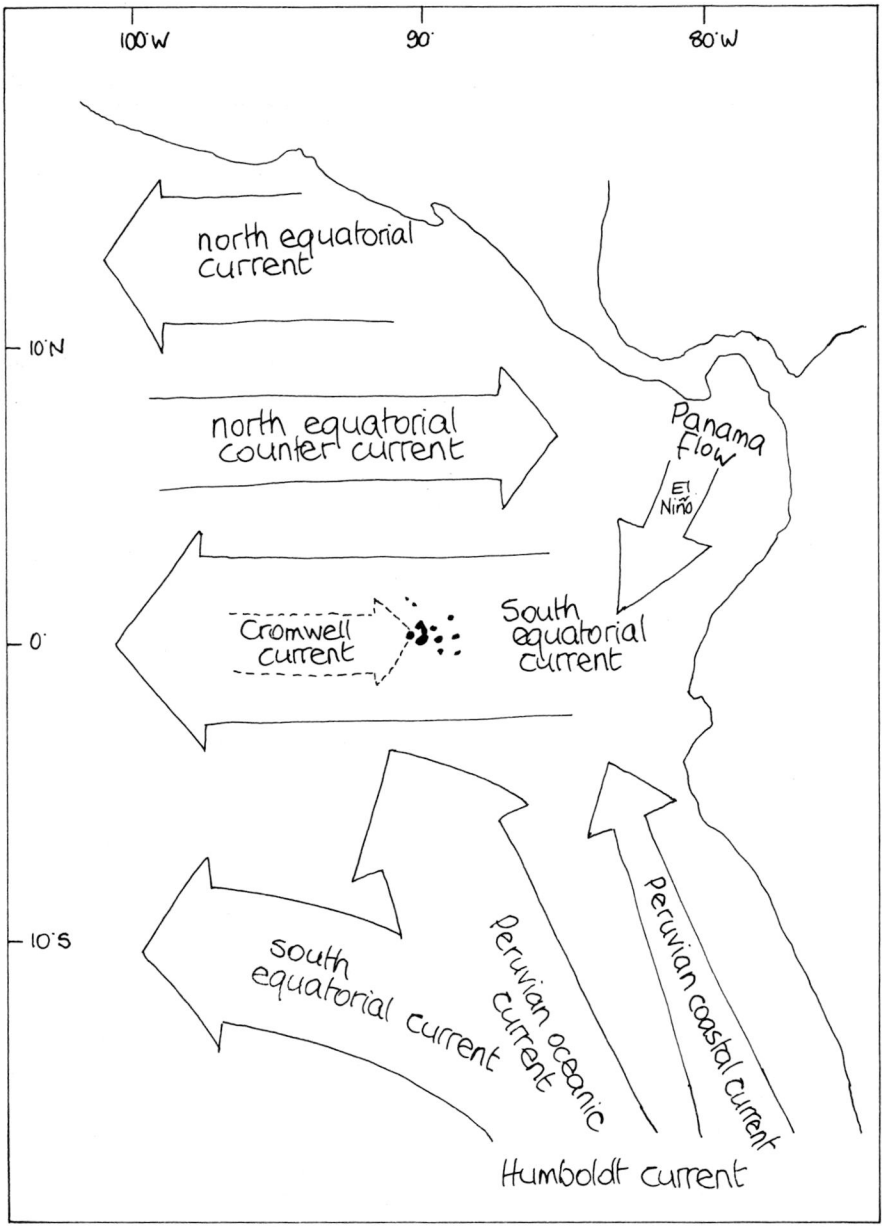

Distribution of the currents ~ Tropical East Pacific.

CHAPTER TWO

Ocean Currents; Seasons and Climate; Temperatures; The 'El Niño'–'La Niña' phenomenon

Oceanic currents and trade winds have a determining action on the Galápagos, for they influence not only the climate but the two resulting seasons, which are:
- The *garua*, or dry season.
- The hot season, or wet season.

Even through they are located on the equator, the islands are classified as 'subtropical' rather than tropical. Nevertheless, the northern islands are almost tropical, because they are less affected by the cold waters of the south. The southern islands are more affected by the cold ocean stream of the Humboldt Current.

Ocean Currents

The confluence of many ocean currents in the Galápagos turned the islands into an unusual geographical spot on the world map. Even though on the equator, they do not have a characteristically equatorial climate and are therefore considered to have a micro-climate.

Logically, the ocean currents are a key to this phenomenon. The oceanic masses come primarily from the southeast, the northeast and the west. Some are cold, such as the Peruvian Coastal Current and the Peruvian Oceanic Current, with a mean temperature of 15° C. Upon arrival in the Galápagos, they surface from a depth of 100 metres.

Another important cold-water current is the Cromwell Current, also called the Sub-equatorial Countercurrent. With a front of 300 kilometres, it comes from the western Pacific, exactly under the equator and under the South Equatorial Current, which in turn flows west. The Cromwell Current is 150 to 200 metres thick, with a temperature of 13° C in its core, and flows at a speed of 25 centimetres per second. It upwells to the west of Fernandina and Isabela islands, then goes around these two islands towards the center of the archipelago, where its action gradually fades away.

From the east, the South Equatorial Current flows at a speed of 50 centimetres per second. This water mass is influenced by the cold waters of the southeastern Pacific (Humboldt Current) and by the warm waters of the northeast coming from Panama (a flow sometimes called 'El Niño'). The border between the subtropical waters of the south and the tropical waters of the north is known as the 'Equatorial Front'. This diagonal line, southeast to northwest, stretches between 4° south latitude and 1° to 3° north latitude.

There is also a convergence of the trade winds, more or less parallel to the Equatorial Front. This is the Intertropical Convergence Zone (ITCZ), where the southeast trade winds and the northeast trade winds meet. This ITCZ is located at 10° north latitude in the dry season, and migrates down to 3° north latitude in the wet season.

Another important current, associated with the Panama flow or El Niño, is the North Equatorial Countercurrent (NECC), which places itself between the South Equatorial Current (SEC) and the North Equatorial Current (NEC), at about 5° north latitude. This superficial current brings warm tropical waters from the western Pacific and ends in the Gulf of Panama, where it splits in two. One part flows up north, along the coast of Central America towards California. The other part flows south, where it meets the SEC. The NECC is the main conveyor of organisms coming from Asia and from the Panama-Colombia area.

The Garua Season

This cool and dry season lasts from May to December. Temperatures are lower than during the rest of the year, and the season brings a subtropical climate, when cold waters come up from the antarctic region.

A frequent mist covers the top of the islands, with some sort of fine rain or 'garua', which is more infrequent on the coast. During the garua season, the cold Peruvian Oceanic Current and Peruvian Coastal Current (known as the Humboldt Current) are dominant. This cold-water mass comes up from Antarctica along the western coast of South America, then heads west to the Galápagos upon reaching the equator. The southeast trade winds, very strong during the garua season, contribute to the process. The temperature of the water is about 18° to 20° C, with a salinity of 35 ppm. The marine fauna is rich. The Humboldt Current is strongest in September, and the sea surface rather rough (see map of Ocean Currents, page 26).

How is the Garua Formed?

The Intertropical Convergence Zone (ITCZ) is well north during the dry season. The southeast trade winds drive the waters of the Humboldt Current north. Warm air migrates over a cold-water current, at an elevation of 100 or 200 metres, cools off upon contact, and becomes bottom heavy and loaded with humidity. An inversion is formed, with hot air above and cold air below. An equilibrium is reached, and the lower layer is saturated with condensed water. A stratus cloud is formed, which will travel horizontally above the ocean surface, with little precipitation.

If this layer meets an elevated island (eg Santa Cruz), an orographic elevation is created, with lower pressure. Hot air will cool off and, since cold air cannot hold moisture as well as warm air, precipitation will pour down in the form of garua.

The Warm Season

It stretches from December to May. The annual rains occur during the first three months of the year. Nevertheless, the temperature is higher, and the sunny days are more numerous than during the garua season. The southeast trade winds vanish, as does the action of the

Humboldt Current. The northeast trade winds become dominant, and warm waters head south from Panama and Colombia. Sea surface temperatures range from 24 to 27° C, with a low salinity of 33.5 ppm, and the waters are poor in organisms. The ITCZ migrates south, to a few degrees north of the equator. The warm waters again meet the Humboldt Current and form the South Equatorial Current, which flows across the Galápagos archipelago.

The climatic 'inversion' created during the garua season disappears, allowing for the formation of cumulus clouds. During the wet season, precipitation occurs as conventional rains—strong, but of short duration.

The 'El Niño'–'La Niña' Phenomenon

Some years the warm-water flow coming from the north is considerably increased. Since it happens around Christmas, it has been named 'El Niño' (after the infant Jesus). It is not a real current. Its action is mainly on the South American mainland, where it triggers heavy rains and disasters in the fishing industry. In fact, it doesn't really affect the Galápagos, where it is manifest every four to seven years.

In 1982–83, an exceptional Niño in the Galápagos brought nine months of continuous rain, an abnormal rate of ambient humidity, suffocating heat and a sea surface temperature of 30° C, followed by tremendous animal mortality. The climatologic effect of that Niño was felt worldwide. Scientists had to study the case seriously. What factors induce such an imbalance? After investigation, it seemed that the phenomenon simply resulted from the dynamics of the Pacific Ocean, and the displacement of considerable oceanic water masses.

During the dry season, the preponderant southeast trade winds push surface waters towards the west, away from the South American mainland. In the Pacific Ocean, the wind action does the same. This brings a conspicuous upheaval of the ocean level in the western Pacific, which means that the water column is higher in the west than it is in the east. Part of the 'return' system is made through the NECC and the Cromwell Current. With the start of the Galápagos' wet season in December, the ITCZ moves south. The water temperature rises with the arrival of warm waters coming from Panama. An enormous amount of warm water returns from the western Pacific towards the east. It is believed that this is what triggered the 1982–83 Niño. These unusual conditions are associated with variations in pressure in the Pacific, allowing equatorial west winds to blow east. This would create surface waves that move across the Pacific, draining warm waters. Hence the floods in Ecuador, the abundant rains and the elevation of the ocean level in the Galápagos by 22 centimetres.

To conclude, the position of the ITCZ is slightly north of the equator, because the dominant winds come from the southeast. Since these bring humidity to the islands, the windward side of the islands is wetter than the leeward side. That is easily seen in the vegetation zones. The arid zone will rise up higher on the leeward side than on the windward

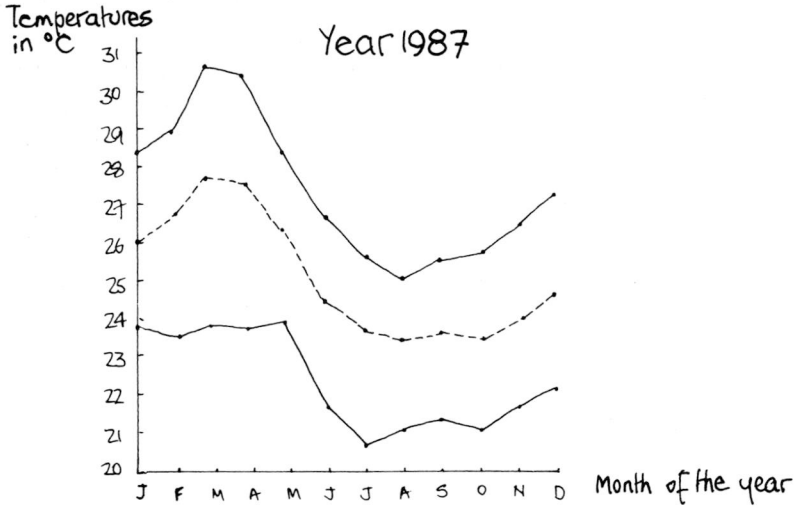

Air temperatures in Puerto Ayora (Santa Cruz), equal to a "Niño" [after "Carta Informativa", CDRS 1988].

Sea surface temperatures Year 1987, for a possible "Niño". [after CDRS, 1988].

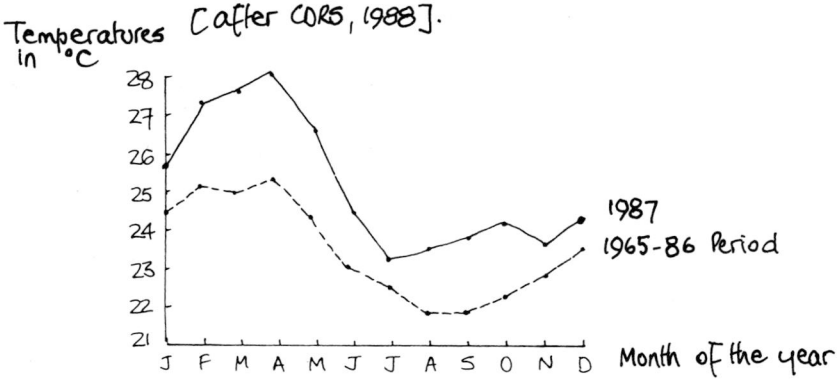

Sea temperatures in °C at 0600 hours

Year	Jan	Feb	Mar	Apr	May	Jun	Jul	Aug	Sep	Oct	Nov	Dec	mean
1981	23.11	24.46	24.87	25.48	24.59	23.28	22.08	20.26	21.10	21.27	21.51	23.31	22.94
1982	24.28	25.39	25.40	24.95	25.29	24.24	23.82	23.17	23.40	24.18	25.94	26.92	24.75
1983	27.57	27.89	28.56	28.54	27.94	27.50	26.75	24.31	22.28	22.41	22.44	23.22	25.78
1984				24.82	23.13	22.09	21.98	21.47	21.76	22.21	22.62	23.16	22.58
1987	25.84	27.37	27.48	27.95	26.59	24.42	22.89	23.00	23.31	23.09	23.60	23.89	24.95
1988	24.15	24.56	24.54	22.68	21.58	19.96	18.96	19.83	20.98	20.25	21.60	22.09	21.77
1996	23.44	24.84	25.59	23.22	22.37	21.35	21.24	20.71	20.09	20.97	21.45	21.27	22.21
1997	23.05	25.36	26.71	27.13	27.03	26.71	26.48	25.91	25.83	25.98	26.65	27.75	26.22
1998	27.87	27.85	28.47	28.46	26.89	25.80	23.09	21.99	20.98	21.05	22.45	21.63	24.71
1999					23.70	22.20	21.20	20.80	20.60	21.60		22.40	21.79

(after Weather Station of CDRS, 2000)

Air Temperatures on the coast in °C, 1200 hours

Year	Jan	Feb	Mar	Apr	May	Jun	Jul	Aug	Sep	Oct	Nov	Dec	mean
1980	27.06	28.26	29.14	28.92	16.82	25.17	23.87	22.77	22.33	23.00	23.97	24.90	25.52
1981	25.98	27.74	28.33	27.70	26.65	24.91	23.21	22.51	21.97	22.70	23.57	25.43	25.06
1982	26.64	28.23	27.97	27.19	26.45	25.10	24.37	24.07	24.87	25.78	27.21	27.68	26.30
1983	29.40	30.12	30.11	29.79	28.79	28.34	27.64	26.25	24.68	24.66	24.70	25.61	27.51
1984	26.63	27.36	28.76	27.10	25.61	23.88	22.66	22.21	22.42	22.74	24.25	25.34	24.91
1985	26.03	26.70	27.75	27.50	24.52	24.22	22.43	21.37	21.51	22.20	23.84	24.63	24.39
1987	27.59	28.61	29.27	29.36	27.70	25.96	24.87	24.39	24.74	25.10	25.62	26.25	26.62
1988	27.43	28.30	28.37	26.26	25.49	23.22	21.64	20.96	21.65	22.01	22.92	24.61	24.41
1996	26.60	28.36	28.70	26.47	25.33	23.79	22.55	21.85	21.40	22.57	23.01	23.54	24.51
1997	26.18	28.29	29.04	28.77	28.13	27.82	27.50	27.19	27.24	26.98	27.62	28.64	27.78
1998	30.27	30.32	30.31	29.40	28.60	27.47	25.42	24.37	23.92	23.96	24.57	25.30	26.99
1999					24.50	23.19	21.60	20.80	20.50	21.40		23.60	22.21

(after Weather Station of CDRS, 2000)

side. Let us take the example of Santa Cruz Island, where the windward side is to the south: the arid zone stretches up from 80 to 120 metres maximum. On the north, leeward face, the arid zone rises up to 200–300 metres. The same applies to the transition zone. This phenomenon is called the 'rain shadow effect'. Fernandina Island is another example, lying in the 'rain shadow' of Isabela Island (see drawing of Vegetation Zones, page 69).

In 1997–98 another El Niño came to Galápagos. Abnormal sea surface temperatures were noticed as early as June 1997. The archipelago was affected and scientists warned that it could be the El Niño of the century. In April 1998, air temperatures were still high, and big waves were coming from afar to wash the south and west shores of the Galápagos islands.

The El Niño phenomenon was already mentioned in old scriptures of Peru in 1525. Incas knew about its existence and built their villages on hilltops; food hiding places would be made in the mountains. Scientists even found geological proof of Niños that occurred 13,000 years ago. The 1997–98 Niño was announced months in advance. The sea level rose 25 centimetres in the East Pacific, off the coast of South America.

The El Niño phenomenon lasts on average 12 to 18 months. For the last 5,000 years, it is recurrent every two to eight years and seems to be more frequent than ever. Global warming for sure is taking its toll. However, El Niño—as it was discovered in the last few years—is part of a remarkable cycle, which has as a consequence a lasting dry period. This cold period, that follows every Niño, has been named 'La Niña' (the small girl).

Since 1965, five major Niños have been identified in the Galápagos: 1975–76, 1982–83, 1986–87, 1993–94 and 1997–98. These have been followed by conspicuous dry times that lasted for two to three years. The scientific community agrees that the 82–83 and the 97–98 Niños were the strongest of the century, with very heavy rains. For the last 34 years, the El Niño–La Niña oscillation has repeated itself every seven years. When the last Niño was over in May 1998, the drought settled in the second half of the year, continued in 1999, and became stronger in 2000. In November of that year, while doing a dive cruise around the islands, I got a shock when I realized that the water temperature was down to 13°C all over the archipelago. Rats!

Fortunately, the marine life, which suffers greatly during the Niño years (death of marine iguanas, sea lions, fish disappear), regenerates amazingly with the arrival of 'La Niña'. Cold waters rich in plankton and in various organisms. Very tonic conditions indeed, I testify!

CHAPTER THREE

The Human History of the Galápagos Islands; Island Names; Darwin and the Galápagos

Well before the Incas—that they ever visited the islands is doubtful—it seems that the first visitors to the islands were Indians who came from Ecuador on balsa rafts. Probably of Mantena or Huancavilca culture, they did not stay long. Pieces of pottery have been found on Santiago Island, on Santa Cruz (Whale Bay) and at Black Beach on the island of Floreana.

Around 1485, Tupac Inca Yupanqui, a prince from Cuzco (who would become the tenth inca), heard rumors about two uninhabited islands far to the west. He was then near the present site of Guayaquil with his army, and decided to build a fleet of balsa rafts equipped with sails. The expedition was gone for nine months to a year. The Inca Yupanqui returned with gold, a bronze seat, and the skin and jaws of a 'horse'. These trophies were kept in the fortress of Cuzco until the arrival of the Spaniards (after Cabello de Balboa, 1586). The two islands were called Nina-Chumbi (Fire Island) and Hahua Chumbi (Outer Island). According to Thor Heyerdahl, the Norwegian explorer, the trophies and the black men could have come from a raid on the mainland, north of the starting point. The skin and jaws of the so-called 'horse' could well have been that of a male sea lion.

The Galápagos bear no archeological remains of dwellings or other structures, so it is quite unlikely that a colony was ever established there, even in remote times.

After the discovery of the Americas by Christopher Columbus in 1492, and the liberation of Spain from the Moors by the Catholic King Ferdinand and Queen Isabella, trips beyond the Atlantic became popular. Conducted with the blessing of the Spanish kings, who were eager to discover new territories, the adventurers' declared aim was the conversion of pagan souls, and their exploits were undertaken under the high authority of the Borgia pope, Alexander VI, who divided the New World for that purpose between Spain and Portugal.

The year 1519 saw the conquest of Mexico by Hernan Cortez. Then in 1532 came the conquest of Peru by Francisco Pizaro, who subdued the Inca empire. Far away from the kingdom of Spain, the conquistadors made their own laws in these new lands and without mercy enslaved all the Indians. Gradually, their thirst for gold and riches (one-fifth was given to the Spanish Crown) brought the conquistadors to quarrel among themselves for supreme power.

It was at that time that Fray Tomas de Berlanga, archbishop of Panama, was given a mission by King Charles V, to report on the anarchic situation in Peru. He and his crew set sail in a caravelle for Lima on February 23, 1535. After seven days of navigation along the coast of South America, the wind dropped for six days. The vessel drifted 800 kilometres west into the Pacific Ocean, carried by the South Equatorial Current. Fray Tomas de Berlanga officially discovered the Galápagos archipelago on March 10, 1535. The bishop

Table of the Names of the Islands

Spanish	*English*
Pinta	Abington
Isabela	Albemarle
Baltra	South Seymour
Santa Fé	Barrington
Beagle	Beagle
Marchena	Bindloe
Tortuga	Brattle
Bartolomé	Bartolomew
Caldwell	Caldwell
Champion	Champion
Floreana, Santa Maria	Charles
San Cristóbal	Chatham
Cowley	Cowley
Crossman	Crossman
Darwin	Culpepper
Wolf	Wenman
Daphné	Daphné
Pinzón	Duncan
Eden	Eden
Enderby	Enderby
Gardner	Gardner (Charles)
Gardner	Gardner (Hood)
Guy Fawkes	Guy Fawkes
Española	Hood
Santa Cruz	Indefatigable
Santiago, San Salvador	James
Rábida	Jervis
Sin Nombre	Nameless
Fernandina	Narborough
Onslow	Onslow
Plaza Sur	South Plaza
Genovesa	Tower
Watson	Watson

wrote to King Charles V, describing the giant tortoises, the iguanas, and the tameness of the birds. To him, the islands appeared very inhospitable.

Eleven years later, in 1546, a Spanish renegade named Diego de Rivadeneira, having deserted the army of Francisco Pizarro, fled with a dozen men on a stolen boat. He got lost just as the bishop had, and drifted away to the islands, where he eventually found water and turtles. He is the first visitor to mention the Galápagos hawk.

After their discovery, the islands still remained without a name. It was much later, during the second half of the 16th century, that quite a number of navigators named them Islas Encantadas or 'Enchanted Islands', for they seemed to appear and disappear on the surface of the ocean by magic. The phantom silhouettes of the volcanoes were always bathed in fog, which made the islands hard to distinguish.

Nowadays, the official name is Archipelago de Colon, and was given to the islands by Ecuador in 1892 to commemorate the 400th anniversary of the discovery of the Americas by Christopher Columbus. The usual name, however, remains 'Galápagos'.

The first marine charts mentioning the islands date to 1570. In 1574, the 'Enchanted Islands' appeared on the map of Abraham Ortelius, with the name 'Archipelago de los Galopegos'. The pirate William Cowley, in 1684, followed by Captain Colnett, in 1793–94, brought English names to the islands. All the names, in English or Spanish, honor kings, admirals, pirates and numerous visitors of the islands.

In 1577, the English pirate Francis Drake cleared Cape Horn and arrived in the Pacific Ocean, where the situation becomes suddenly explosive. 'There is no peace beyond the line,' said he, referring to the boundary line drawn by Pope Alexander VI, which stretched north to south, 1,800 kilometres west of the Cape Verde Islands. Hostilities were declared between England and Spain. These would last from 1593 to 1710.

In the 17th century, English, French and Dutch pirates waged a war against Spain and used the Galápagos as a refuge. From there, they could easily attack the Spanish galleons sailing from the South American coast and sack the coastal ports of Guayaquil and Lima. Buccaneer's Cove and James Bay, on Santiago Island, became favourite hideouts of the pirates. There, they would collect water, wood and giant tortoises. The unfortunate reptiles that were piled in the hulls of the boats could survive a year without drinking water. The most famous of the English pirates were Cowley, Dampier, Davis, Wafer, Cook and Eaton. Among the French were Groguiet, l'Escuyer, Desmarais, Le Picard and Rose. The most visited islands were Santiago and Floreana, where volcanic caves served as primitive dwellings as well as a place to hide bounty and food.

Another famous man who came to the Galápagos was 'Robinson Crusoe'. Alexander Selkirk was his real name. He was freed in February 1709 from his lone island—Juan Fernandez, off the coast of Chile—by Captain Woods Rodgers, another pirate. After four years and four months, Robinson Crusoe, who had been master of the ship *Cinque Ports*, was taken aboard Woods' ship. Three months later, he was in the Galápagos. There, he was given the command of a ship, and later on, he took part in the sack of Guayaquil, a port on the coast of Ecuador. Two years later, in 1711, he returned to England, where he became famous, thanks to *Robinson Crusoe* by Daniel Defoe.

Between 1780 and 1860, the waters of the Galápagos became a favourite place for British and American whalers. During the 19th century, thousands of fur sea lions were butchered. Captain Benjamin Morell confessed to having skinned 5,000 sea lions in two months. Thousands of turtles left the islands at that time, piled alive in the hulls of the boats, from which they were extracted periodically for their meat and their fat. In 1793, a postal 'barrel' was erected on Floreana Island to enable passing ships to collect and deposit mail. The barrel was put there by Captain James Colnett of the British Royal Navy, and officially marked the beginning of the era of the whaling industry. It is still in place today, at Post Office Bay.

The first man to live in the archipelago was Irish, and his name was Patrick Watkins. Nobody knows whether he was a castaway or if he deliberately chose to live on Floreana, in 1807. Anyway, he survived by growing vegetables, which he traded for rum with the passing whalers. His only wish was to drift permanently in the vapor of alcohol. Captain Porter of the navy frigate USS *Essex* described Watkins as a monster with devilish looks:

> *The most dreadful that can be imagined: ragged clothes, scarce sufficient to cover his nakedness, and covered with vermin; his red hair and beard matted, his skin much burnt from constant exposure to the sun, and so wild and savage in his manner and appearance that he struck everyone with horror.... But this man, wretched and miserable as he may have appeared, was neither destitute of ambition, nor incapable of undertaking an enterprise that would have appalled the heart of any other man; nor was he devoid of the talent of rousing others to second his hardihood.*

Two years later, in 1809, Watkins seized a whaling ship, the *Black Prince,* while the crew was on land in search of fresh water and turtles. He took with him five sailors that had landed on Floreana. Unable to find a way out without Watkin's help these five men became his 'slaves'. Watkins eventually made his way to Guayaquil on his own and no one ever discovered what became of his companions, whether he ate them or threw them overboard.

In 1813, the famous Captain David Porter of the USS *Essex,* who hated the English, captured the British whaling fleet in the Galápagos, taking 12 ships in five months. Porter wrote many interesting notes on the Galápagos environment. After Watkins, the islands were more or less uninhabited until 1832, when Ecuadorian General José Villamil founded a prosperous colony on Floreana. The population was mainly composed of convicts, political prisoners and other unwanted people, who traded meat and vegetables with the whalers. In February 1832, two years after the creation of the young republic, Colonel Ignacio Hernandez took official possession of the archipelago in the name of Ecuador. Spanish names were given to the islands, in addition to existing English names. After Villamil departed to San Cristóbal, the colony of Floreana was turned into a penitentiary and fell into chaos. In 1869, a cruel and tyrannical man named Manuel Cobos founded the penal colony of El Progresso on San Cristóbal Island. He regularly abused the wives of his men, and was eventually murdered with a machete by a Colombian convict in 1904.

Many colonies were established over the years, and nearly all collapsed. One succeeded, founded in 1893 by Don Antonio Gil, an honourable citizen of Guayaquil, in Puerto Villamil, on the southern coast of Isabela Island. People survived by selling cattle and by the exploitation of the sulphur mine of Sierra Negra volcano. A Norwegian colony settled on Floreana Island in 1926. Just like its predecessors, the attempt quickly went awry and the island was deserted.

Some years went by. In 1929, a strange German doctor, Friedrich Ritter—dentist, vegetarian and philosopher—arrived on the island with his female assistant, Dore Strauch. They built a house named 'Friedo' in the highlands of Floreana, near a freshwater spring, then created a cosmogonic orchard, following the elaborate theories of Dr Ritter. For the next three years, he wrote many articles for the press, which became well known in Europe. In 1932, the Wittmer family decided to settle on the island too, to practice agriculture and to lead a peaceful life. Floreana became so fashionable that luxurious yachts used to call in, and rich Americans dropped anchor at Black Beach to pay a visit to the 'Robinson Crusoes' of Floreana.

This was tremendously pleasing to the Baroness von Wagner de Bousquet, a young German woman who had a notion to build a hotel for 'millionaires' on the same island. With her two lovers, Lorenz and Philipson, she disembarked in 1932 and built the 'Hacienda Paraiso', a mere shack of planks and corrugated iron. Soon after, she proclaimed herself the 'Empress of Floreana' by virtue of the gun and the whip. Of course, this was not to the liking of Dr Ritter or the Wittmer family. Tensions rose.

The story ended in 1934, after the disappearance of the baroness and Philipson, and the tragic death of Lorenz, who was caught in a storm in a small boat and cast away on the shore of Marchena Island, where he died of thirst with a Norwegian sailor. Dr Ritter died too, poisoned by tainted chicken. Dore Strauch left the island and returned to Germany, where she wrote a book entitled *Satan Came to Eden* before she fell to the curse of Ritter some years later. Only Margret Wittmer survived this untold drama and the mystery lived on. She lived at Black Beach on Floreana, and turned 90 on July 12, 1994. Her book, *Floreana, Poste Restante,* an extraordinary adventure tale of life at the end of the world, was published in 1961 and became a bestseller. She died in Floreana in March 2000.

During the Second World War, an American Air Force base was built on the strategic island of Baltra (north of Santa Cruz Island), from where it was possible to defend the Panama Canal (see the Chronology of Events, page 291). Nowadays, Floreana and Isabela

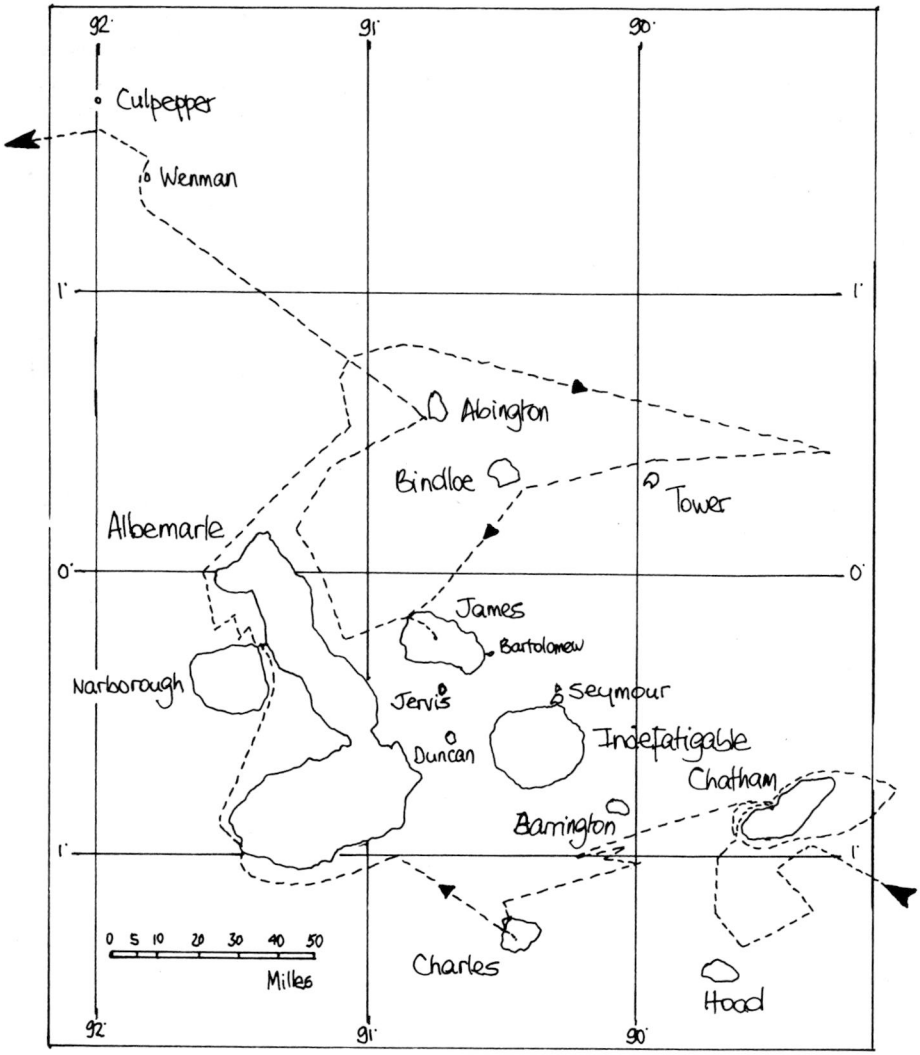

The Route of Charles Darwin
aboard HMS Beagle [Sept. 17 ~ Oct. 20 1835].

islands are inhabited, and bigger communities have been established on Santa Cruz and San Cristóbal. On Santa Cruz, the most central of all, two villages are occupied with agriculture in the tropical highlands. Puerto Ayora, in Academy Bay, is the touristic capital of the Galápagos. Puerto Baquerizo Moreno, on San Cristóbal, is the administrative capital and Ecuador's second naval base.

In 1981, the population of the islands was estimated at about 5,000 people. It reached 10,000 people in 1988, and was around 20,000 people in 1994 (see Appendix 3, page 304).

Darwin and the Galápagos

Without any doubt, the most famous visitor to the Galápagos is Charles Darwin. His short stay in the archipelago has proved enormously significant for science and for the study of evolution (see map: the Route of Charles Darwin, page opposite). At the age of 26, the young British naturalist travelled around the globe on the HMS *Beagle* with Captain Fitzroy. Towards the end of 1835, he sailed from Tierra del Fuego, along the coasts of Chile and Peru, and arrived in the islands for the most unforgettable five weeks of his life. One morning, after dropping anchor in a cove at San Cristóbal, he disembarked and would later (1845) write:

> *The entire surface of this part of the island seems to have been permeated, like a sieve, by the subterreanean vapours: here and there the lava, whilst soft, has been blown into great bubbles; and in other parts, the tops of the caverns similarly formed have fallen in, leaving circular pits with steep sides. From the regular form of the many craters, they gave to the country an artificial appearance, which vividly reminded me of those parts of Staffordshire, where the great iron-foundries are most numerous. The day was glowing hot, and the scrambling over the rough surface... was very fatiguing; but I was well repaid by the strange Cyclopean scene. As I was walking along I met two large tortoises, each of which must have weighed at least two hundred pounds: one was eating a piece of cactus, and as I approached, it stared at me and slowly walked away; the other gave a deep hiss, and drew in its head. These huge reptiles, surrounded by the black lava, the leafless shrubs, and large cacti, seemed to my fancy like some antediluvian animals. The few dull-coloured birds cared no more for me than they did for the great tortoises.*

As he observed the fauna of the archipelago, one of Darwin's major discoveries was to realize that the species were not 'unchangeable', but that they were exposed to the irreversible process of evolution. Natural selection, adaptation to the environment, and genetic mutation, became keywords that helped him to elaborate—thanks to the finches mainly—the celebrated theory of 'The Origin of the Species', which came to light in 1859, 24 years after his journey to the enchanted islands. A new revolution in the scientific mind was born.

CHAPTER FOUR

Arrival and Establishment of the Flora and Fauna

The first thing to consider is the difference between two fundamental concepts: 'continental island' and 'oceanic island'. A continental island is an island that has, at some time in the past, been connected to the continent by a land bridge, and which, therefore, possesses flora and fauna typical of the continental mass from which it originated. By contrast, an oceanic island is born from a submarine volcano which has emerged from the ocean without any life on it. The great distance between an oceanic island and the continent make if difficult for land organisms to reach it, even those having good means of dispersal. Logically, groups of plants and animals having an easy means of dispersal have a greater chance of reaching an oceanic island and thriving, if the conditions are favorable.

The consequence of this phenomenon is an unbalanced flora and fauna in comparison to the continental mass. The word 'disharmonic' is used to define this condition. The Galápagos Islands are therefore a good example of biotypic disharmony. The vertebrates are well represented by birds and reptiles; native mammals are poorly represented, while amphibians and freshwater fishes are totally absent. Among insects, only butterflies and beetles are well represented. A good number of land birds are totally absent in the archipelago.

Among plants, lichens, ferns, grasses, sedges and the Compositae family are well represented, whereas gymnosperms and palm trees are absent, and monocotyledons almost nonexistent. Very few trees are native to the islands. Orchids (11 species), Labiatae (mint family), Acanthacae (grasses, shrubs) are appreciated by the pollinating insects.

Groups of animal and plants well represented in the archipelago are therefore those most likely to cross an ocean frontier of hundreds of kilometres. Such a crossing could be made in three different ways:

- free floating on the sea, or on a natural raft.
- dispersal by wind, or in the air.
- transport in the body of another organism, by air or by sea.

Arrival

Let us consider first transport by sea. Seeds can be carried away passively by flotation. Legumes, even though intolerant of immersion, have an empty space between the embryo and the external shell of the seed. The Galápagos cotton *(Gossypium darwinii)* can withstand a lengthy stay in salt water, and may float for 10 weeks or longer (Stephens, 1958). The Humboldt and South Equatorial currents may carry these cotton seeds from the coast of Peru in less time than that.

Turtles have also a great capacity for flotation, for they have a pocket of air between the upper back and the shell. The second type of passive transport is 'rafting', by natural raft. These vegetation rafts have been seen drifting hundreds of kilometres from the coast, pushed by the sea winds towards the Galápagos from Peru to Ecuador by the Humboldt or Panama currents. Even palm tree logs can carry various insects: ants, larvae, beetles. In 1892, Agassiz saw large rafts drifting from Panama to Cocos Island and the Galápagos, at a speed of about 130 kilometres (75 miles) a day. Such a raft could reach the archipelago in two weeks. Reptiles have a completely waterproof skin, and drink very little water. In 1880, a boa constrictor was seen (alive) in the Caribbean, coiled around the log of a cedar tree, floating 300 kilometres from Trinidad. Sea lions and fur sea lions also travel with the help of the currents. They came from the north (California) and from the southeast (Antarctic), and colonized the archipelago after a group migration.

The second type of transport is transport by air. Aerial dispersal is the best means by which insects reach the islands. It can be passive, as with spiders taken in air currents at an elevation of about 3,000 metres. Likewise, the seeds of orchids and spores of ferns, mosses and mushrooms, which can resist very low temperatures, are dispersed this way. When they arrive above the islands, the spores drop with the condensation of the air. The poor representation of butterflies in the Galápagos is due to the fact that adults have fragile wings, and the larvae are very sensitive.

Transport via other organisms, or active transport, is mainly carried out by birds. Seagulls, for example, come from areas with abundant vegetation. They carry seeds in their stomachs, between their feathers or under their wings, even in the mud stuck to their feet. Seeds collected from riverbanks or swamps can be carried away in such a fashion.

Among 607 species of plants found in the Galápagos, it has been estimated that 59 per cent of them were transported as seeds by birds, 32 per cent by the wind, and nine per cent by ocean transport. If one considers the influence of man, then 40 per cent were transported by birds, 32 per cent by man, 22 per cent by wind and 6 per cent by flotation.

Establishment and Survival

Once on the island, the organism has to establish itself, and before anything else it must find food to survive. Reproduction of the species comes later. The establishment is as vital as the arrival in order to colonize the island with success. Two major reasons explain why a group of animals or plants can be absent from an island:

- The organism has not reached there at all.
- After arriving, the organism has not been able to establish (importance of the season).

An airborne organism—unlike one carried by sea—is not conditioned to land on a particular island. It can drop on the soil of any habitat, and therefore has a greater chance to become established. Once the difficulties of arrival are overcome, the living being has to reproduce to ensure the survival of the species.

Hermaphroditic plants have no problems in reproducing, for the male and female principals are located on the same flower. By contrast, in dioecious plants, male and female principals are on different plants, as is the case with most animals, for whom reproduction is possible only if the complementary individual is present.

In the Galápagos, three plants are dioecious: *Castela* and *Croton*, which are shrubs of the arid zone, and *Bursera*, also called palo santo, which is a tree with white bark.

Lindsay (1966) thinks that the first plants introduced to the islands were self-reproducing. Later on, the presence of a wasp, as well as of some other pollinating insects, was important in the reproductive process of the plants. To illustrate the action of the wind in reproduction, studies have shown that 32 per cent of the flora are pollinated by the wind in Hawaii, 34 per cent in Juan Fernandez in the southeastern Pacific and 29 per cent in New Zealand.

Some factors are essential for a plant to establish. The majority of land plants need a soil rich in humus, and will not establish on an island where the soil is poor. Exceptions include the lichens *Archicera*, which can fix themselves upon lava on the shore.

Finally, animals are dependant on plants for food, therefore the plants must be established before the animals. We may talk about the vegetarian vertebrates, such as turtles, or marine iguanas, which need a good cover of vegetation to survive. Some sea birds need material to build their nests. The optimum moment chosen by an organism (eg a bird) to arrive is important when related to the arrival of another competing species. The 'ecological niche' (that is, all conditions necessary for survival and reproduction) of an arriving species may be already occupied by another organism which established itself earlier in the community. A morphological transformation will then take place. Otherwise, one of the two species is doomed to extinction. The arrival of an organism in an already overpopulated island is only possible if another species is going extinct or has already disappeared. The island reaches equilibrium when immigration is balanced by extinction. When they are near to the mainland, big islands have a high immigration rate and a low extinction rate, which means that they are soon saturated. Faraway islands, with a low immigration rate (even more if they are small), will be saturated less quickly. This is also due to a faster extinction rate.

MacArthur and Wilson (1963), authors of the equilibrium theory, take the example of Krakatoa Island, where fauna took 36 years to reach equilibrium after the devastating volcanic eruption. As a matter of fact, Krakatoa is very interesting, for it is a similar example to the Galápagos.

Krakatoa, a volcanic island of Indonesia, between Sumatra and Java, emerged from the ocean after a memorable explosion in 1883. In 1886, three years later, there were 11 species of ferns, two species of *Compositae* and two grasses. In 1894 (11 years later), the interior of the island was bedecked with grassy vegetation and a few shrubs. The year 1903 saw luxurious vegetation on the island. In 1908, 25 years after the eruption, one could find 13 species of birds, a species of monitor lizard, one gecko, and 192 species of insects: ants, flies, beetles, dragonflies and butterflies; spiders and scorpions were also present.

The Galápagos followed the same pattern of population, and are today the home of unique organisms, including land and marine iguanas, giant tortoises, mockingbirds, lava gulls, Darwin's finches, the Galápagos dove, the flightless cormorant, the waved albatross and the Galápagos penguin, which are found nowhere else in the world.

Geographic Affinities

Logically, most of the animals in the Galápagos originated from North, Central and South America and the Caribbean.

- from North America: some land birds like the 'yellow warbler' and the California sea lions.
- from the Caribbean: pink flamingos, Darwin's finches (the ancestor on St Lucia Island was transported by winds to Costa Rica, and later on to Cocos Island, before reaching the Galápagos).
- from South America: land iguanas, giant tortoises, pelicans, flightless cormorants, vermilion flycatcher.
- from the Antarctic: fur sea lions and penguins.

CHAPTER FIVE

THE THEORY OF EVOLUTION AND THE GALÁPAGOS

The Galápagos archipelago has been called the 'showcase of evolution', and truly, for the biologist, the islands are a living laboratory for the study of evolution. The closest example to the Galápagos is perhaps Hawaii, which, at 20 million years old, is six times older than the assumed age of our archipelago.

Evolution is the central topic of biology. Before Darwin, the creationist theory declared that life appeared on earth on Sunday 23 October 4004 BC, at nine in the morning. Darwin had been brought up to become an Anglican clergyman. He left England for a five-year journey around the planet, questioning himself for a long time, testing his ideas. He recognized variation within species and also that a gradual change was sometimes affecting a species. The word evolution means change in the characteristics of living beings, which cannot be inherited. A living being is recognized by five essential characteristics, which are:

- the ability to reproduce.
- the ability to memorize information in their genes (in a molecular sense).
- control of their environment.
- excitability, or ability to respond to a stimulus.
- excitability by/in producing energy.

A living organism knows how to adjust to specific conditions and is able to 'modify' itself. These evolutionary changes may be an answer to natural selection. Those which fail are doomed; those which succeed must change and evolve. 'The survival of the fittest', said Darwin. According to the theory of evolution, all living organisms have a phylogenetic heritage, in other words, a genetic heritage linked to the development of the group (Grzimek, *Encyclopedia of Evolution,* 1972). This phylogenetic process is stimulated by two factors: genetic variation and natural selection.

If organic evolution is a change in genetics, natural selection should not be mistaken for evolution. Evolution refers to temporal changes of all sorts, whereas natural selection brings about a particular way through which these changes are made (E.R. Pianka, 1974).

Another definition of evolution is: non-cyclic changes in the genetic pool (sum of the allele genes in a population). Two ideas come up next: the 'genotype' and the 'phenotype'. The genotype is the genetic asset of an individual as inherited from its parents' DNA. The phenotype is its morphology, physiology and real behavior after interaction of the genotype with the environment.

The evolutionary space-time (or time-free) frame of evolution is the mutation. Mutations within a population, and within a given time, play an important role in the future evolution of this population. Evolution is induced by mutations and natural selection. Mutations favor genetic variety. Natural selection, on the contrary, limits the genetic variety. Evolution is a continuum; it is not a number of species following one another. 'Speciation', or multiplication of the species, occurs when a genetic pool is divided in two isolated parts. This is to say that members of a given population become reproductively isolated from the other members of that population. Once evolution reaches such a level, where two populations cannot mate, then each turns into a unique species. The evolution process is so unique that the complex relationship between an organism and its environment changes with time. Three examples will bring some light to this idea:

- Evolution may occur when the biological entity (animal) stays within its habitat and does not substantially change its lifestyle.
- Organisms, having gone through mutations, even minor ones, may conquer a new habitat (a new ecological niche) by modification of their behavior, but still keeping their old structure. In other words, structures may accomplish new functions.
- Another possible evolution links the two cases mentioned above. Anatomic changes and new functions may occur simultaneously in the evolution of an animal group.

The original organism, having gone through the effects of natural selection, is transformed in such a way that its body is able to meet the functional demands of the environment. It evolves so that the last forms of individuals have more chances of survival and a higher rate of reproduction success than the earlier forms.

To conclude, let us quote Haeckel: 'Ontogeny recapitulates phylogeny', which means that the development of the individual within the egg sums up the development of the animal group to which it belongs. In the Galápagos, one important factor to consider is insularity. Islands differ from the continental landmass by their isolation, which implies not only the role of selection, but also that of the 'chance' factor in the evolutionary process. Mayr (1963) has shown the extreme importance of geographic isolation in speciation. Darwin is known for his famous saying: 'The survival of the fittest', which can be compared with 'the death of the weakest'. Considering fitness or adaptability, natural selection stresses an answer to the conditions of the environment.

For an animal, a change in behavior brings about a change in physiology, therefore a morphological change. Natural selection is the means through which organisms become gradually better adapted to their environment. Even though the majority of the species are doomed to extinction without the creation of a new evolutionary way, it is not impossible that a particular species can become a pioneer of evolution. Without differentiation of the species, there would not be any diversity in the organic world, and very little progress in evolution. The species is then the 'key' to evolution.

For insular populations, two common factors induce fragmentation and speed up speciation:

- the tendency for a well-established population to move out of the marginal habitats towards more central habitats, therefore minimizing the capacity of dispersal of the population.
- the fact that island organisms have a tendency to form restricted and localized populations.

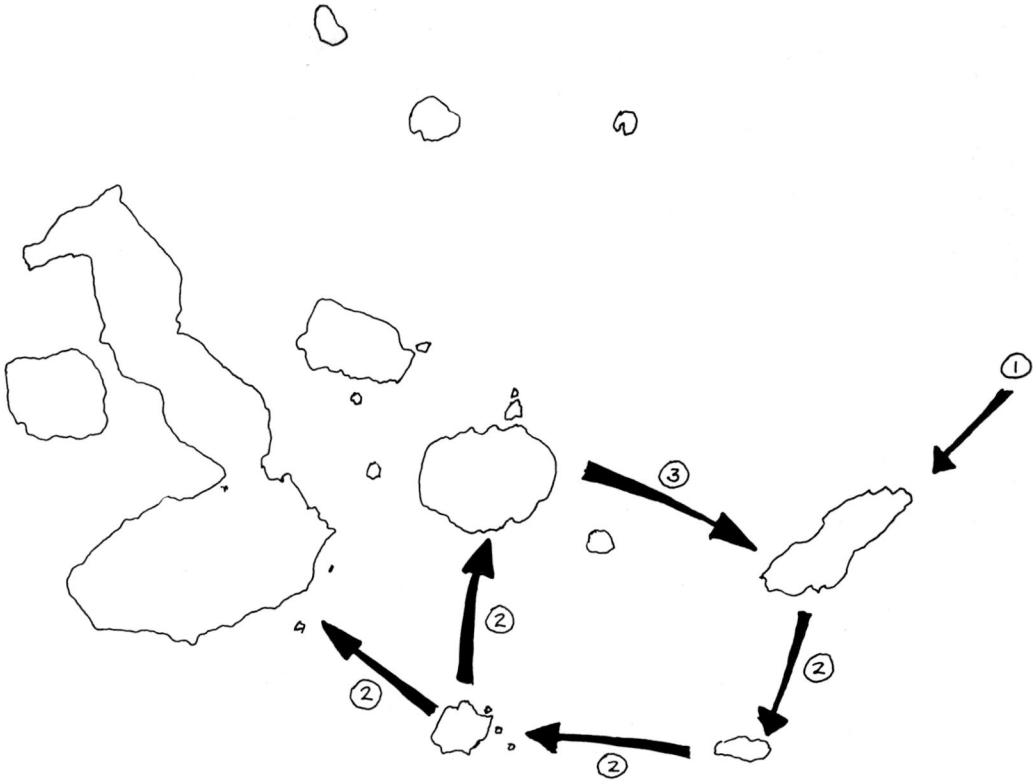

Allopatric model of the distribution of the species
e.g. the speciation of Darwin's Finches [after Peter Grant, 1981].

Darwin's Finches

Archipelagos are ideal for geographic isolation and speciation. In the Galápagos, 13 species of finches (in fact 14, counting the one on Cocos Island) have evolved from one original species, which migrated from Costa Rica. *Melanospiza richardsoni,* on St Lucia Island in the West Indies, is the nearest species.

For populations in isolation, various selective pressures on different islands lead to evolution and divergent adaptations. Occasional interactions between islands favour 'competition' which promotes the diversity of the 'niches'. (Niche: all the necessary conditions for an animal to survive and to reproduce in a given environment.) The competition may be 'interspecific', ie, between different species, or 'intraspecific', within the same species. The more individuals, the greater the competition. For the niches of the original island, the increasing population leads to the departure of a number of individuals towards other habitats. Each newly colonized island will later yield as many unique species, adapted to a specific environment with adequate functions. The 'adaptive radiation' of the finches in the Galápagos has created four distinct genera, which differ by the following factors:

- where they feed
- how they feed
- what they feed on

For the Darwin finches, the morphological changes are seen in the size and shape of the beak: ground finches, tree finches, cactus finches, vegetarian finch, warbler finch, sharpbill ground finch, carpenter finch... Some of these individuals migrate in the opposite direction, towards islands already colonized by their ancestors, and live in perfect harmony with other species, each with its specific function and proper habitat. There would be no more competition for food. The 'allopatric' model of speciation (Peter Grant, 1981) explains the 'adaptive radiation' in four successive steps:

1) Colonization of an island in the Galápagos by a population coming from the continent (Central America), after crossing an oceanic barrier.

2) The population develops on the initial island. Some individuals migrate to nearby islands. Genetic changes occur in the new environment. The second step may be repeated many times, resulting in the establishment of allopatric populations of one single species on many islands.

3) A secondary contact between the original population and the second population occurs. It is important to know how different the two groups are at the time of contact. If the differences are minor, the interaction goes freely and the two groups fuse. If the differences are moderate to wide, the individuals of the two groups may show a slight tendency to mix,

and those which do so will leave offspring less fit than those which mate within the same group. Natural selection will favour those which reproduce in the tradition.

Differences between the new groups will be greater in the signals and responses related to mating. The result is that the reproductive isolation between groups initiated in 'allopatry' (ie, on different islands) will be perfected in 'sympatry' on the same island. In the end of the third step, two species have been produced out of one. Their coexistence is dependent on sufficient ecological differences: the selective process is similar to the one mentioned above. Selection acts against individuals of the two incipient species, which look so alike that they will certainly develop a competitive spirit for resources such as food. The consequence will be the divergence between the characters to exploit the resources.

4) The final step is the simple repetition of this cycle of events. This is how the 13 species of Darwin's finches were established (see the 'Allopatric model', page 46).

Endemism

An organism, species or group, living and evolving in a specific place, which is found nowhere else, is called endemic. It is important to remember this word, since it will be used frequently in the description of the flora and fauna of the archipelago. Oceanic islands have a high rate of endemism because of their isolation. If the island is small, such as Cocos Island, northeast of the Galápagos, speciation will not be as great as in an archipelago. The Cocos finch is endemic, but that is the only species. On bigger islands, where possibility for isolation is greater, differentiation may occur. In the Galápagos, 14 endemic races of tortoises, distinct and subspecific, have evolved on 11 islands. On the island of Isabela alone, five races were distinguished—one on each volcano. It is quite likely that these five volcanoes have been separate islands in the past, since in the Quaternary ice ages the level of the ocean rose and fell considerably.

Land iguanas have evolved on the central islands of the archipelago, and one distinct species has been recognized on Santa Fé Island. The lava lizard has distinct forms on Floreana, Española and San Cristóbal, as well as on the northern islands such as Marchena and Pinta. One single species is found on the central islands, with the exception of Pinzón, which has an endemic species.

The four species of mockingbirds have an easier dispersal ability than reptiles. They inhabit all islands, except on Floreana where they are extinct.

Examples of Adaptation to the Environment

The flightless cormorant—whose ancestor came from equatorial America—lost its ability to fly. Without any predators, its wings became useless. The flightlessness is also due to the action of strong winds, which may take birds far away from the islands against their will. For

Aerial view of Tortuga Island, Isabela

Aerial view of the crater of Beagle Lake, Isabela 1990

'Embarcadero', Puerto Villamil, Isabela 2002

Horse riding on Sierra Negra, Isabela

The "pahoehoe" lava field of Sullivan Bay, Santiago 1990

Ropey lava on a "pahoehoe" surface, Sullivan Bay 1982

Hornito, Sullivan Bay 1990

Bartolomé Island 1995

Cerro Ballena, Isabela Island 2002

The garua on the rim of Sierra Negra volcano, Isabela 1988

Sulphur fumaroles, Sierra Negra, Isabela 1986

Punta Vicente Roca, the sea lions' lagoon, Isabela 1990

Tuff cliffs, Punta Vicente Roca 1988

Volcan Ecuador, Isabela 1992

The blowhole of Punta Suarez Espanola 1989

Lava tube, Santa Cruz 1988

Darwin's Arch, Darwin Island 1993

The "Grottos", James Bay, Santiago 1990

Cathedral of tuff, "Leon Dormido" Cristobal 1992

Lava flow at Cape Hammond, Fernandina Island 1995

Salt mine and tuff cones, James Bay, Santiago 1992

Mangroves in "Divine's Bay", Puerto Ayora, Santa Cruz 1984

Opuntia *cacti and* sesuvium *flowerbeds in the dry season, Plaza 1993*

Giant opuntia *cactus, Buccaneer's Cove, Santiago 1990*

Flower of the opuntia *cactus, Punta Moreno 1986*

Jasminocereus *cactus, Punta Moreno 1988*

Sesuvium flowerbeds, Punta Pitt, San Cristóbal 1992

Red mangrove, Santa Cruz 1980

Jasminocereus *cacti, Darwin Station 1988*

Brachycereus *(lava cactus), Punta Espinosa 1990*

Nolana galapageia, *Floreana 1993*

Carpenter bee on Parkinsonia aculeata *1994*

Arid zone of the palo santos, Genovesa 1993

Agriculture zone of Santa Cruz, Santa Cruz 1993

Scalesia *forest, Los Gemelos, Santa Cruz 1993*

Scalesia *forest, Santa Cruz 1993*

Tree ferns, Sierra Negra, Isabela 1988

Lava lizard (female), Espanola 1992

Lava lizard (male), Punta Pitt, Cristóbal 1992

Lava lizard (female), Punta Pitt 1992

those which keep their wings, the flight technique is to fly low above the ground. Marine iguanas feed on chlorophyllian algae encrusted on the rocks, and may dive to a depth of 20 metres without breathing for half an hour. Some finches on Wolf Island suck blood from the wings of masked boobies. At first, finches were probably interested in the parasites on the boobies (such as horseflies) hidden between the feathers and around the neck of the seabirds.

In the tropical forest of the islands, the carpenter finch uses a wooden stick as a tool to dig larvae out of old stumps. Well-known reptiles such as tortoises and land iguanas feed on vegetation and not on insects. On the islands where these reptiles are found, opuntia cacti, with conspicuous pads, grow up like trees and develop a trunk, as tall as possible, to avoid being eaten by the reptiles. On islands where these reptiles are absent, opuntia grow close to the ground. It is amazing to realize that the cactus has developed an ability to 'think'—no more than a survival reaction—that some may call a 'conservation instinct'.

The Uncertainty of the Future

Living organisms in the Galápagos are doomed to possible extinction. Islands deteriorate due to the erosion of wind, rain, sea. The worst factor, though, has been the arrival of man, who introduced unwanted species into the fragile ecosystem of the Galápagos: goats, rats, pigs, dogs and cats. These animals, at first domestic, turned feral and became a threat to the native species of the archipelago. Goats are very competitive and eat the food of the reptiles; dogs prey on iguanas; wild pigs on tortoise nests and young; fire ants destroy the population of invertebrates and become a plague.

CHAPTER SIX

Flora and Vegetation Zones

We mentioned earlier that the disharmony of the flora in the Galápagos is supported by the fact that the islands have never been connected to the continent. There are no native gymnosperms (cone-bearing trees), and 'monocotyledons' are poorly represented. Ferns represent a high percentage of the flora. Lichens are pioneer plants, which do not need any soil to grow.

Orchids, with only 11 species in the archipelago (as opposed to 3,000 species on the continent), are poorly represented. Their survival is limited by elevation, and they require a pollinating insect to ensure reproduction. The absence of such a pollinating insect considerably reduces the number of families and plants present on the islands.

In the Galápagos, 607 species of plants are found (or 736 taxa, if one considers species, subspecies and varieties). Out of that number, 412 species are native, and 195 species were introduced by man (32 per cent). Among natives, 242 species are indigenous and 170 species are endemic (34 per cent). If we consider the taxa, 312 taxa are indigenous, 229 are endemic, 195 are introduced. The number of introduced species rises with immigration of Ecuadorian settlers. In 1986, the new number of introduced plants was 240 species. Following a survey by the Charles Darwin Station in 2004, the number of introduced plants on inhabited islands, passed 650 species.

The distribution of plants on various islands is influenced by climate and soil. Larger islands, high in elevation, have many vegetation zones and therefore a greater number of species. The number of species depends therefore on surface and elevation, but more on elevation.

	PINTA	MARCHENA	ESPAÑOLA	SANTA FÉ
Surface	60 km^2	30 km^2	58 km^2	24 km^2
Altitude	650 m	343 m	213 m	244 m
Number of Species	200	60	110	70

Ninety-nine per cent of the flora of the Galápagos originated in South America, and only one per cent comes from Central America and Mexico. As we said earlier, the transport of seeds is carried out by birds (60 per cent), wind (31 per cent) and rafting (nine per cent).

Ferns, with spores dispersed by wind, are best represented in the archipelago (but endemic species are few). Lichens, grasses and mosses are also important due to their dispersal ability. Flowering plants of the *Compositae* family are very well represented (daisies and sunflowers belong to that family). With an excellent dispersal, they are pioneer plants in the colonization of faraway islands. In taxonomy, one considers:

- Phylum
- Class
- Order
- Family
- Genus
- Species
- subspecies } Taxa
- variety

Seven endemic genera of plants are found in the Galápagos:

- *Scalesia*	(16 species)	Compositae family
- *Lecocarpus*	(3 species)	Compositae family
- *Darwiniothamnus*	(3 species)	Compositae family
- *Macrea*	(1 species)	Compositae family
- *Jasminocereus*	(1 species, 3 subspecies)	Cactae family
- *Brachycereus*	(1 species)	Cactae family
- *Sicyocaulis*	(1 species of vine)	Cucumber family

Research for conservation of native plants in 2004, revealed a new population of the strange *Lecocarpus* plant on San Cristóbal.

Scalesia

This genus is spread out and has adapted to different zones: arid, humid, and cliffs. It is distinguished by the shape of the leaves, and flowering heads.

- *Scalesia pedunculata* (central islands) is a tree of the humid zone (ex: Santa Cruz). Branches have small flowering heads (see photo, page 63).
- *Scalesia dentatae*: shrub with large flowering heads (*Scalesia affinis* on Santa Cruz).
- *Scalesia lobatae* (*Scalesia helleri*) : shrub of the arid zone on Santa Cruz Island.
- *Scalesia foliosae*: shrub with flowering heads and arrow-shaped leaves.

A new population of *Scalesia* was discovered in Santa Cruz, in 2004.

Cacti

Two endemic genera: *Jasminocereus* and *Brachycereus*, and one endemic species: *Opuntia echios*.

- *Jasminocereus thouarsii*, also called the candelabra cactus, is a tall cactus found in the arid zone, and resembles Mexican organ pipe cacti (see photo, page 59).
- *Brachycereus*, is a small cactus with white spines, 50–60 centimetres high, which grows directly on lava surfaces (see photo, page 60).

- *Opuntia* is the most common species of the arid zone. Rather small like a shrub, or tall like a tree with a trunk rising up to five metres, and spines at the base to discourage herbivores. The most impressive *Opuntiae* are found on Santa Fé Island, where the circumference of one trunk reached three metres (see photo, page 59).

Vegetation Zones

Seven vegetation zones are distinguished in the archipelago, but only big islands like Santa Cruz have them all (see drawing, page 69). From the bottom to the top, we may consider:

1) the Coastal or Littoral Zone
2) the Arid Zone
3) the Transition Zone
4) the Scalesia Zone
5) the Brown Zone
6) the Miconia Zone
7) the Pampa or Fern Zone

The Littoral Zone

A very narrow stretch a few metres wide, which is found on the coast or around saltwater lagoons. The vegetation is influenced by salt, and is made of shrubs and small trees. Mangroves are dominant, with four species:

- Red mangrove — *Rhizophora mangle* (see photo, page 60)
- Black mangrove — *Avicennia germinans*
- White mangrove — *Laguncularia racemosa*
- Button mangrove — *Conocarpus erectus*

The four mangroves are easily recognized by the shape of the leaves: oval in the white mangrove, elongated and pointed in the black mangrove. The red mangrove has bigger, arrow-shaped leaves and has stilt roots sticking out of the water. The button mangrove is distinguished by conspicuous white buttons at the base of the leaves, at the end of the branches.

The saltbush: *Cryptocarpus pyriformis* is a bush with fat, green leaves, very common in the islands, which may reach two metres in height. Local name: *monte salado.*

Sesuvium edmonstoneï or *Sesuvium portulacastrum,* of the succulent family, are very colourful annual plants which may cover large areas of the ground. Leaves are small sugar-almond type, red or green according to the dry or wet season. Flowers are pink or white, according to the species: *Sesuvium portulacastrum* (pink) or *Sesuvium edmostoneï* (white).

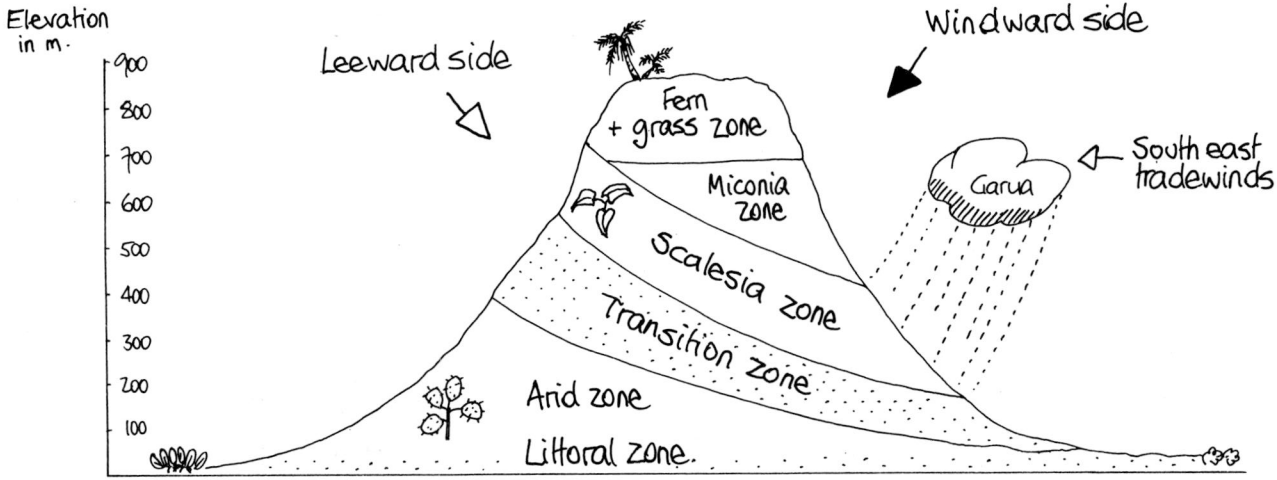

Vegetation zones e.g. Santa Cruz
[after Van Straelen Hall, Darwin Station].
Piroco 1994

The Arid Zone

This rather large zone spreads up to an elevation of 80–120 metres. Dominant vegetation is represented by three cacti: *Opuntia, Jasminocereus* and *Brachycereus*. Most of the plants have a xerophytic adaptation (ie, adaptation to dry land), which is characterized by small leaves, a high rate of photosynthesis, spiny shrubs (eg *Scutia pauciflora*), deep roots (eg *Parkinsonia aculeata*), and leaves that may orient themselves towards the sun (eg *Maytenus octogona*).

The arid zone is also the country of the palo santo, *Bursera graveolens* (see photo, page 62), a tree with white bark which has leaves only during the wet season. It is characteristic of the arid zone and found everywhere. Acacia are also seen, as shrubs or small trees (*Acacia rorudiana*), with tiny leaves, flowers like small yellow balls and a fruit like a brown bean. The almost identical *Prosopis juliflora* has bigger oblong leaves, typical of the acacias.

Chala: *Croton scouleri* is a shrub with grey stems, leaves are orange to yellow-green, and the fruit looks like a capsule. The sap of this plant stains clothes.
Manzanillo: *Hippomane mancinella* is a tree that develops at first near the ground, then grows quite tall. The fruit, green or yellow, resembles a small apple, but it is highly toxic, and may burn the skin and the eyes. If eaten, very painful stomach cramps may result.
Muyuyo: *Cordia lutea* is a nice tree with yellow flowers which is found frequently in Academy Bay, Santa Cruz Island.

During the wet season, the arid zone blooms with 'annual plants'. These plants are ephemeral.

The Transition Zone

This zone climbs up between 100 and 200 metres in elevation, but may rise up to 500 metres on the leeward side. There again, palo santos are found. The characteristic plant of this zone is pega pega (*Pisonia floribunda*), a tree with a short stem and spread-out branches. The coarse bark is covered with lichens. The local name pega pega means 'stick stick', because the leaves of this tree will 'grab' your fingers.

Guayabillo: *Psidium galapageium* is also spread out and conspicuous. The bark of this tree is soft and pinkish grey. Leaves are leathery and the fruit is similar to the guayaba (*Psidium guayava*) introduced to the islands, yellow and round with a pink flesh. The transition zone is intermediate between the arid and the humid zone.

The Scalesia Zone

From 200 to 400 metres. A very humid zone with constant precipitation. This is where the garua concentrates during the dry season. Ferns, grasses and mosses are abundant, but the predominant species is *Scalesia pedunculata* (local name: lechoso). This sunflower tree may reach ten metres in height, and concentrates in dense forests, with mosses hanging from the branches and with flowers looking like white daisies. The scalesia forest climbing up the slopes of Santa Cruz volcanoes is a beautiful sight.

The Brown Zone

This part ends the scalesia zone. Liverworts are the characteristic plants. Liverworts are epiphytes, which cling to the tree but do not depend on it. These brown mosses fall from the branches of scalesia, thus the name 'brown zone'.

The Miconia Zone

Above the former zone, it rises up to 1,000 metres. This zone is represented by miconias, leafy bushes two to four metres tall. Leaves are long, rather oval shaped, and distinguished by three parallel central ribs. *Miconia robinsoniana* is also called 'cacaotillo', because the leaves resemble cacao. Flowering heads are pink or violet. The species is endemic, and is found only on Santa Cruz Island (Media Luna) and on San Cristóbal, towards San Joaquin volcano.

The Pampa Zone

The pampa finishes the scale of the vegetation zones and ranges from 650 metres' elevation up to the summit of the island. This windy and misty land with no trees is represented by ferns, grasses, sedges and other plants adapted to water; swamps and peat bogs are common. Waterholes within small collapsed lava tubes are often like greenhouses, where mosses, ferns and four species of orchids grow. The only tree present is the tree fern, *Cyathea weatherbyana*, which may reach three metres in height. The moist pampa is a microclimate in itself (see photo, page 63).

The Introduced Species

By 1986, 240 species of plants had been introduced by man to the Galápagos. In 2004, less than 20 years later, the number passed 650 species. These were found in the colonized, agricultural zone. The arrival of farmers and settlers on San Cristóbal, Floreana and Santa Cruz, as well as in the south of Isabela, has created a few ecological disorders in the scalesia and miconia zones. As a matter of fact, many introduced species are taking over the native species.

Twenty per cent of the introduced species originate from North America or Europe. At least 10 species are aggressive in their active dispersal ability, ie, the ease with which they invade vegetation zones, to the detriment of the indigenous or endemic species. This is a major concern of the Galápagos National Park Service, in its efforts to protect and conserve the islands.

For two years the SPNG has used herbicides against guayaba, but the problem remains. No one knows exactly how much poison should be used to eradicate it efficiently. An attempt has been made to plant fast-growing teck or scalesia to counteract the slow-growing guayaba.

The Ten Principal Introduced Species of Plants

FAMILY	SPECIES	LOCAL NAME	USE
Agavaceae	*Furcraea cubensis*	Cabuya (cactus)	Hedges
Crassulaceae	*Kalanchoe*	Pinnata	Ornamental
Lauraceae	*Persa americana*	Avocado, aguacate	Fruit
Mytaceae	*Psidium guayaba*	Guayaba	Fruit
Mytaceae	*Eujenia jambos*	Pomarosa	Fruit
Rustaceae	*Citrus spp*	Limon, Toronja	Fruit
Verbenaceae	*Lantana camara*	Lantana	Hedges
Poaceae	*Digitaria decumbens*	Pangola	Pasture
Poaceae	*Pennisetum purpureum*	Pasto elephante (elephant grass)	Pasture

PART TWO

FAUNA OF THE GALÁPAGOS

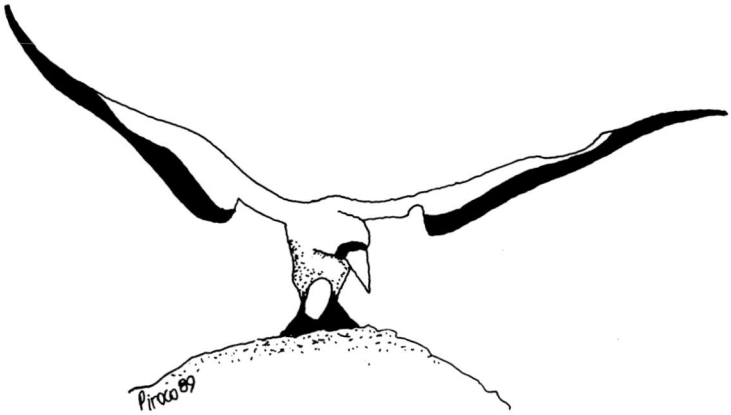

CHAPTER ONE

Reptiles: Geckos, Snakes, Lizards, Marine and Land Iguanas, Marine Turtles, Giant Tortoises

In the Galápagos archipelago, the dominant quadrupeds are reptiles. This is the reason that the islands were long considered a refuge for prehistoric, antediluvian beasts. These reptiles, related to South American forms, are represented by iguanas, lava lizards, geckos, snakes, and of course giant tortoises, which gave fame to the Galápagos. Sixty three per cent of the reptiles (17 species of 27) are endemic to the Galápagos.

Geckos

Geckos are small lizards of the Geckonidae family. Three genera are found in the archipelago, and six species are endemic, all of the genus *Phyllodactylus:*

- *Gonatodes caudiscutatus* (one species, on San Cristóbal only.)
- *Phyllodactylus* (six endemic species, on Santa Cruz, Isabela, Baltra, Floreana, San Cristóbal)
- *Lepidodactylus lugubris* (one species, on Santa Cruz, Isabela, San Cristóbal).

The gecko is five centimetres long, with sand-coloured skin, and may climb smooth and vertical surfaces (such as windowpanes) thanks to the adhesive pads on its toes. With a vertical slit in its black eye, it is an essentially nocturnal reptile, but it may be seen during the daytime under rocks and in cracks. One or two eggs are laid in October and November. Geckos have permanent eyelids, like contact lenses. After eating, they lick their eyes with their tongue. They also swallow their dead skin after moulting. Some species change color, like chameleons. Geckos have the ability of autotomy, ie they are able to part from their tail if necessary. Geckos are found in the central islands of the Galápagos.

Snakes

Two snake species, a land snake and a sea snake, are found in the Galápagos:

The Galápagos Land Snake

This small, diurnal constrictor may catch prey up to 1.5 metres in length. Posteroglyphous, hardly venomous, it belongs to the family Colubridae and to the genus *Philodryas,* originating from the West Indies (Caribbean). Eight subspecies were identified in the Galápagos:

- *Philodryas biserialis* (Española, Cristóbal)	3 subspecies
- *Philodryas slevini* (Central islands, except for Santa Fé)	2 subspecies
- *Philodryas dorsalis* (Central islands)	3 subspecies

Brown with yellow stripes, or grey-black with yellow spots in a zigzag pattern, it measures about 1.2 metres in length. It feeds on lizards, insects, small birds and young marine iguana hatchlings. The Galápagos snake is found on all islands, except in the five northern islands.

The Yellow-bellied Sea Snake *(Pelamis platurus)*
Belongs to the family Hydrophiidae. Dorsally black, ventrally yellow, with spots on the tail section. It measures up to 85 centimetres in length. Its venom is stronger than the cobra's. Rare, except during the Niño years when waters are warmer. Common from the west coast of Central America westward.

Lava Lizards

family: Iguanidae
genus: *Microlophus*

This genus is found only in South America and the Galápagos. Seven species are endemic to the archipelago (one on each island). The biggest lizard is found on Española island, where it grows up to 25 centimetres. The smallest is half that size and is found on Floreana (south of the archipelago) (see photo, page 64). The male is bigger than the female, greyish black in colour with specks. The female has a conspicuous red-orange throat; sometimes, on Española, for example, the whole head is red.

Lizards feed on insects, seeds, flowers and leaves, and show a preference for vegetarian food. They love to bask in the sun on lava rocks, and have an excellent thermo-regulating system; by standing on all fours the are able to reduce their body temperature. At night, *Microlophus* retreats to its cosy nest, made of soil and leaves, in lava cracks.

Lizards are very territorial, but their aggressiveness is shown only to individuals of the same sex. In cases of conflict, males challenge each other by push-ups on their forelegs. They do not face each other, but sideways—displaying their spiny crest—and in opposite directions. They circle one another, sometimes biting each other on the mouth, spilling blood, but that is as far as it goes. Lava lizards have the ability of autotomy (the ability to cast off parts of the body), only once, but the tail will grow up again. This is a self-defense mechanism against predators.

Sexual maturity in the female is from nine months to one and a half years. For the male, it starts at three years. The mating season coincides with the hot season. The male mates with two or three females, after the garua season, in December. The female digs a shallow burrow, where she lays two to six eggs. The hatching will take place two to three months later. Lava lizards can live up to ten years.

Predators of the lava lizards are snakes, hawks, owls, herons and mockingbirds. Lava lizards are absent on Genovesa, Darwin and Wolf.

Marine Iguanas

genus: *Amblyrhynchus*
species: *cristatus*

An endemic genus with one species and seven subspecies. The age of the iguana could be nine million years or more if we consider the fact that it is older than the islands existing today. It is descended from a land iguana from the South American mainland. It most probably reached the Galápagos via vegetation rafts that were drifting on the surface of the ocean. Consequently, it had to adapt to a strictly vegetarian seafood diet.

The only marine iguana in the world, the Galápagos species is found along shore on lava rocks. These creatures of another era gather in herds of a fantastic aspect, individuals packed one on top of another. The length, including the tail, ranges from 60 centimetres for the smallest variety (Genovesa Island) to one metre for the largest (Isabela Island). The tail is half the size of the body. A spiny crest runs along the back, from the top of the head to the tip of the tail (see photo, page 81).

The sooty-black skin—a mimetism with the black lava substrate—is a camouflage against predators and enables the iguana to absorb more heat during its exposure to the sun. Very lazy, even ugly to some people, the marine iguana spends most of its time warming up on the rocks. Flat in the morning, the body, with a prominent abdomen, changes orientation towards the sun as the day progresses. When it is too hot, the iguana raises the front of the body above the ground and allows the breeze to circulate under the stomach.

Like many reptiles, the marine iguana is poikilothermic; ie it may adapt to great temperature variations. It is also ectothermic, ie directly influenced by external heat (mammals, by contrast, are endothermic). Despite an optimal ambient temperature of 35–37° C, these cold-blooded reptiles may have an extreme body temperature 40° C at the hottest hour of the day, helping out in the digestive process, but at night its temperature drops to 24° C.

The iguana feeds on 'Ulva', a chlorophyllian alga, and sometimes on the faeces of sea lions or of its own species. Marine iguanas may also eat the leaves of the *Sesuvium* plant when in need. More surprisingly, as a renowned vegetarian, it has been recently filmed catching a live octopus (Stevie Divine, December 2004) in Puerto Ayora, proving that these reptiles can live on fresh seafood. It may easily dive to a depth of 20 metres (over 60 feet) to look for food on the rocks, and spend as much as one hour under water at a time. The compressed tail is well adapted to swimming, above or under water, and while doing so the legs have no use and stick to the sides of the body. The iguana tends to feed at low tide, when the ulva algae are exposed. They frequently eject a salt excess through the nostrils. The spray is thrown 50 centimetres, and may be used to warn off potential predators.

Extremely territorial, iguanas use their tongue and their olfactory sense to recognize their territory. They are sexually mature at around six to eight years, and have a life expectancy of 25 to 30 years. The mating season spreads over November and December, eggs are laid in February and March and will hatch in May or June. Females lay once every two years.

During the mating season, males—always larger than females—take on a red coloration (especially on Española, the southernmost island of the archipelago) and a green color appears along the back, on the forelegs and hind legs. Males become very aggressive, and defend territories of one to two square metres. After mating, females are in competition to find the right nesting area. Sometimes a female waits for another one to finish a nest, then will try to take it over by force. Head to head fights are spectacular, and the strongest wins. On South Plaza Island, eggs are laid between early February and the end of March; two or three eggs will be left in a burrow of volcanic soil. On Española Island, where soil is scarce, iguanas dig their burrow under the pebbles of the beach. (The operation may be tragic at times, when a rock collapses over the animal and it dies in the nest). After covering the nest with soil, the female will guard it for ten days.

Eggs have a thin white shell, and weigh from 80 to 100 grams. The gestation lasts about three months (between 84 and 91 days). Predators of the marine iguanas are hawks, herons, snakes and feral dogs.

During the disastrous Niño year 1982-83, the green ulva algae disappeared, leaving only a toxic brown alga. This increased the mortality rate of the marine iguanas to 60 per cent. The population is estimated today at about 200,000 to 300,000 individuals (Eibl-Eibesfeldt).

Land Iguanas

genus: *Conolophus*
species: *subcristatus* or *pallidus*

This endemic genus has officially two species, but may have one more if one considers the possibility of an endemic species on Fernandina Island.

Yellow-orange to brown, the land iguana differs from the green iguana, *Iguana iguana,* of South America and the Caribbean, ancestor of the Galápagos iguanas, by a lack of fear towards man. In the Galápagos, two species of land iguanas have been identified:

- *Conolophus subcristatus*: on Santa Cruz, Plaza, Isabela and Fernandina (yellow-orange in color). Extinct on Santiago Island (see photos, page 85).

- *Conolophus pallidus*: on Santa Fé (whitish to chocolate brown). This is the biggest land iguana; the male weighs six to seven kilograms, the female three kilograms. The eyes are often red, as if injected with blood (see photos, page 87).

Land iguanas do not have a square nose like marine iguanas but a pointed one. Their length is about 1–1.2 metres. *Conolophus* feeds on grass, centipedes and annual plants in season, but its favorite food consists of the pads of the opuntia cactus: especially the fruits and the yellow flowers, during the hot season. On Fernandina Island, at an elevation of 330 metres, 90 per cent of the food of the iguana is composed of the fruits and flowers of the creeping vine *Ipomea alba* (morning glory). Sometimes land iguanas feed on sea lion's afterbirth, grasshoppers or even dead birds. On Santa Fé island, a Galápagos mockingbird was seen landing on a land iguana's head, picking ticks from around the eyes and mouth and cleaning it, while the iguana raised itself on all fours (November 2008).

Males have an impressive dorsal crest, more conspicuous than the female's, and are larger. Their body temperature ranges from 32.2° C (dry season) to 36° C (wet season). Females are sexually mature at 6 to 10 years. Land iguanas may reach 60 to 70 years old.

Land iguanas form small colonies. They keep to the driest part of the islands and dig burrows in the soil, sometimes under rocks (25 centimetres deep, 15 centimetres long). During the mating season males are territorial, and protect areas of 10 to 20 metres in diameter. Females choose the males. A male may have up to seven females. Each of the females comes back to the same nesting area. After a pair begins courtship the female stays in or around her mate's burrow while he keeps intruders away. After copulation, the female leaves the male for the nesting area, and digs several false nests before laying eggs in the right burrow—females fight over nesting sites. When ready to lay her eggs the female backs into the nest, partially sealing herself into it, and stays there for 24 hours. Thinner after emerging, she leaves the burrow and closes it; for the next week she will defend the nest.

On Fernandina Island, the females nest inside the caldera, near the fumaroles. From the coast, the round-trip takes 32 days. Egg laying peaks during the first two weeks of July. Nests are one to two metres deep. The ground temperature is 32 to 34° C. Clutches consist of 7 to 23 eggs, of a size smaller than those of the marine iguanas (50 grams).

Egg laying occurs during the hot season on Isabela and Plaza islands, and during the dry season on Fernandina, Santa Cruz and Santa Fé. Gestation lasts for three to four months, and the number of eggs ranges from 6 to 20, soft shelled.

Predators of the eggs are beetles; hawks, herons and snakes prey on hatchlings. The survival rate of a young land iguana in the wild is less than ten per cent.

Egg-laying of the Land Iguanas in the Galápagos

	Mating	Hatchings	Clutch	No. of eggs (average)
Isabela	January	May-June	10 to 25	14
Fernandina	June/July	Oct/Nov	8 to 22	10
Santa Cruz	September	January	5 to 17	12
Plaza	Jan/March	May/July	1 to 9	6
Santa Fé	Oct/Nov	Feb/March	7 to 10	8

On South Plaza Island, where marine iguanas are also present, Heidi and Howard Snell think that marine and land iguanas did at one time interbreed, producing hybrid offspring: 'Weirdo' in 1980 and 'Zebra' in 1985. On that particular island, it was common to see land iguanas climbing on shrubs and relaxing on the branches. The last hybrid iguana died of hunger in August 1993.

A symbiotic relationship exists between the small ground finch and land iguanas, in which the birds eat ticks off the iguanas. When the finch comes, the iguana stands on all fours, allowing the bird free access as it hunts for the pests.

Since 1976, and following the attack of wild dogs on the land iguana colonies of Conway Bay (Santa Cruz) and Cartago Bay (Isabela), the Galápagos National Park and the Charles Darwin Research Station have started a programme to protect and conserve the species. Eggs were brought to Puerto Ayora to be incubated, and young to be bred in captivity. Since 1980, more than 250 young iguanas have been returned to Cartago Bay (SPNG, 1988). The repatriation on Conway Bay started in 1987.

In 1991 and 1992, 50 land iguanas were reintroduced onto Baltra Island by the SPNG, after a 40-year absence. The initial source came from North Seymour, through the reproduction centre of the Darwin Station. In January 2009, a new species of land iguana, known as 'Rosada', was identified by scientists (Gentile et. al.) on the slopes of Wolf volcano on Isabela island. It had been seen earlier in 1986, but wasn't then recognized as being unique.

Marine Turtles

family: Chelonidae
genus: *Chelonia*
species: *agassizi*

There may be eight species of marine turtles in the world, but only four species have been seen in the Galápagos (see drawings, page 101).

- *Dermochelys coriacea*	Leatherback
- *Lepidochelys olivacea*	Olive ridley
- *Eretmochelys imbricata*	Hawksbill
- *Chelonia mydas*	Green turtle

The last-named is the only turtle common on the islands. It is a distinct dark form, known as the 'black turtle', *Chelonia mydas agassizi*, found in the eastern Pacific region from Baja California to the Galápagos. In the view of some specialists, it is a separate species. (See *National Geographic*, February 1994).

The Black Turtle

This turtle feeds on ulva, the chlorophyll alga, on the roots of mangroves, as well as on the leaves of the red mangrove. Males are smaller than the females, with a concave plastron, claws on the bend of the front flippers (to grasp the carapace of the female) and a long tail. The concave plastron facilitates copulation. Females have a convex plastron (see photo, page 91). Sexual maturity is reached at 20 to 25 years. The mating season starts with the hot season, and the peak reproduction and egg laying occur in December–January. Group mating is easily seen in the lagoon of Tortuga Negra (north of Santa Cruz) in November.

Egg laying takes place generally between January and June, but may occur all year-round. The female comes out of the water after dark, and starts digging on the beach (high on the dune) with her hind flippers. After about 20 minutes of digging, she lays 80 to 120 eggs about the size of ping-pong balls at the bottom of the nest. The hardest part is still to come, for she has to work another 30 to 60 minutes covering the nest with sand. Turtle tracks may be observed on the beach the following morning, if the tide has not erased them during the night.

Gestation lasts for about two months (55 days). The hatchlings have a soft black shell, five centimetres long; the carapace (shell) of the adult is 84 centimetres long, but this measurement will decrease over the years. The temperature of incubation influences the sex of the individual. If it is over 30° C, the egg produces a female; below that temperature, the tendency is towards males. The egg-laying frequency is every two to three years. The main predators of the marine turtles are sharks, orcas and crabs (which feed on hatchlings), and the beetle *Trox suberosus* (which preys on eggs). A few sea birds and shore birds such as herons, frigates and lava gulls also prey on the young as they are crossing the beach towards the sea. This is why the nest usually comes to life after dark, because as soon as the day breaks, the baby turtles are blinded by the sunlight and cannot find their way to the ocean. This is when they become an easy catch for predators.

Between 1975 and 1980, a special programme that marked 7,400 green turtles proved that migrations occur from Costa Rica, Panama, Colombia, Peru and Ecuador.

Giant Tortoise or 'Galápago'

family: Testudinidae
genus: *Geochelone*
species: *elephantopus*

Only two island groups in the world are inhabited by giant tortoises: Aldabra Island in the Seychelles, and the Galápagos Islands. Giant tortoises would have to have reached the Galápagos by floating from South America, which seems unbelievable. The most likely ancestor, *Geochelone chiliensis*, originally came from Argentina, but nothing explains its arrival in the archipelago, which remains a total mystery. No one knows what size these tortoises were in the beginning.

In the Galápagos, female tortoises can weigh up to 50 kilograms and males up to 250 kilograms (see photo, page 88). In the past, the population of tortoises was estimated at about 250,000 individuals; In 1980 only 15,000 remained. Before man reached the islands in the time of the pirates, the tortoises had no predators. For the past four centuries, man has been responsible for the destruction of these reptiles. Now the danger comes from other introduced species.

The scientific name of the giant tortoise is *Geochelone elephantopus*. Zoologists have numbered 14 races or subspecies, but only 11 survive today (in fact, the real figure is ten

Portrait of marine iguana (male), Floreana 2001

Colony of marine iguanas and crabs (zayapas), *Punta Espinosa, Fernandina 1990*

Marine iguanas in the ventilated position, Punta Espinosa 1989

Marine iguanas of Espanola 1989

Track of a marine iguana, James Bay 1988

Track of a marine iguana, Las Bachas 1990

Marine iguana of Espanola, Punta Suarez 1992

Galápagos snake coiling around lava lizard, Isabela 2005

Swimming marine iguanas, Punta Espinosa 1990

Land iguana on South Plaza

Land iguana (male), Urvina Bay, Isabela 1986

Iguana iguana, *green iguana of South America, Guayaquil 1989*

Land iguana (male), South Plaza 1993

Land iguana under Opuntia *cactus, South Plaza 2002*

Iguana eating a cactus pad, Plaza 1993

Land iguana, Santa Fé 1990

Mockingbird cleaning parasites off land iguana, Santa Fé

Land iguana on its way, Santa Fé 2002

Giant tortoise, Volcan Alcedo, Isabela 1985

Giant tortoise digging a burrow against the sun, Alcedo 1988

Giant tortoise, Urvina Bay, Isabela 1992

Giant tortoise on the rim of Alcedo volcano 1992

Giant tortoises in the rainy season, Alcedo 1991

Female giant tortoise on a volcano trail, Alcedo 1991

Giant tortoises, Alcedo 1991

Dome-shaped tortoise, Santa Cruz 1993

Saddle-shaped tortoise of Espanola, Darwin Station 1992

The black marine turtle, Chelonia agassizi, *Bartolomé 1993*

Black turtle after laying eggs, Floreana 1993

Marine turtle underwater, Gordon Rocks 1993

Galapagos penguins, Bartolomé 1990

Flightless cormorants in courtship display, Punta Espinosa, Fernandina 1992

Flightless cormorants, Fernandina 1986

Flightless cormorants, Punta Albemarle, Isabela 1986

Flightless cormorants, Punta Espinosa 1986

Swallowtail gull, South Plaza 1986

Lava gull, Tortuga Bay 1992

Swallowtail gulls mating, Genovesa 1990

Young swallowtail gull, Genovesa 1993

Albatrosses mating, Espanola 1989

Albatross, Punta Suarez, Espanola 1993

Young albatross, Espanola 1993

since Lonesome George, the only survivor of Pinta Island, now lives at Darwin Station in Puerta Ayora on Santa Cruz island. The $10,000 reward offered to whoever could provide a female of the same species brought no results, and George will remain an old bachelor. The giant tortoise is extinct on Fernandina, Floreana, Santa Fé. Contrary to what was once thought, there were never tortoises on Rábida.

In early 2009, a rumour was spread—probably by the Galápagos National Park's Department of Communication—that 12 unhatched eggs were found in Lonesome George's 'den' on Pinta Island. This is incorrect, and a joke aimed at boosting the Galápagos' image, as usual. In fact the eggs were found in the corral of Lonesome George, in Puerto Ayora (Santa Cruz Island) near the Darwin Station. The famous tortoise had finally agreed to mate with a submissive female of another species, after 10 years of unsuccessful trials. The eggs were brought to the incubator, but soon proved to be infertile and dead.

Isabela Island, with more than 6,500 individuals, remains the island with the largest giant tortoise population. More than 4,000 Galápagos live in the caldera of Alcedo volcano; 1,000 survive on Wolf volcano, 700 on Cerro Azul, 500 on Darwin, and 400 on Sierra Negra (see map of Isabela). On Santiago Island, the western population was destroyed, and the eastern population numbers 500. There is still a strong population in the east and south of San Cristóbal (despite competition from feral goats), and 250 individuals on Española (compared with 15 in 1960), saved from extinction by the SPNG.

Very independent animals, the giant tortoises live mostly on the summits of the islands. Three groups are distinguishable, based on the shape of the shell:

Saddleback Type (Española, Pinzón, Pinta and Fernandina)
The carapace is raised in the front, and the neck and legs are very long. By its morphology, this type of tortoise looks for food (cactus pads or leaves) high above the ground, extending its long neck forward like a periscope (see photo, page 90). It is found in the arid zone of the lowlands.

Dome-shaped Type (Santa Cruz, Isabela)
Heavier and more voluminous than the former type, this tortoise grazes grass directly on the ground. It is found on islands with rich vegetation, in the highlands, around the rim of the volcanoes and in the calderas (see photo, page 90).

Intermediate Type
This is a variation of the dome shape, including the other races (except those on Wolf volcano and Santa Fé).

Tortoises can survive in dry areas as they are able to conserve water and fat in their internal cavities. This ability was first noticed during their long survival on pirate boats. Nobody

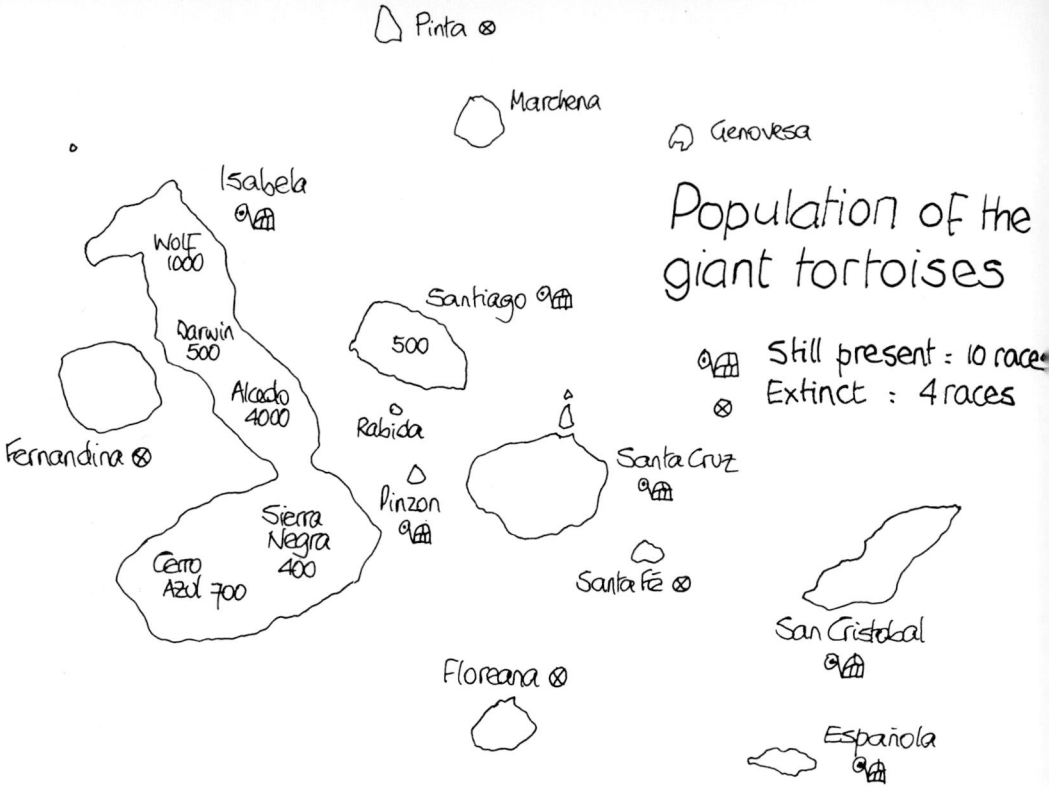

Identification marks on tortoises

here : n° 2054

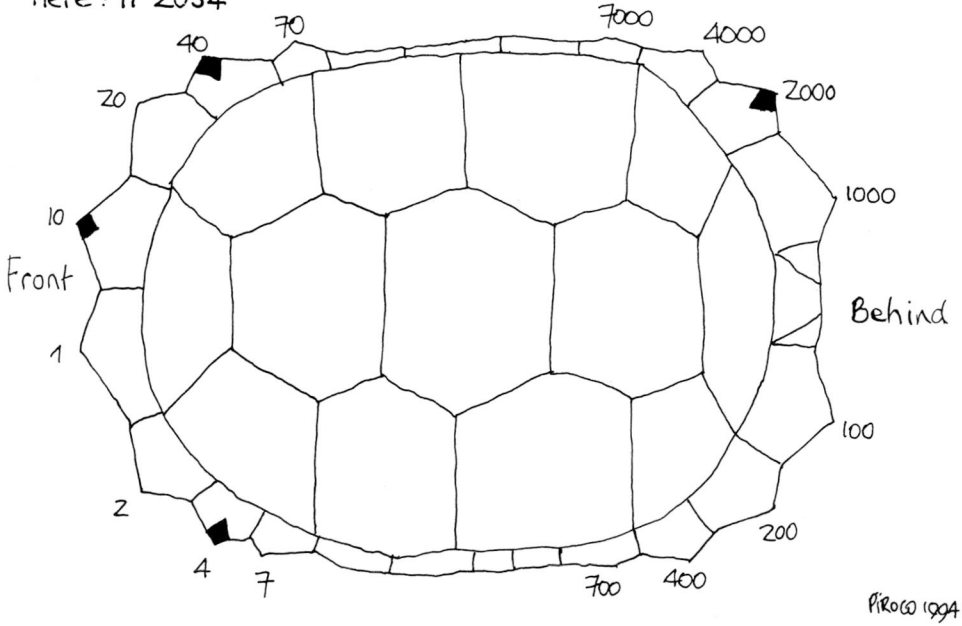

knows the maximum age of these land turtles. In the corral of the Darwin Station, the oldest individual may be as much as 170 years old (and would have known Darwin himself).

Tortoises have a peaceful life. Throughout the year, they eat great quantities of grass, leaves, lower parts of bushes, and the cactus pads of the opuntia. Most of the time they sleep in open spaces, or wade in mudponds during the wet season. At night, they hide under the shrubs. When threatened, their first reaction is to retract head and legs under the shell with a conspicuous hiss. If, by misfortune, one is rolled upon its back, it is difficult for it to get back on its legs. Then it becomes vulnerable.

The mating season coincides with the wet season. Males engage in mock fighting, then look for a female. Later on, between February and May, females start the long journey downhill to the coast, and will look for the right nesting area, in the arid zone, about 20 metres above sea level. Egg laying lasts from June to December. The female digs a nest 30 centimetres deep and 20 centimetres wide, which will be cemented by a lid made of urine and excrement. This jelly is then covered with sand. The construction of the nest takes eight to 12 hours of work on Española, and four to five hours on Santiago Island.

The gestation period lasts from three to eight months, depending on the location of the nest. If it is at low elevation, it will take 120 days; if the elevation is high, then the incubation period may take as long as 200 days. The number of eggs depends on the species: 12 to 15 eggs on Santa Cruz, four to five eggs on Española and Pinzón.

Observation and research carried out by Linda Cayot at the Darwin Station has shown that the temperature of incubation influences the sex of the giant tortoise. If the temperature is higher or equal to 28.5 or 29° C, embryos turn into females. Below that temperature, the eggs produce males. The hatch occurs between mid-January and March. The clutch is of three to eight eggs for the saddleback tortoises and up to 16 eggs for the dome-shaped tortoises. According to some scientists, the sexual maturity of the giant tortoise could be reached at 20 to 30 years.

Predators are numerous. The black rat (*Rattus rattus*), introduced by the pirates, preys on eggs after digging out the nests. Wild pigs do the same. Feral dogs attack small tortoises after hatching (south of Isabela), and dig up the nests (San Cristóbal). As for feral cats, they do not harm tortoises, except in the south of Isabela.

Various means have been adopted by the Galápagos National Park to protect the nests:

- against the rats on Pinzón Island: nothing much can be done but to destroy the rats themselves. This was done in 1989 by the SPNG.
- against feral pigs: by building a stone wall around the nest.
- the incubation of eggs and the breeding of young tortoises at the Darwin Station, which helps to develop the existing population.

Feral dogs are the 'plague' of the moment.

Programmes of protection, conservation and breeding of giant tortoises have begun at the Galápagos National Park and at the Darwin Station in 1960. At the time, 13 individuals (11 females and two males) from Española Island were the last survivors of a race doomed for extinction. By 1988, 200 saddleback tortoises had been reintroduced on Española, following the successful incubation programme.

Each year, park guards collect tortoise eggs on different islands. These are brought back and incubated at the Darwin Station, where the young will be raised for four years and then returned to their original island. Today, more than 1,000 tortoises have been reintroduced to various islands of the archipelago.

In July 1996 reports of nine dead and 11 sick tortoises were made at El Chato reserve in the highlands of Santa Cruz. Toxicological analysis led by Dr. Linda Cayot of the CDRS were negative, but coliform and anaerobic bacteria were found, as was fungus. The diet of the giant tortoise has been oriented towards the *maracuya*, or passion fruit. The likelihood of *maracuya* poisoning is under investigation, as is the possibility of pond infection by dead tortoises.

Marine Turtles

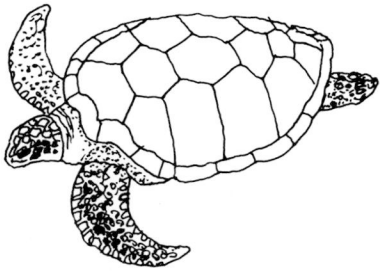

Black turtle
(Chelonia agassizi)

Hawksbill turtle
(Eretmochelys imbricata)

Leatherback turtle
(Dermochelys coriacea)

Olive midley
(Lepidochelys olivacea)

Pirosco 89

CHAPTER TWO

Sea Birds; Shore and Lagoon Birds

The bird life of the Galápagos is unique and diversified. In the beginning, migrating sea birds came from Ecuador, Peru, Colombia, and the Caribbean. Trade winds also helped introduce these migrants to the archipelago. Dependent not on the land but on the sea, sea birds were probably the first animals to colonize the islands. Half of the resident population of birds is endemic to the archipelago, but only five species of sea birds (of 19) are unique to the Galápagos: the Galápagos penguin, the flightless cormorant, the lava gull, the swallowtail gull and the Galápagos waved albatross. Therefore, 25 per cent of the sea birds are endemic to the islands.

Galápagos Penguin

Spheniscus mendiculus

Endemic. Belongs to the order Sphenisciformes, birds that cannot fly, and in which the wings evolved for use as fins (see photo, page 92).

The Galápagos penguin is related to the Magellan penguin, *Spheniscus magellanicus,* an ancestor thought to be found in southern Chile. It is also related to the penguin of the Falkland Islands and islands near Antarctica. This penguin came to the Galápagos by means of the Humboldt Current. In the islands, its population was 13,000 before the 1982–83 Niño, concentrated around Bartolomé, Rábida, Sombrero Chino, Floreana, the west coast of Isabela and the Bolivar Channel, as well as on the coast of Fernandina, the westernmost island.

The Galápagos penguin swims with its front fins, and its feet help in steering. Swimming slowly at the surface, it moves very fast underwater and sometimes leaps above the water happily; in dolphins, this behavior is known as 'porpoising'. On land the Galápagos penguin walks, hops from rock to rock, and goes 'tobogganing'. Before jumping, it stretches its neck forward as if studying the terrain.

Head and beak movements can be an appeasement response to threatening behavior. They are also a way of greeting without triggering aggression. Crossing beaks is done for the same purpose. During the mating season, Galápagos penguins preen one another's heads, and also slap themselves gently with the front flippers.

Galápagos penguins are opportunistic reproducers. They nest in cavities, where two eggs will be laid three to four days apart. On Fernandina, egg laying occurs in September. Incubation lasts from 38 to 40 days. Very shy animals, penguins nest in groups. They sleep on land and look for food during the day, returning to the shore between 4 and 6:30 pm. In the early morning, they can be seen in the water between 5 and 7 am. They leave a wake behind them, just like ducks.

The disastrous 1982–83 Niño year caused a loss of 77 per cent of the population. By 1985, their number had been slowly recovering and was estimated at 2,000-3,000 individuals. Predators of the Galápagos penguin include red crabs, rice rats, Galápagos snakes, short-eared owls and Galápagos hawks. A survey in 2004, indicated a population of 1500 individuals.

In late 1996, two penguin nests were found on Isla Floreana. In May of the same year a 'Penguin Expedition' spent five weeks on the northwest coast of Floreana from Post Office Bay to Black Beach. A pair of penguins was found at the base of Cerro Daylight and a single adult was found at the islet of Piedra Dura. A second nest was found at Cerro Daylight the following August. A herd of six goats and a cat were also seen.

Flightless Cormorant

Nannopterum harrisi

Endemic. Belongs to the order of Pelicaniformes. It is a large dark bird with atrophied wings and a strong, long beak with a hooked end. Adults are black above, brown underneath, and have turquoise-blue eyes. The young are black all over, with dull eyes. Males are larger than females (see photo, page 93).

Cormorants are often seen above the tideline, with wings spread out to dry in the wind. This is an ancestral habit which is useless, since the bird cannot fly. A lack of predators has influenced its flightlessness.

Like a penguin, it swims underwater and uses its webbed feet. It feeds on fishes, eels and octopus. This sedentary bird emits a grunt and nests in small colonies on rocks or sheltered beaches. The mating season lasts from November to March, but may be throughout the year since the flightless cormorant is an opportunistic breeder. The male chooses the female. Between March and September, she lays two or three big white eggs in a nest of twigs, algae and marine grass. The incubation time is about 35 days.

Being endemic to the Galápagos, it is one of the rarest birds in the world. A survey carried out in 2004 indicated a population of 1500 individuals. It is found on the shore of Fernandina and on the west coast of Isabela, where the nutrient-rich Cromwell current from the central Pacific brings an abundance of fish.

The largest colonies of flightless cormorants are located at Cape Douglas (37 nests), Cape Hammond (28 nests) on Fernandina and at Cape Berkeley (30 nests) on the northwest of Isabela. Visitor sites are Punta Espinosa (Fernandina), Punta Moreno, Punta Garcia and Punta Albermarle (Isabela).

Lava Gull

Larus fuliginosus

Endemic. Belongs to the order Charadriiformes and to the family Laridae (see photo, page 94). The population of this bird was once estimated at 400 pairs, but it is found everywhere in the Galápagos. Adults are sooty grey with a white ring around the eyes. Feet and beak are black. The lava gull has the funny habit of staring between its feet, head bent down. This submissive attitude means 'good intentions' to the protagonist. It also has a loud shriek that can be mistaken for a human laugh.

Frequently encountered in ports, the lava gull feeds on crabs and small marine iguanas, but mainly on dead fish and waste like sea lions' afterbirth. It is a scavenger. Solitary, it nests in rocky overhangs and at the bottom of cliffs near the waterfront. Two olive-green eggs speckled with brown are laid in a nest of twigs. Adults are very protective of the nest, and will scare off any intruder (even bigger than themselves), using their feet to hit the aggressor.

Swallowtail Gull

Creagrus furcatus

Endemic. The only other gull present in the Galápagos. It is differentiated from the lava gull by a black and white spotted swallowtail and a red eyering. The body is pale grey on its back, ventrally white. The beak is black with a white tip, and the feet are red (see photo, page 94). The white marks at the base and tip of the beak help the chick in the nest to see the arrival of its parent at night. Consequently, to obtain food, it will just knock on the beak of the adult. Big black eyes are characteristic of the swallowtail gull, which feeds only at night. Its nocturnal vision is made possible by the red eyering which serves as a sort of sonar. It feeds offshore, looking for fish and squid. This night-feeding habit has developed in response to competition from other sea birds during the daytime, in particular the tropicbird, which feeds during the day on the same food.

The swallowtail gull nests in cliffs and lays only one egg—white speckled with brown—which is easily mistaken with the composition of the nest, which is made of pieces of white coral and black lava gravels. Prosperous couples mate once every nine or ten months.

Swallowtail gulls are often seen at dawn and at dusk when they go or come back from fishing. Their cry is unique and resembles a clanking whose possible function may be compared to echolocation.

In the Galápagos, other gulls may be seen occasionally migrating such as the Franklin's gull and the laughing gull (Genovesa, March 1995).

Waved Albatross

Diomedea irrorata

There are 13 species of albatross in the world. The albatross belongs to the order Procellariformes, which is recognized by the tube-nose on the top of the beak. This order comprises two families, which feed on plankton: the Diomedeidae (albatross) and the Procellaridae (petrels and puffins).

One of the most majestic birds in the archipelago, the waved albatross is endemic not only to the Galápagos, but also to the island of Española (Hood Island), for this is the only place in the world where it reproduces. This cousin of the petrels and the puffins, has a population of nearly 24,000 individuals. Weighing four kilograms, and with a wingspan of 2.5 metres, this is the largest bird in the Galápagos (see photo, page 96).

The back, wings and tail are light brown, contrasting with the whiteness of the head, neck and belly. Its big yellow beak looks like a tube, hooked at the end.

With sufficient wind, the albatross in flight is a tremendous glider, but in calm weather it has to move its wings harder than other birds. It feeds offshore, on fish, squid and other invertebrates, and may also steal from boobies occasionally. Nevertheless, its feeding habits are nocturnal, and its big black eyes are the proof of it. It feeds on the surface of the water.

The waved albatross is found in the Galápagos only during the dry season, on Española; it arrives around mid-April and leaves around mid-December. It returns to its island to reproduce after six months spent in the open sea of the Pacific Ocean, and as far as Japan. Every year, the ritual is repeated: males arrive first to reconnoitre the terrain and the nesting site; when the females arrive a few days or weeks later, one may see a kind of collective rape. Afterwards, serious matters start, and pairs are formed. Albatrosses are faithful to their mate for their whole life (see photo, page 95).

Generally, the courtship of the female by the male does not happen in the same year as nesting, but in two different seasons. The courtship display is remarkable. In their dance, albatrosses cross beaks as two fencers in a duel, then go for a 'sky-pointing display', with the beak opening and loudly snapping shut, and start the love fight again. This display is repeated over and over.

The mating occurs over a period of five days. The single egg, as large as a billiard ball, is laid between mid-April and mid-June. The whole colony reproduces at the same time. The eggs hatch between mid-June and mid-August, after an incubation of 63 days. Curiously, the waved albatross will roll its egg quite a distance between the rocks, pushing it with the beak, as if to give it exercise. Sometimes the egg breaks.

The albatross chick is a big, ugly, brown fluffy thing. It will take 167 days before it flies. The nesting site is abandoned between the end of November and mid-January.

The waved albatross of Española is sexually mature at the age of five or six years. Its lifespan may reach 30 to 40 years. Some albatrosses abandoned at Española have been found as far away as the shores of Japan. There was a massive abandonment of the nests during the Niño year 1982–83. The estimated population in 1994 was 15,000 pairs.

GALÁPAGOS SHEARWATER

Puffinus subalaris

Formerly known as the 'Audubon's Shearwater', it was discovered to be a new species in April 2005. Belongs to the order Procellariformes and to the family Procellaridae. The Galápagos subspecies is endemic. Dorsally dark brown, ventrally white, the Galápagos shearwater is originally from the Antilles, but it is also found in the Pacific and Indian oceans (see drawing, page 107). The Galápagos shearwater is easily mistaken with the Hawaiian petrel, which is larger and has a white patch on the forehead.

Active during the day, it feeds on plankton and crustaceans. It often fishes in group and flies low above the water. It may dive to a depth of two metres, and uses its wings to swim after small fish.

The Galápagos shearwater is an opportunistic breeder. On south Plaza Island, the reproduction cycle is nine months. One white egg is laid with an incubation time of 49 days. The juvenile may fly 75 days later. The population in the Galápagos is estimated at 10,000 pairs. Its predator is the short-eared owl.

HAWAIIAN PETREL

Pterodroma phaeopygia

Dorsally black, ventrally white (see drawing, page 107). Two subspecies are found in Hawaii and in the Galápagos respectively. This black bird with a white forehead and white underwings may be seen in the highlands of Santa Cruz, San Cristóbal, Floreana, Santiago and Isabela, where the vegetation is dense. The Hawaiian petrel nests on the ground, under rocks and in volcanic caves.

The reproduction season differs according to the island:

	Floreana	Santa Cruz	Santiago
Arrival:	end November	May	January
Egg laying:	end December/April	June/September	February/June
Hatch:	end February/June	August/November	April/August
Takeoff:	June/September	December/March	July/November

Sexual maturity is reached after eight years. The reproduction cycle is annual, and only one egg is laid. The incubation time is 51 days, and 120 days are necessary for the juvenile to take off. It feeds on fish and squid, offshore.

The predators of the Hawaiian petrel are rats and cats (which pilfer eggs and chicks), feral dogs and feral pigs. These are a major problem in the Galápagos National Park, which has led a campaign for protection and conservation of the species in Floreana since 1982. Its population has been estimated at between 10,000 and 50,000.

Hawaiian Petrel
Galápagos shearwater
Storm Petrels
Castro's storm petrel
Galápagos storm petrel
Elliot's storm petrel
MCCO 89

Storm Petrels

Belong to the Procellariformes, easily recognized by the tube nose. Three species are found in the Galápagos:

- Castro's storm petrel (*Oceanodroma castro*)
- Galápagos storm petrel (*Oceanodroma tethys*)
- Elliot's storm petrel (*Oceanites gracilis*)

Plankton feeders, these small black petrels skip across the surface of the water, fluttering about like butterflies. They are each differentiated by the white markings at the base of the tail (see drawing, page 107).

Castro's Storm Petrel

Oceanodroma castro

Subtropical Atlantic and Pacific distribution. Conspicuous white band on the tail. Nests in cliffs, among rocks and under ledges, on Plaza Island, Daphne Mayor, Guy Fawkes, Cowley's Island, Devil's Crown, Isla Pitt and Genovesa (Tower Island).

This pelagic bird feeds at night, as well as during the day, on small fish and squid. Castro's storm petrel is an annual breeder; two seasons are distinguished: eggs are laid between March and June, or December-January (Plazas). A single white egg is laid. The incubation time is about 42 days.

Its predator is the short-eared owl, mostly during the cold season.

Galápagos Storm Petrel

Oceanodroma tethys

Distinguished by the white cuneiform (wedge-shaped) mark at the base of the tail. Pelagic, its feeding habit is nocturnal, on the surface. Annual reproduction; one single egg is laid between May and June. The population of Galápagos storm petrels is about 200,000 pairs, nesting on Genovesa, Isla Pitt and Roca Redonda.

Elliot's Storm Petrel

Oceanites gracilis

Among all petrels, this is the most common. A white lens-shaped mark is conspicuous at the base of the tail. It feeds inshore. One single egg is laid between April and September.

The population of Elliot's storm petrels is several thousand pairs.

Brown Noddy

Anous stolidus

Also known as the noddy tern. The resident subspecies is endemic. Color is sooty grey to brown, with the top of the head white. The black eye is circled in white (see photo, page

113). The noddy builds its nest of twigs in the cliffs. It feeds on the surface of the water, inshore. It may enter the water, but generally hovers low above fish schools. It often associated with Audubon shearwater and brown pelicans; by sitting on the heads of these larger birds it can wait for the small fish they catch.

Known as the 'noddy' because of its courtship display, nodding its head in front of the mate, it is an opportunistic breeder. The noddy tern nests in caves and rocky overhangs. One single egg is laid.

The following terns are present but rare: The royal tern, *Sterna maxima,* is white with the top of the head black and an orange beak. The sooty tern, *Sterna fuscata,* nests only on Darwin Island in the north of the archipelago.

Great Frigatebird

Fregata minor

Belongs to the order of Pelicaniformes, which are recognized by reduced or absent external nasal slits.

Frigates, or 'vultures of the sea', are specially designed for life aloft. Their wingspan is as big as that of the albatross. This bird, having lost the waterproofing of its black plumage, never lands on the sea. The uropygial gland, which normally oils the feathers, is atrophied and useless.

Frigates spend time gliding in circles in the sky. When in pursuit of other birds—especially boobies, for example, which they frequently harass for food—they may be very fast. This is called 'cleptoparasitism'. Frigates may also catch small fish on the surface of the water with the mere swipe of the hooked beak.

Males are black with a greenish sheen. Wings are long and pointed, and the tail is scissorlike. During the courtship display, the male inflates a huge leathery red pouch under his throat. This seduces and attracts the female to the nest, which the male has already prepared for the purpose of mating. This amazing ritual may be observed in March and April on Frigatebird Hill (San Cristóbal) or on Genovesa Island (Darwin Bay), or throughout the year on North Seymour Island.

Females also have black plumage, but the throat and breast are white (see photos, pages 114 and 115). The eye-ring is conspicuously red on the female, while the male's is bluish green. Frigate chicks are all white at first, then the head and neck turn hazelnut in color.

The reproduction cycle of the frigate is one and a half to three times longer than that of any other member of the order Pelicaniformes. Ten to 20 days of courtship display are necessary before mating. Frigatebirds reproduce in colony. One single egg is laid in a nest of twigs, always in a tree or a bush. The annual reproduction differs on various islands. Eggs are laid between February and August on Genovesa Island, between April and November on Española Island. The incubation time is 55 days. Maturity takes 130 to 160 days (even 180 days sometimes), before the juvenile can fly. The slow growth of the young, and its ability to fast, are remarkable adaptations to the irregularity of the food supply. The great frigate is therefore a 'tropical breeder', which means that it has a long reproduction cycle. Apparently the frigate reproduces every two years. It always returns to the same nesting site and does not show any sign of territorial aggressivity to other birds of the same species.

The great frigate is an 'offshore feeder', foraging far away from the coast and from the islands, thus avoiding competition with the magnificent frigate, which is an 'inshore feeder' feeding closer to the islands. The great frigate feeds on fish caught on the surface, and also 'hijacks' other sea birds (such as boobies), catching them by the tail and forcing them to regurgitate food in the air. Frigates also prey on turtle eggs and recently hatched young.

Great frigatebirds are found throughout the archipelago on the periphery of the islands. Main colonies are located on Genovesa, Darwin, Wolf, Española, Floreana (Gardner), Tortuga Island, Isla and Punta Pitt. The great frigate is pantropical.

Magnificent Frigate

Fregata magnificens

Very similar to the great frigate, but the male has a purple sheen on its black plumage, and the female has a black triangle on the white patch of the throat. The eyering is bluish green on both sexes. Unlike the great frigate, the magnificent frigate is an 'inshore feeder', and feeds near the islands. On North Seymour, where it is easily seen, courtship displays are observed throughout the year. It is also a 'tropical breeder', with long reproduction cycles. Only one egg is laid, with an incubation time of 55 days.

The magnificent frigate nests on the salt bush, *Cryptocarpus pyriformis* (North Seymour) or in the palo santos (San Cristóbal). The main colonies are found on Seymour, Darwin, Wolf, Isabela (Punta Moreno), San Cristóbal (Wreck Bay) and Genovesa.

Magnificent frigates are also found in the Caribbean, on the west coast of Central America and in the north of South America.

Tropicbird

Phaethon aethereus

Belongs to the order Pelicaniformes and to the family Phaethontidae, which comprises one genus and three species: the red-billed (the species here), the red-tailed, and the white-tailed tropicbird. All three are pantropical (but the red-tailed does not breed in the Atlantic).

This beautiful white bird with short wings has two long and narrow feathers extending from the tail. A black line runs through the eyes, and the bill is coral red in adults. The juvenile lacks the two tail feathers. Its food being pelagic, the tropicbird is an 'offshore feeder'. It feeds on fish and squid by plunge-diving during the daytime.

The tropicbird reproduces in colonies, and lays only one red-brown, spotted egg in a crack of a cliff or between rocks (see photos, page 116). There is a noticeable difference between reproduction cycles of the tropicbirds on South Plaza, Genovesa and Daphné Island:

South Plaza:	annual reproduction, three eggs are laid between August and February
Genovesa:	eggs laid between July and November
Champion, Onslow, Enderby:	egg laying between August and December (islets of Floreana)
Daphné:	eggs are laid any time of the year. Severe intraspecific competition for the nesting sites. Opportunistic breeders, incubation time: 42 days.

Even though three eggs may be laid, only one usually develops into maturity. Chicks are fed until their first flight. They receive fish of an average size (20 centimetres) and squid.

Colonies of tropicbirds are found on Plaza, Seymour, Daphné, Rábida, Sombrero Chino, Tortuga and Floreana (Champion, Enderby, Caldwell, Gardner, Onslow). This bird does not like cold waters, and is therefore rare on Fernandina and Isabela.

Brown Pelican

Pelecanus occidentalis

One of the largest birds in the archipelago. Adults are grey-brown with the top of the head white. The nape is reddish hazelnut during the mating season. Young do not have these colors and are brown overall. Feet are webbed and grey-black. The beak is very long and hooked at the tip. The lower jaw has a large pouch, which inflates with water after plunge-diving.

The pelican fishes along the shore. It will take in a few liters of saltwater, which is ejected later through holes in the beak, before it swallows its fish (see photo, page 117).

In flight, the pelican gives a few strokes of its wings, then glides for a long time. It often flies in formation with other pelicans.

This opportunistic breeder nests in the mangroves, or on the salt bushes. The reproduction cycle of nine months occurs during the hot season. Two or three chalk-white eggs are laid on a platform of twigs. A few juveniles die young after they learned how to fly, usually when they have not mastered the fishing technique.

The brown pelican nests on all central islands, but more easily on Marchena and Española.

BOOBIES

Sula

Boobies are very common in the islands. Three species are seen in the Galápagos: the blue-footed, the red-footed and the Nazca booby (formerly masked booby, see page 130). All have an aerodynamic body and a long, pointed bill.

All three live in colonies, but with various habitats. The name 'booby' may derive from the fact that—once they have seen fish while flying—they drop on it like arrows from a height of fifteen metres. Unfortunately, they react in the same way towards fishing lures, plunge- diving on the surface of the ocean behind the boat.

Boobies belong to the family Sulidae, and the order Pelicaniformes (pelicans, frigates, cormorants, tropicbirds). All have webbed feet. The family Sulidae is divided into two groups:

- the genus *Morus* ..... three gannets
- the genus *Sula* ..... six boobies

The six boobies belong to the genus *Sula*. Three of these are common to the Galápagos. The three others are the Peruvian booby (creator of guano), the brown booby (pantropical) and the Abbott's booby (found on Christmas Island, near Java in Indonesia).

Blue-footed boobies are found north to the Gulf of California and south to the coastal islands of northern Peru. The two other boobies of the Galápagos are pantropical. Great concentrations of Sula exist in the regions of cold waters, which are rich in nutrients and organisms. The Humboldt current supports the booby colonies of the archipelago.

Well adapted to extensive flight when looking for food, boobies have the ability to plunge-dive and move underwater, when fishing.

Boobies incubate their eggs with their webbed feet and not with an abdominal pouch.

RED-FOOTED BOOBY

Sula sula

This is the lightest booby, with a weight of about one kiogram. Colour is light brown, with a bluish beak. There is also a white variety, called the 'morpho blanco'. The red feet are adapted to gripping branches; thus it is the only booby to nest in trees (eg palo santos or in the bushes) (see photos, pages 118 and 119). The reproduction season depends on the availability of food . The chicks may easily die of hunger during the first weeks of their life. Despite the high mortality rate, only one egg is laid. The time necessary to breed young does not allow an annual cycle of reproduction. Consequently, a period of 14 months elapses before the red-footed booby nests again.

The largest colony of red-footed boobies is on Genovesa Island. The population of the archipelago is 250,000. The red-footed boobies are the largest community of boobies in the Galápagos.

Noddy terns, Punta Vicente Roca 1992

Great frigate (male), San Cristóbal 1981

Pair of great frigates, Genovesa 1990

Female great frigate and chick, Genovesa 1992

Young great frigate, Genovesa 1993

Young great frigates in flight 1988

Colony of great frigates in the salt bushes, Genovesa 1993

Tropicbird, Punta Suarez, Espanola 1984

Tropicbird in flight, Espanola 1984

Brown pelican (adult), Puerto Ayora 1984

Pelican and young, Punta Moreno, Isabela 1988

Pelican nesting, Rabida 1989

Pelican feeding its young, Rabida 1990

Red-footed booby, Genovesa Island 2008

Red-footed booby, Morpho blanco variety, Genovesa 1990

Red-footed boobies (young), Genovesa 1990

Blue-footed boobies, Espanola 1980

Blue-footed booby (young), Espanola 1985

Nest of excreta of the blue-footed booby Punta Pitt 1993

Courtship display of the blue-footed boobies, Espanola 1984

Blue-footed booby and chicks, Espanola 1993

Nazca booby, Espanola 1992

Pair of Nazca boobies, Daphné 1993

Nazca booby, Espanola 1981

Ventilation posture of a booby, Daphné 1992

Great blue heron, Floreana 1990

Lava heron (juvenile), Bartolomé 1990

Yellow crowned night heron, Genovesa 1993

Cattle egret, Santa Fé 1990

Common egret, Urvina Bay 1992

Oystercatcher with eggs, Fernandina 2001

Flamingo, Punta Cormorant, Floreana 1992

Young flamingoes, Floreana 1992

Young flamingo, Floreana 1992

Common stilt, Santa Cruz 1991

Bahama pintail, Hotel Galapagos 1991

Whimbrel, Puerto Egas, Santiago Island

Ruddy turnstone, Fernandina 1992

Sanderlings, Seymour 1992

Ruddy turnstones feeding on a sea lion's afterbirth, Seymour 1993

Blue-footed Booby

Sula nebouxii

This is the most common booby. The Galápagos subspecies is endemic. Its lifespan is about 15 to 20 years. Unlike its red-footed relative, the blue-footed booby fishes inshore. It nests on the coast. The nesting site, on the ground, is marked by sprays of ejecta which draw a radiant white sun on the volcanic sand. Food is usually abundant, and allows two or sometimes three eggs to be laid.

The male is lighter than the female (1.28 kilograms and 1.80 kilograms respectively) and plunge-dives more easily than the female. It is recognized by the black pinpoint pupil of the eye, while the dark iris coloration of the female gives the impression that her pupil is larger. The male whistles, and the female honks (see photo, page 120).

During the mating season, the booby dances with its turquoise-blue feet, spreads out its wings, bring its tail up, point its bill to the sky and whistles loudly. This ceremony is known as 'sky pointing display'. Meanwhile, the female moves about, retracts her beak towards the body, and seems to respond 'no, no'. Sometimes a jealous pretender intrudes on the pair's courtship, trying its luck with the female. But conflict soon erupts, and very noisy beak fighting follows.

The second egg hatches five to seven days after the first, which puts the younger of the two chicks at a great disadvantage. If food is sufficient, the two chicks will be bred together. Otherwise, the stronger firstborn will survive and will kick its sibling out of the nest. Exposed to the fierce equatorial sun, or to the marauding frigates, the abandoned chick will die quickly.

The sexual dimorphism of the blue-footed boobies allows a partial division of activities. The small size and long tail of the male favour its mobility underwater. Consequently, it will be the one fishing while the female sits on the nest. In any case, a parent will always remain with the nest. The feet of the boobies are well irrigated with blood, and their thermo-regulating function insures perfect incubation.

An opportunistic breeder, the blue-footed booby avoids nesting in the hot season, between December and April. It prefers the cold season between May and December, for it needs dry and clear ground which is not covered with vegetation. Once the egg hatches, after one and a half months of incubation, the parent will stay with the chick until it is able to fly, giving it shade and protection. Finally, the juvenile must learn to plunge-dive and to fish. This takes 50 days for the blue-footed booby, and three months for the red-footed booby.

Since their food is abundant, blue-footed boobies may have more than one clutch a year. Nine months' time will be necessary, for the limiting factor is the moult.

The light weight of these birds allows them to build a nest inside a crater (eg Daphné Mayor), from where they may take off easily. Of the three boobies, the blue-footed is the only one to do this.

The population of the blue-footed boobies has been estimated at 10,000, but it may be much more. Large colonies are found on Española (Punta Suarez), Daphné, Tagus Cove and Punta Vicente Roca (west coast of Isabela), Cape Douglas (Fernandina).

Nazca Booby

Sula granti

Formerly known as the masked booby but discovered to be a new species in 2001. Heaviest of the three boobies, males weigh 1.63 kilograms, while females are larger at 1.88 kilograms. The plumage is white, wings are fringed with black, and the beak is orange yellow. The conspicuous black mask on the eyes makes it easy to recognize (see photo, page 122).

Like the blue-footed booby, the white or Nazca booby nests directly on the ground and surrounds its nest with waste. It chooses the site on clifftops, where the air streams allow it to take off easily. The fishing zone is intermediate between those of the other booby species, ie between islands. This adaptation to the environment illustrates the idea of the 'ecological niche'.

In Nazca boobies, sexual dimorphism is slight. Two eggs are laid five days apart. The incubation time is 43 days, but the clutch is quickly reduced to one chick following an unavoidable fratricide. Food sources are not as abundant as they are for the blue-footed boobies.

The season for reproduction is stable. On Genovesa Island, the Nazca booby mates from September to November, on Española Island, from November to February.

The population of Nazca boobies is about 25,000. The largest colonies are found at Punta Suarez (Española Island), where the nests are on the southern cliffs, at Darwin Bay (Genovesa Island), as well as on Wolf and Darwin Island in the north of the archipelago, where they are preyed upon by the sharpbill ground finch, also known as the "vampire finch". This species of finch, originally interested in the parasitic horsefly found in between the feathers around the neck of the boobies, ended up drawing blood and apparently got addicted to it.

Shore Birds and Lagoon Birds

Great Blue Heron

Ardea herodias

Greyish blue, with a lighter head and neck, this tall wader nests in the mangrove. Frequently seen at Puerto Ayora (Santa Cruz Island), and around the kitchen of the Hotel Galápagos (an old one with a broken wing). They can be observed at Tortuga bay, strolling down the beach at low tide and looking for small fish. Preys on baby turtles as well (see photo, page 123).

Lava Heron

Butorides sundevalli

Small grey-black heron, with yellow or red feet, which stalks on the shore and around tide pools. Young may be lighter, with a striated back and yellow legs. On the rocks near the waterline, lava herons look for crabs and small fish, and stand still for long spells, with an amazing stare (see photo, page 123).

Night Heron

Nyctanassa violacea

Of intermediate size between the two former species, this heron is streaked grey-brown. It has a black head with yellow and white feathers. Two thin white feathers run behind its head from the top of the skull. This nocturnal wader is found at night under the street lamps of Puerto Ayora (Santa Cruz Island), and can also be frequently seen during the daytime at the entrance of caves or under rock ledges overlooking tide pools, as in Darwin Bay (Genovesa Island) or Puerto Egas (Santiago Island) (see photo, page 124).

Cattle Egret

Bubulcus ibis

A little white heron, very majestic in flight, with black legs (juveniles) or yellow legs (adults). It is found on the shore at low tide, or even in the arid zone, where it catches lizards and grasshoppers. The nest is made in the mangrove.

It is found in the highlands of Santa Cruz, where it is seen in the company of cows. It also comes near sea lions in search of flies, which is not always to the liking of these mammals! (See photo, page 124).

Common or Great Egret

Casmerodius albus

A great white heron with a yellow bill and black legs. It concentrates in the central islands, on the coast, and nests in the mangroves, laying two eggs. The common egret feeds on fish, lizards, grasshoppers and other insects (see photo, page 124).

Oystercatcher

Haematopus ostralegus

A brown bird with a white belly, a black head and a red eyering. The bill is long, pencil-like, orange or red. The oystercatcher is the same size as the lava heron. It is found on the littoral (Punta Suarez, Española, Puerto Egas, Santiago Island), but is not common, due to the lack of proper habitat. Feeds on abalone, conical shaped shells fixed on the rocks of the intertidal zone, as well as on pencil sea urchins (see photo, page 125).

Shore and lagoon birds (1)

Shore and lagoon birds (2)

Northern phalarope

Ruddy turnstone

Common gallinule

Purple gallinule

Pirdo 89

Flamingo

Phoenicopterus ruber

Rare in the Galápagos, it is found in seven saltwater lagoons, behind the mangroves of the littoral. Flamingos may only reside in places where the water is not too deep for wading (less than one metre).

Swinging its neck right and left, it searches for food in the silt, thanks to a sonar in the bill which enables it to detect organisms. These are mainly a small pink shrimp (*Artemia salina*), the water-boatmen (*Trichocorixia reticulata*), larvae of coleoptera and diptera, organisms belonging to the ostracidae family and algae. Flamingos feed for seven to 12 hours a day. The tongue sucks the sediment and salt water; everything is filtered through sievelike plates inside the beak, then pumped out of the sides.

Mud nests, like small towers, are erected on the border of the lagoon. These are sometimes destroyed by floods or by wild pigs.

The flamingo reproduces at the age of five to six years, and mates every three to four years. A single egg is laid with an incubation time of 28 days. Only about 50 per cent of the hatchlings will survive. Of this number, 73 per cent will reach adulthood. Chicks are fluffy white, with big black legs. At the age of two months, they know how to filter food. At four months they become adults. Juveniles are preyed upon by hawks, suffer during floods or get lost. A mortality rate of 20 per cent occurs during the first year.

Flamingos have a lifespan of 18 to 24 years. Easily disturbed, they take flight if approached noisily. Common stilts, usually present in the area, always warn flamingos of any potential danger.

The population in the archipelago is estimated at 400 to 600. Flamingos may be observed at Espumilla Beach (Santiago Island), Rocas Bainbridge, and lagoons of Villamil (Isabela Island), Punta Cormorant (Floreana Island) and Rábida Island (see photo, page 125).

Common Stilt

Himantopus himantopus

Another bird of brackish lagoons, which feeds on small animals caught in the silt with its long thin black bill. The common stilt is a slender bird, black dorsally, white ventrally and up to the underparts of neck and head. Legs are long and red. Common stilts share the lagoon with flamingos and white-cheeked pintail ducks (see photo, page 126).

Bahama White-cheeked Pintail

Anas bahamensis

Also known as the Bahama duck. This brown duck has white cheeks and a red mark at the base of the beak. It is the only duck to reproduce in the Galápagos. Blown to the islands by the northeast trade winds, this species originated in the Caribbean and is now found in freshwater pools and brackish lagoons (see photo, page 126).

WHIMBREL

Numenius phaeopus

This shoreline wader is distinguished by its long curved bill. Brown with white spots, it has a dark streak on the eye and other bands on the top of the head. Found on rocks and on beaches at the border of retreating waves. A very shy bird and easily frightened, it takes off with a conspicuous repetitive shriek (see photo, page 127).

WANDERING TATTLER

Heteroscelus incanus

A slate-grey bird with white eyebrows. Ventrally white or speckled, a long thin black bill, and long yellow legs. Usually found on the rocks of the shore at low tide (see drawing, page 132).

SEMI-PALMATED PLOVER

Charadrius semipalmatus

A small bird of the littoral. The back and top of head are brown. Ventrally white, with orange legs. A conspicuous black ring is noticeable around the neck. The bill is short and black, with an orange base. Walks quickly on the beach along the waterline, or on rocks (see drawing, page 132).

SANDERLING

Calidris alba

Dorsally grey speckled with white, ventrally white up to the throat. A long, pointed black bill, and black legs. Walks very fast on the beach along the waterline, after the retreating waves (see photo, page 128).

RUDDY TURNSTONE

Arenaria interpes

Dorsally brown, speckled with black and white, ventrally white. A conspicuous black collar under the throat. The legs are orange. The bill is small, sharp and curved upward. Its cry is a deep crackling. When in search of food, it turns over shells and rocks. It has also been observed feeding on sea lions' afterbirth, and sucking blood avidly (Seymour, December 1993). Usually found on the rocks near the water (see photos, pages 127 and 128).

NORTHERN PHALAROPE

Phalaropus lobatus

Dorsally streaked, grey-blue and orange. The head is blue-grey, the throat is white, and a brown-red collar appears during the mating season. Ventrally white with black legs (see drawing, page 133; photo, page 161).

Common Gallinule

Gallinula chloropus

A bird of brackish lagoons. Black to metallic blue, with a yellow-tipped red bill. Big yellow legs. A shy bird, quite rare. When it swims, the head moves back and forth. Feeds on plants and aquatic invertebrates. It may be observed in the lagoons of Puerto Villamil (Isabela Island) (see drawing, page 133).

Purple Gallinule

Porphyrula martinica

Purple-blue on the top of the head and ventrally. Dorsally brownish green. The forehead is turquoise-blue. The bill is red and yellow tipped. Big yellow legs. Found in lagoons with abundant vegetation (see drawing, page 133).

CHAPTER THREE

Land Birds; Darwin's Finches

In the Galápagos, the endemism rate of land birds (76%) is three times higher than the endemism rate of sea birds (25%). This is easily explained by the fact that sea birds are migrants, and land birds are rather sedentary. The latter are also more shy towards man than sea birds.

All land birds in the Galápagos originated in North, Central or South America. They arrived in the islands by chance with the northeast or southeast trade winds. The impossibility of returning to the mainland forced them to adapt to their new environment. Later on, competition and natural selection brought diversification and speciation for some genera. Through evolution, some species became endemic, with no other possible choice (except extinction).

Endemic Species

Nowadays, 29 species of land birds can be identified in the Galápagos, 22 of which are endemic and seven non-endemic.

Among the endemic species: 13 species of Darwin's finches, four species of mockingbird, one dove, one flycatcher, one hawk, one martin, one rail. Among the non-endemic species are: one crake, one cuckoo, two owls, one ani, one warbler, one flycatcher (see Appendix 2, Geographical distribution of the land birds). Since the avifauna come mainly from South America, the distribution of the species is disharmonic. The 1,000 kilometres of the Pacific Ocean between the islands and Ecuador pose an almost impossible barrier to migrations.

Examples of Disharmony:

	Number of species in world	Number of species in Ecuador	Number of species in Galápagos
Hummingbirds	319	120	0
Parrots	315	44	0
Eagles and Hawks	208	46	
(genus *Buteo*)		12	1
Flycatchers	347	153	2
Mockingbirds	31	6	4 + 7 subspecies
Finches	436	47	13

For some groups, the quality of the environment is the most important. For example, hummingbirds look for big flowers, and parrots look for succulent fruits, all of which are nonexistent in the Galápagos.

All the land birds in the Galápagos breed during the rainy season, at the beginning of the year (January). All, that is, except for one species, the Galápagos rail, which breeds in the cold season, between June and December. The rainy season brings plant growth and thus abundant food for the land birds. This immediate response to the presence of food is called 'opportunistic breeding'.

No land bird species has gone extinct throughout the islands, whereas in Hawaii the islandwide extinction rate is 40%. In the Galápagos, extinctions are localized. Three species have disappeared on Floreana: the mockingbird, the large-bill ground finch, and the barn owl (killed by man). The Galápagos hawk is also extinct on San Cristóbal (because of man), but a few pairs are left on Santa Cruz.

Galápagos Mockingbird

Nesomimus

The ancestor of the Galápagos mockingbird is the longtail mockingbird, *Mimus longicaudatus,* from Ecuador (see photo, page 161). In the Galápagos, the four species and six subspecies of mockingbirds are all endemic:

- Galápagos mockingbird (on all islands except Pinzón)
- Hood mockingbird (endemic to Española and Gardner)
- Cristóbal mockingbird (endemic to San Cristóbal Island)
- Floreana mockingbird (only found on the satellite islands of Floreana: Champion and Gardner).

These noisy birds, very curious by nature, are greyish brown dorsally and cream-coloured ventrally. The beak is black and curved downward.

Predatory birds, they feed on small finches, lava lizards, centipedes and insects. They also crave the eggs of sea birds, such as boobies and albatrosses. Very social birds, they have no fear of man, and are quite common to the archipelago.

Out of the breeding season, mockingbirds establish communities, with up to nine individuals on Genovesa Island and up to 40 individuals on Española Island. All associate for the defense of the territory and for the search of food. Serious fights may occur at the border of two territories. Two rows of antagonists face one another, and the fighting is fierce between the opposing parties.

Galápagos Dove

Zenaida galapagoensis

Endemic. This little dove, dorsally reddish brown, ventrally beige to pink, has a conspicuous turquoise-blue ring around the eye. Very tame towards man, as the pirate William Dampier related in 1684: 'One could easily kill a few dozen with a stick, during the morning.' Obviously, this would not be possible nowadays.

The Galápagos dove feeds on the ground, on seeds, usually of the opuntia cactus and of the croton shrub (of which fruits are also eaten), and on caterpillars.

The optimal time of breeding is during the wet season. The Galápagos dove nests on the ground of the arid zone, sometimes under lava rocks. It uses also old nests of mockingbirds. During the breeding season, ritual fights and nodding ceremonies occur. Two eggs are laid.

The Galápagos dove is found on Genovesa, Española, Santiago, Rábida, but it became rare on the inhabited islands of Santa Cruz, Floreana and Cristóbal (see photo, page 162).

Vermilion Flycatcher

Pyrocephalus rubinus

A very colorful bird, red on the head and on the belly, dorsally black. It has a conspicuous black mask on the eyes. Vermilion flycatchers are found in the humid (scalesia) forest of the highlands, mostly in the central islands. Absent on Genovesa and Española. The female is yellow ventrally, black dorsally, as is the juvenile male, which turns to red in a later phase.

Originally from South America, it is now found up as far as Mexico and southern California. Known locally as 'brujo' or sorcerer (see photo, page 162). Some observers consider the Galápagos populations as one—even two—separate endemic species: *Pyrocephalus nanus*, *Pyrocephalus dubius*.

Large-billed Flycatcher

Myiarchus magnirostris

Endemic. May be observed in the highlands, and also in the transition and arid zones. Larger than the former species, it has a yellow belly and a grey throat. Dorsally brown, the top of the head may have a slight crest at times. Inquisitive by nature, it has the habit of collecting human hair for the construction of its nest (see photo, page 163).

Yellow Warbler

Dendroica petechia

Originally from the North American mainland, and found from Alaska to southern Peru. This small, insect-eating bird is entirely yellow; the male has a reddish brown patch on the top of the head. The bill is sharp and pointed. Yellow warblers often enter houses to search for flies against the windowpanes.

Common to all these islands, it is found in mangroves, in arid zones and humid zones with dense vegetation. Confined to the Galápagos and Cocos Island (see photo, page 164).

Galápagos Martin

Progne modesta

Endemic. Distributed in small groups on central islands. Resembles a big dark swallow. The male is bluish black; the female is light grey. Although rare, it may be observed circling in the sky. Its flight alternates between quick wing flapping and periods of gliding.

The Galápagos martin nests in the holes of cliffs, in calderas and on the rim of volcanoes (Sugar Loaf, on Santiago Island and Daphné Island).

Dark-billed Cuckoo

Coccyzus melacoryphus

This is a rare bird. Twice as big as the yellow warbler, it is mainly speckled grey, with the top of the head black, and a long tail. Dorsally dark brown, ventrally pale. Widely distributed in South America, it arrived in the Galápagos recently, where it can be observed mainly in the highlands. Very frequent in the lowlands during the Niño year 1982/83. Related to the black-billed cuckoo of North America (see drawing, page 141).

Smooth-billed Ani

Crotophaga ani

Reached the Galápagos recently from Ecuador. It was probably introduced by settlers in 1962 to protect cattle from ticks. This black bird has a feathery black tail, and a smooth broad black bill humped on the top. Poorly adapted to long-distance flight, it was discovered on Genovesa Island, 90 kilometres away from Santa Cruz.

Anis are gregarious. They are found in the humid highlands, where they are company to cattle, from which they eat ticks and other parasites. The smooth-billed ani belongs to the Cuculidae family (cuckoos and anis). (See drawing, page 141.)

Galápagos Rail

Laterallus spilonotus

Endemic. About 15 centimetres long, dark colour with hazelnut markings and white spots on the wings. Feeds on insects and other invertebrates on the ground, and on dead leaves. Omnivorous, it lost its ability to fly, due to its feeding habits. Nevertheless, it may fly ten to 15 metres. The rail lives in the highlands between 350 and 600 metres (San Cristóbal, Santa Cruz, Santiago, Isabela, Floreana, Pinta and Fernandina).

It is the only land bird to breed in the cold season between June and December. The incubation period of the egg is 23 to 25 days.

Land birds

Smooth billed Ani

Dark billed cuckoo

Galápagos rail

Paint-billed Crake

Pikoco 89

PAINT-BILLED RAIL

Neocrex erythrops

Slightly larger than the Galápagos rail, it is distinguished by dark plumage with no markings, a yellow and red bill, and red legs.

A poor flier, it was discovered in 1953 in the agricultural zone of Santa Cruz and Floreana Island (see drawing, page 141). It is found in Peru and other parts of the continent.

GALÁPAGOS HAWK

Buteo galapagoensis

Endemic. This magnificent predator was for a time extinct on Santa Cruz. But recently (Gemelos, November1993) the author observed the return of the hawks to the highlands of that island. Practically extinct on Floreana and San Cristóbal, due to hunting by the settlers. The hawk is common to Pinzón Island (for a long time infested with black rats), and to Santiago and Isabela islands.

The adult has dark brown plumage, a tail striped with white, and yellow legs. Juveniles are lighter and speckled with white. This bird of prey is unique, having no predators itself, and is therefore on the top of the 'food chain'. With its sharp eyesight, the hawk may detect prey—mainly lizards, iguanas, snakes, finches, boobies, flycatchers and young goats—from a great distance. It will also eat dead animals, such as sea lions, sea birds, marine iguanas, goats and fishes.

The Galápagos hawk builds its nest in trees and on rocks. Two or three eggs are laid, and the chicks may be bred simultaneously. The reproduction system, known as 'cooperative polyandry', is unusual. A female hawk will mate with up to four males and make four different nests. Each male will take care of a nest. The female is larger than the male. The reason for this polyandry may be due to the difficulty in finding an appropriate territory, or to the limited number of available territories (see photo, page 165).

SHORT-EARED OWL

Asio flammeus

Endemic subspecies. Present on all islands except Wolf. This diurnal hunter is seen in the highlands and close to the sea bird colonies. Short-eared owls feed on rats, land birds and sea birds such as storm petrels. It has no fear of man whatsoever, provided it is not approached too closely.

On Santa Cruz, it hunts early morning from 5 to 10 am, then in the evening from 4 to 10 pm. It nests on the ground, among high grasses. When hawks and barn owls inhabit the same island, the short-eared owl is rare (see photo, page 166).

Barn Owl

Tyto alba

Endemic subspecies. Unlike the short-eared owl, the barn owl is a nocturnal predator, feeding on rats and mice only. It is found on the big central islands: Fernandina, Isabela, Santiago, Santa Cruz and San Cristóbal. The barn owl is not afraid of man.

It nests in rock caves, holes in trees and in abandoned houses. The population is about 8,500 pairs (see photo, page 166).

Darwin's Finches

The theory of evolution brought fame to Darwin's finches. The dark-coloured birds are about the size of a sparrow and are distributed on all the islands. They are often very noisy birds and have no fear of man.

Although they belong to the finch family, they make a subfamily called Geospiznae, which is found only in the Galápagos and on Cocos Island to the northeast. Thirteen species are endemic to the archipelago; all originated from an original species, *Melanospiza richardsonii*, found on St Lucia Island in the Caribbean.

All the finches are strikingly alike, and it takes the trained eye of a specialist to distinguish them perfectly. The diversity of structure apparent in this little group of birds aroused Darwin's interest in 1835. He came to understand, long after his journey, that a mother species had modified to different ends and for specific functions (1845).

Finches may be classified in different genera, following the characteristic shape of their beak and feeding habits. Four main groups and six genera are distinguished, with the Cocos finch:

- Ground finches (Geospiza, 6 species)
- Vegetarian finch (Platyspiza, 1 species)
- Tree finches (Camarhynchus, 3 species; Cactospiza, 2 species)
- Warbler finch (Certhidea, 1 species)

Classification of the 14 Darwin's finches

Cocos finch	*Pinaroloxias inornata*
Cactus finch	*Geospiza scandens*
Large cactus finch	*Geospiza conirostris*
Small ground finch	*Geospiza fuliginosa*
Medium ground finch	*Geospiza fortis*
Large-billed ground finch	*Geospiza magnirostris*

Sharpbilled ground finch	*Geospiza difficilis*
Small tree finch	*Camarhynchus parvulus*
Medium tree finch	*Camarhynchus pauper*
Large tree finch	*Camarhynchus psittacula*
Carpenter finch	*Cactospiza pallida*
Mangrove finch	*Cactospiza heliobates*
Vegetarian finch	*Platyspiza crassirostris*
Warbler finch	*Certhidea olivacea*

Lack and Bowan, two scientists who studied finches after Darwin, each have their own views on their evolution. Lack thinks that isolation and competition were important factors in the evolution of the finches. Bowan thinks that only differences in food brought about a particular adaptation. Therefore, there was no competition between species. Ground finches are distributed in the dry arid zone, and look for seeds on the ground. Tree finches are more often in the humid zone. The medium tree finch is only found on Isabela Island. The sharpbill ground finch, also known as the 'blood-sucking' finch or 'vampire' finch (on Wolf Island), draws blood from the base of the feathers of Nazca and red-footed boobies. The cactus finch appears in the coastal and transition zones. The large cactus finch is only found on Genovesa and Española islands. The carpenter finch, which uses a stick as a tool, is found from the arid zone to the highlands. The mangrove finch is found in the elevated mangroves of Isabela and Fernandina islands.

Finches lay four eggs after the mating season. The incubation time is 14 days (see photos, pages 167–69). See Appendix 2: Distribution of the land birds according to vegetation zones.

Darwin's finches

1 Large billed ground Finch
2 Medium ground Finch
3 Small ground Finch
4 Sharpbilled ground Finch
5 Cactus Finch
6 Large cactus Finch
7 Small tree Finch
8 Medium tree Finch
9 Large tree Finch
10 Carpenter Finch
11 Mangrove Finch
12 Vegetarian Finch
13 Warbler Finch

CHAPTER FOUR

Mammals: Bats, Rats, Sea Lions

Like most oceanic islands, the archipelago is poor in native mammals: two species of bats, a few species of rats and, of course, sea lions.

The paucity of native mammals in the islands is explained by the fact that the islands were never connected to the mainland. Today the only existing land mammals, apart from the bats and rice rats, are those introduced by man: goats, dogs, cats, donkeys, horses, pigs and the black rat (see pages 276–279).

Bats

Lasiurus

Two species are present. They inhabit the mangroves, the crowns of opuntia cactus, and the hollow tree trunks introduced by man, such as the guayabillo (*Psidium galapageium*).

One of these bats, *Lasiurus brachyotis*, is endemic, related to the red bat of South America, but smaller and with short ears. The other species is the hoary bat (*Lasiurus cinereus*), with whitish grey hair and light brown fur. Feeding on insects, these bats are found on Santa Cruz (coast and highlands), on San Cristóbal, Floreana and West Isabela (mangroves).

Galápagos Rice Rats

Oryzomys

Endemic to the Galápagos Islands, these rodents belong to the genus *Oryzomis*, distributed on the American mainland. This small brown rat with big bulging black eyes has no fear of man. It digs nests under the rocks of the arid zone, as well as in the highlands. The rice rats are omnivorous. Seven species have been identified.

The Galápagos rice rats have been studied by Brosset (1963), a Frenchman, who divided them into two categories:

1) genus *Oryzomis*: two endemic species: *Oryzomys galapagoensis*, found on San Cristóbal, and *Oryzomis bauri*, on Santa Fé. The latter, mainly vegetarian, feeds on seeds and vegetation.
2) genus *Nesoryzomis:* four species, found on Fernandina and Santiago Island. Extinct on Baltra, Santa Cruz and Isabela.

A third genus, now extinct, was found in the highlands of Santa Cruz and Isabela. It is known as *Megaoryzomys*, the giant rice rat. The endemic rice rats of the Galápagos has been disappearing since the introduction of the black rat (*Rattus rattus*) during the time of the pirates. Three factors speed its extinction: competition and disease.The natural predators of the rice rat are the short-eared owl, the barn owl and the Galápagos hawk.

Sea Lion

Zalophus wollebacki

In early 2000, the Galápagos sea lion—once called the California sea lion (*Zalophus californianus)*—was found to be an endemic species to the Archipelago. Belonging to the family Otaridae the Galápagos sea lion is related to the California sea lion, but is smaller, and is different from the Peruvian sea lion (*Otaria flavescens*), which is from a more southern distribution.

Abundant in the archipelago, sea lions gather in colonies on sand or on the rocks. The male is polygamous, but there is no such thing as a 'harem' in the strict sense of the word, for the female is free to come and go as she pleases, in and out of the group. The male is distinguished from the female by its huge size and by a conspicuous hump on the forehead, while the female has a smooth forehead.

The male becomes adult at the age of ten years and weighs up to 250 kilograms. The female matures at around six to eight years and weighs up to 120 kilograms.

The male is very territorial, especially at the beginning of the mating season, and patrols on the beach or in the water constantly to chase occasional intruders. He keeps an eye on the young, which may wander off too far from the safety of the beach, and may be attacked by sharks.

The mating season occurs between May and January, more or less the time of the garua. It stretches over a period of six to eight months, with a peak from September to November. The male defends a territory of 40 to 100 square metres with a group of up to 30 females. Those which do not have territories gather in 'bachelor clubs'. This is often a voluntary retreat, following a tiring period of holding a territory. A territorial male has very little time to feed, and he keeps his territory for about 14 to 29 days before it is taken over by another male.

Mating occurs in the water. The female gives birth on land—after retiring to a chosen site—and walks away from the afterbirth, with the pup in her mouth. Frigates, gulls, hawks, mockingbirds and ruddy turnstones have been seen feeding on the afterbirth. The newborn sea lion pup weighs about five to six kilograms; one year later it will weigh 20 to 30 kilograms.

Mother and pup recognize one another by cry and smell. The female stays five to six days with the young and teaches it to suck from her four teats. Then the mother goes back to the sea. The pup will lose its first fur five months later, and will have its adult pelt. It will suckle the female for one to two years maximum, before it is left on its own.

Four weeks after giving birth, the female mates again, but the fertilization of the new egg will be effective only two months later. This is known as the 'delayed implantation'. The next birth will occur after a gestation of nine months.

The Annual Cycle of the Galápagos Sea Lion

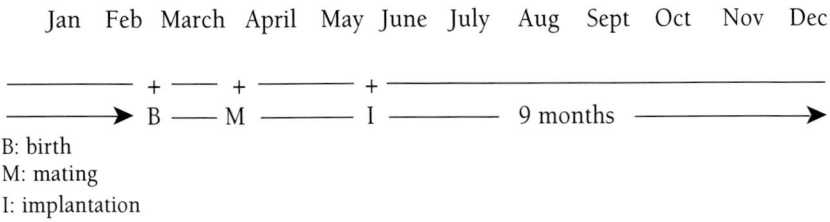

Seventy per cent of the sea lion's diet is composed of sardines. The sea lion may dive to a depth of 30 to 60 metres, and dives down to 100 metres have been recorded. It feeds during the day, as opposed to the fur sea lion, which feeds at night.

One of the sea lion's favourite games is surfing a big wave as it is about to crash on the shore (eg on North Seymour Island). Another game is 'water polo', using a marine iguana instead of a ball. The unfortunate reptile is caught by the tail and gleefully thrown up in the air.

The lifespan of sea lions is 18 to 20 years. Females are sexually active after three years. Males become sexually active at about six or seven years, when they can defend a territory against other males or challenge a dominant male.

Sea lion colonies are found on South Plaza, Santa Fé, Rábida, James Bay (Santiago Island), Española, San Cristóbal, Isabela. The global population is estimated at 20,000 to 50,000 individuals.

Since 1970, a viral disease, the 'seal pox', has affected sea lions, contributing to a loss of 50 per cent of the population. The disease is evidenced by an infection of the eyes and purulent warts all over the body. The natural predators of the sea lions are sharks and orcas (see photos, pages 170–72).

Fur Sea Lion

Arctocephalus galapagoensis

Whatever people may tell you, there are no fur seals in the Galápagos, but only fur sea lions. This species originated in the Southern Hemisphere, and reached the islands via the Humboldt current. The mother species is *Arctocephalus australis*, and the existing Galápagos subspecies, *Arctocephalus galapagoensis*, is endemic. Another branch of the genus *Arctocephalus* is found in South Africa and on the west coast of Namibia, *Arctocephalus capensis*, the Cape sea lion, which enjoys the cold Benguela current—the equivalent of the Humboldt current in the eastern Atlantic. *Arctocephalus pusillus*, the New Zealand fur sealion, is found in New Zealand and South Australia.

The fur sea lion of the Galápagos was near extinction at the beginning of the 20th century, following the plundering of their numbers by whalers and other skin hunters. It is the only tropical species of the genus, which was at first subantarctic. It is also the smallest (see photo, page 172).

Differences between seals and sea lions include the following:
- seals do not have external ears, sea lions do.
- seals cannot support themselves on their front flippers, and creep on the ground.
- seals swim with their posterior flippers, sea lions with the front flippers. Sea lions possess strong front flippers, on which they stand and which they use to swim.

The fur sea lion may be easily distinguished from the sea lion by its smaller size, its pointed nose, and big round sad eyes with a glossy glare. Most of the time it lies under rocks or in lava cracks, hiding from the sun. Males weigh up to 75 kilograms and females up to 35 kilograms.

Fur sea lions feed at night on squid and schools of small fish. They may dive to depths of 40 to 100 metres. Mating occurs on land during the garua season, between mid-August and mid-November. Many pups are born in early October. The female is sexually mature at the age of three years, and takes care of the young for two or three years. The pup changes skin and fur at the age of six months.

As in the California sea lion, there is a delayed implantation, three months after the birth of the first pup, making for an annual breeding cycle. Males hold territories for between 27 and 51 days. Since they do not have time to feed, they lose up to 25 per cent of their original weight. For males defending a territory, the mortality rate is 30 per cent the first year. After the birth of the pups, the territorial structure disappears, and the males leave, exhausted.

These *lobos de dos pelos* ('double-fur sea wolves'), as they are known locally, are found in Puerto Egas (Santiago Island), on Fernandina Island and on the northern islands of Marchena, Pinta, Isabela, Wolf and Darwin.

At present, the global population is stable, with 30,000 to 40,000 individuals. The two species of sea lions suffer shark attacks, especially on full-moon nights. Therefore, these marine mammals avoid going out on these nights!

CHAPTER FIVE

Marine Life: Fish, Whales, Dolphins; List of the 484 Species of Fish and Marine Organisms

The Galápagos are bathed by three currents—the cold Humboldt and Cromwell currents, and the warm Panama flow (or El Niño)—providing the islands with a rich, diverse and unique underwater fauna. Organisms originated from three main regions or oceanic provinces:

- the southeastern Pacific, on the Peru-Chile coast
- the eastern Pacific, stretching from Panama to Baja California
- the western Pacific, or Indo-Pacific region, for the tropical species of warm waters.

In 1978, the number of species of fish was estimated at 306 (McCosker, Taylor and Warner). Of this number:

51 species,	or 17%,	are endemic to the Galápagos
177 species,	or 58%,	belong to the Panamic region
43 species,	or 14%,	belong to the Indo-Pacific province
21 species,	or 7%,	belong to the Peru-Chile province
7 species,	or 2%,	are insular endemic: Galápagos, Cocos, Revillagigedos, Malpelo
4 species,	or 1%,	belong to the Atlantic province

The number of fish above is far from exhaustive. According to the most recent research by Jack Grove and Dr. Lavenberg, of the Los Angeles County Museum in California, in their publication 'The Fishes of the Galápagos Islands' (1997) the number came up to 460 species; including 112 families, 304 genera, 41 endemic species and 9.2 per cent of endemism in group. The research of Dr. Philippe Bearez, of the French Museum d'Histoire Naturelle in Paris (2004), revealed a total of 938 species of fish for Ecuador, in which 488 species belong to the waters of the mainland only, 162 species belong to the Galápagos waters only and 288 belong to both Ecuador and Galápagos. Thus a total of 450 species of fish were recorded in the Galápagos Islands, and 776 species of fish recorded for Ecuador. The Galápagos' rate of endemism is therefore confirmed at 17% within Ecuador, or 36 per cent within Galápagos waters (endemism shared with Malpelo, Cocos, Revillagigedos Islands). In September 2005, 'Fish Base' indicates a total number of 465 species for Galápagos, including 86 species endemic.

Among the numerous fish found in the archipelago, there are 18 species of morays, five species of rays (stingrays, golden ray, marbled ray, spotted eagle ray and manta rays). There are also about 28 species of sharks, which so far have not been harmful to man. No serious incidents have occurred, although some shark attacks have been reported from Pinzón Island. The dangerous great white shark is not an inhabitant of the archipelago; it is found farther north and away from the islands. The most common sharks are the white-tip reef shark, the black-tip reef shark, two species of hammerheads, the Galápagos shark, the grey reef shark, the tiger shark, the hornshark and the whale shark (Gordon Rock, 1984; Darwin Island).

Among the cetaceans, at least 16 species of whales and seven species of dolphins have been identified. Of the latter, the most common are the bottle-nosed dolphin (*Tursiops truncatus*) and the common dolphin. Whales include the sperm whale, the humpback whale, the pilot whale, the orca and the false killer whale, Sei whale, Minke whale, Bryde's whale, Cuvier's beaked whale and other beaked whales. All these whales are distributed throughout the archipelago and are easily observed in the west of Isabela and Fernandina due to the 'upwelling' of the Cromwell current, rich in organisms and plankton. Another species of whale was added to the list in 1993; a few sightings of blue whales were reported by the research sailboat *Odyssey* to the north of Isabela and Fernandina (David Day).

The littoral is also rich in various organisms such as sea stars and cushion stars, sea urchins, sea cucumbers and red crabs (*'zayapas'*) with turquoise blue colorations. A few coral reefs—hermatypic hexacorallians and octacorallians—are present to the west of Santiago, south of Genovesa and Santa Cruz (Tortuga bay), north of Floreana. Ahermatypic solitary corals are also found. Corals need particular conditions for their development: clear water with a minimal temperature of 18° C to 20° C, and an optimal depth of 20 metres (see map and drawing, pages 186–87).

Among shells we may mention: cones *(Conidae)*, mitre shells *(Mitridae)*, cowries *(Cypraeidae)*, nerites *(Neritidae)*, periwinkles *(Littorinidae)*, creepers *(Cerithiidae)*, strombs *(Strombidae)*, helmet shells *(Cassidae)*, murex shells *(Muricidae)*, horse conches.

A list of marine invertebrates follows on pages 183–185 and 188.

Classification of the Cetaceans in Galápagos

Order of marine mammals

Size	SUBORDER OF MYSTICETI (Baleen whales)	
	Rorquals (Family Balaenopteridae)	
19 metres	Sei whale	*Balaenoptera borealis*
15 metres	Bryde's whale	*Balaenoptera edeni*
10 metres	Minke whale	*Balaenoptera acutorostrata*
19 metres	Humpback whale	*Megaptera novaeangliae*
30 metres	Blue whale	*Balaenoptera musculus*
	SUBORDER OF THE ODONTOCETI (Toothed whales)	
	Sperm whales (Family Physeteridae)	
21 metres	Sperm whale	*Physeter catodon*
3.7 metres	Pygmy sperm whale	*Kogia breviceps*
2.7 metres	Dwarf sperm whale	*Kogia simus*

Classification of the Cetaceans in Galápagos *Order of Marine Mammals*

Size		
	Beaked whales (Family Ziphiidae)	
7 metres	Cuvier's beaked whale	*Ziphius cavirostris*
5 metres	Beaked whales: Blainville's	*Mesoplodon densirostris*
	Lesser	*Mesoplodon peruvianus*
	Gingkotoothed	*Mesoplodon gingkodens*
	Marine dolphins (Family Delphinidae)	
10 metres	Orca, killer whale	*Orcinus orca*
2.7 metres	Pygmy killer whale	*Feresa attenuata*
6 metres	False killer whale	*Pseudorca crassidens*
7 metres	Shortfin pilot whale	*Globicephala macrorhyncha*
	Longfin pilot whale	*Globicephala melaena*
2.8 metres	Melon-headed whale	*Peponocephala electra*
2.4 metres	Fraser's dolphin	*Lagenodelphis hosei*
4.5 metres	Risso's dolphin or Grey grampus	*Grampus griseus*
2.6 metres	Common dolphin or White-bellied dolphin	*Delphinus delphis*
4 metres	Bottle-nosed dolphin	*Tursiops truncatus*
2 metres	Spotted dolphin	*Stenella attenuata*
2.7 metres	Striped dolphin	*Stenella coeruleoalba*
2 metres	Spinner dolphin	*Stenella longirostris*

(List of Cetaceans, after David Day, *Noticias de Galápagos*, April 1994).

List of the fishes, whales, dolphins and other marine animals of the Galápagos (492 species)

(E) = Endemic

1/ **Cornetfishes, trumpetfishes, pipefishes:**	
Reef cornet fish	*Fistularia commersonii*
Trumpetfish	*Aulostomus chinensis*
Fantail pipefish	*Doryrhampus melanopleura*
Sailor pipefish	*Bryx veleronis*
Spotjaw pipefish	*Bryx coccineus*
Pacific seahorse	*Hippocampus ingens*
2/ **Needlefishes, halfbeaks, flying fishes:**	
Pike needlefish	*Strongylura exilis*
Silverstripe halfbeak	*Hyporhampus unifasciatus*
Ribbon halfbeak	*Euleptorhamphus longirostris*
Longfin halfbeak	*Hemirhampus saltator*
Sharpchin flying fish	*Fodiator acutus*
Spotted back flying fish	*Cheilopogon dorsomaculata*
Barbel flying fish	*Exocoetus monocirrhus*
Sailor flying fish	*Prognichthys seali*

Baleen whales

Toothed whales

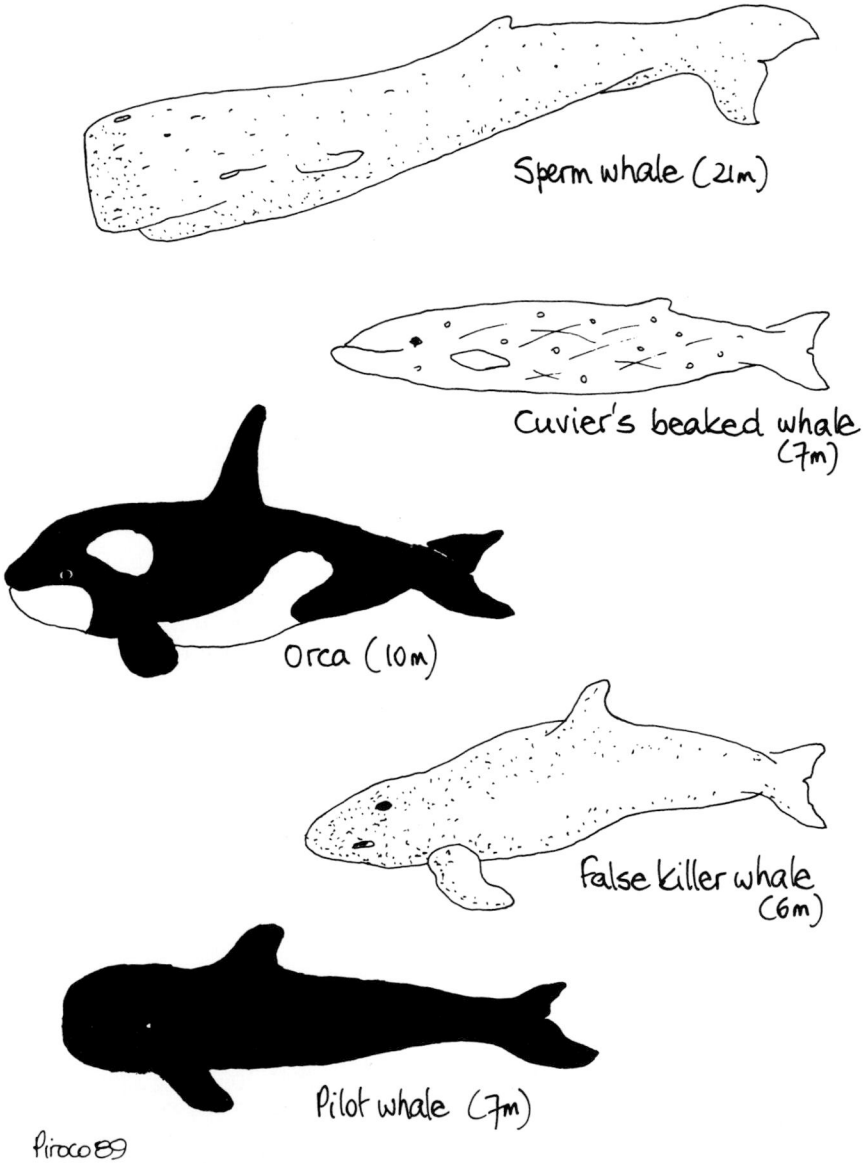

3/ **Parrotfishes, wrasses:**

Bluechin parrotfish	*Scarus ghobban*	
Bumphead parrotfish	*Scarus perrico*	
Bicolor parrotfish	*Scarus rubroviolaceus*	
Azure parrotfish	*Scarus compressus*	
Loosetooth parrotfish	*Nicholsina denticulata*	
Mexican hogfish	*Bodianus diplotaenia*	
Harlequin wrasse	*Bodianus eclancheri*	
Cortez rainbow wrasse	*Thalassoma lucasanum*	
Sunset wrasse	*Thalassoma lutescens*	
Chameleon wrasse	*Halichoeres dispilus*	
Spinster wrasse (or goldspot wrasse)	*Halichoeres nicholsi*	
Dragon wrasse	*Novaculichthys taeniourus*	
Peacock wrasse	*Xyrichthys pavo*	
Surge wrasse	*Thalassoma purpureum*	
Galápagos sheephead	*Semicossyphus darwini*	
Pacific beakfish, Tigris	*Oplegnathus insigne*	

4/ **Surgeonfishes, angelfishes, damselfishes, butterflyfishes:**

Yellowtail surgeonfish	*Prionurus laticlavius*	
Gold-rimmed surgeonfish	*Acanthurus glaucopareius*	
Yellowfin surgeonfish	*Acanthurus xanthopterus*	
Convict tang	*Acanthurus triostegus*	
Spotted unicorn	*Naso brevirostris*	
Vlaminck unicorn	*Naso vlamingii*	
Moorish Idol	*Zanclus canescens*	
King angelfish	*Holocanthus passer*	
Cortez angelfish	*Pomacanthus zonipectus*	
Barberfish	*Heniochus nigrirostris*	
Scythe butterflyfish	*Chaetodon falcifer*	
Three-banded butterflyfish	*Chaetodon humeralis*	
Meyer's butterflyfish	*Chaetodon meyeri*	
Raccoon butterflyfish	*Chaetodon lunula*	
Threadfin butterflyfish	*Chaetodon auriga*	
Duskybarred butterflyfish	*Chaetodon kleinii*	
Longnose butterflyfish	*Forcipiger flavissimus*	
Panama sergeant major	*Abudefduf troschelli*	
Night sergeant	*Nexilarius concolor*	
Rusty damselfish	*Nexilosus latifrons*	
Yellowtail damselfish	*Stegastes arcifrons,*	(E)
Acapulco damselfish	*Eupomacentrus acapulcoensis*	
Galápagos whitetail damsel	*Stegastes leucorus beebei*	
Giant damselfish	*Microspathodon dorsalis*	
Bumphead damselfish	*Microspathodon bairdii*	
Whitespot chromis	*Chromis atrilobata*	
Blackspot chromis	*Azurina eupalama*	(E)
White striped chromis	*Chromis alta*	

5/ **Puffers, porcupinefishes, boxfishes:**

Galápagos pufferfish, concave puffer	*Spheroides angusticeps*	(E)
Concentric pufferfish, bullseye puffer	*Spheroides annulatus*	
Oceanic puffer	*Lagocephalus lagocephalus*	
Saddled puffer	*Canthigaster valentini*	
Honeycomb puffer	*Canthigaster janthinoptera*	
Spotted puffer	*Canthigaster amboinensis*	

Longnose puffer	*Spheroides lobatus*	
Guineafowl puffer	*Arothron meleagris*	
White-spotted puffer	*Arothron hispidus*	
Spotted sharpnosed pufferfish	*Canthigaster punctatissima*	
Balloonfish	*Diodon holocanthus*	
Porcupinefish	*Diodon hystrix*	
Galápagos blue porcupinefish	*Chilomycterus affinis galapagoensis*	
Yellow spotted burrfish	*Cyclichthys spilostylus*	
Pacific boxfish	*Ostracion meleagris*	
6/ **Triggerfishes, filefishes:**		
Yellow bellied triggerfish	*Sufflamen verres*	
Black triggerfish	*Melichthys niger*	
Pink tail triggerfish	*Melichthys vidua*	
Blunthead triggerfish	*Pseudobalistes naufragium*	
Finescale triggerfish	*Balistes polyepsis*	
Red tail triggerfish	*Xanthichthys mento*	
Blue-striped triggerfish	*Xanthichthys caeruleolineatus*	
Scrawled filefish	*Aluterus scriptus*	
Vagabond filefish	*Cantherines dumerlii*	
Pacific leatherjacket	*Oligoplites saurus*	
7/ **Blennies, clinid blennies (klipfishes), combtooth blennies, gobies:**		
Large-banded blenny	*Ophioblennius steindachneri*	
Sabretooth blenny	*Plagiotremus azaleus*	
Castro's blenny	*Acanthemblemaria castroii*	(E)
Red-spotted barnacle blenny	*Hypsoblennius brevipinnis*	
Galápagos four-eyed blenny	*Dialommus fuscus*	(E)
Bravo clinid	*Labrisomus dentriticus*	(E)
Large mouth blenny	*Labrisomus xanti*	
Jenkins clinid	*Labrisomus jenkinsi*	(E)
Porehead blenny	*Labrisomus multiporosus*	
Galápagos triplefin blenny	*Enneapterygius corallicola*	(E)
Blenny sp.	*Malacoctenus afuerae*	
Belted blenny	*Malacoctenus zonogaster*	(E)
Throatspotted blenny	*Malacoctenus tetranemus*	
Galápagos blenny	*Starksia galapagensis*	
Ophidiid	*Ogilbia galapagoensis*	(E)
De Roy's ophidiid	*Ogilbia deroyi*	(E)
Tagus goby	*Chriolepis tagus*	(E)
Blackeye goby	*Coryphopterus urospilus*	
Goby species	*Eleotrica cableae*	(E)
Galápagos blue-banded goby	*Lythrypnus gilberti*	(E)
Spotcheek blenny	*Lythrypnus rizophora*	(E)
Red clingfish	*Arcos poecilophtalmus*	(E)
Banded cleaner goby	*Elacatinus nesiotes*	
?	*Gobisoma* species	
8/ **Groupers, seabasses, grunts, mojarras, snappers, seachubs:**		
Flag cabrilla	*Epinephelus labriformis*	
Spotted cabrilla grouper	*Epinephelus analogus*	
Panama graysby	*Epinephelus panamensis*	
Mutton hamlet	*Epinephelus afer*	
Pacific mutton hamlet	*Alphestes immaculatus*	
Leather bass	*Epinephelus dermatolepis*	
Snowy grouper	*Epinephelus niphobles*	

Norteno grouper	*Epinephelus cifuentesi*	
Sideblotch bass	*Serranus stilbostigma*	(E)
Misty grouper, mero	*Epinephelus mystacinus*	(E)
Rainbow basslet	*Liopropoma fasciatum*	
Bacalao, yellow grouper	*Mycteroperca olfax*	(E)
Camotillo, white spotted seabass	*Paralabrax albomaculatus*	(E)
Barred serrano	*Serranus fasciatus*	
Creolefish	*Paranthias colonus*	
Cortez soapfish	*Rypticus bicolor*	
Black soapfish	*Rypticus nigripinnis*	
Gray threadfin seabass, plumero	*Cratinus agassizi*	
Galápagos grunt	*Orthopristis forbesi*	(E)
Sheephead grunt	*Orthopristis cantharinus*	
Brassy grunt	*Orthopristis chalceus*	
Grey grunt, Golden-eye grunt	*Haemulon scudderi*	
Graybar grunt	*Haemulon sexfasciatum*	
Burrito grunt, yellowtail grunt	*Anisotremus interruptus*	
Peruvian grunt	*Anisotremus scapularis*	
Black-striped salema	*Xenocys jessiae*	(E)
White salema	*Xenichthys agassizi*	(E)
Bigeye salema	*Xenichthys xanti*	
Silver mojarra	*Eucinostomus dovii*	
Pacific flagfin mojarra	*Eucinostomus gracilis*	
Spotfin mojarra	*Eucinostomus currani*	(E)
Yellowfin mojarra	*Gerres cinereus*	
Stripe-tail aholehole	*Kuhila taeniura*	
Machete	*Elops affinis*	
Blue and gold snapper	*Lutjanus viridis*	
Yellowtail snapper	*Lutjanus argiventris*	
Mullet snapper	*Lutjanus aratus*	
Pacific dog snapper	*Lutjanus novemfasciatus*	
Golden snapper	*Lutjanus inermis*	
Barred pargo	*Hoplopagrus guentheri*	
Jordan's snapper	*Lutjanus jordani*	
Dusky chub	*Girella fremenvillei*	(E)
Cortez sea chub	*Kyphosus elegans*	
Blue bronze chub	*Kyphosus analogus*	
Rainbow chub	*Sectator ocyurus*	
Shiner perch	*Cymatogaster aggregata*	
9/ **Squirrelfishes, bigeyes, cardinalfishes:**		
Crimson soldierfish	*Myripristis leiognathos*	
Big eyed soldierfish	*Myripristis murdjan*	
Whitetip soldierfish	*Myripristis* species	(E)
Sun squirrelfish	*Sargocentron suborbitalis*	
Glasseye	*Priacanthus cruentatus*	
Popeye catalufa	*Pseudopriacanthus serrula*	
Tail spot cardinalfish	*Apogon dovii*	
Pacific cardinalfish	*Apogon pacificus*	
Pink cardinalfish	*Apogon parri*	
Blacktip cardinalfish	*Apogon atradorsatus*	(E)
Percelle	*Cheilodipterus species*	
10/ **Scorpionfishes, hawkfishes:**		
Spotted scorpionfish	*Scorpaena plumieri mystes*	

Rainbow scorpionfish	*Scorpaenodes xyris*	
Bandfin scorpion	*Scorpaena histrio*	
Red scorpionfish	*Pontinus furcirhinus*	
Mottled scorpionfish	*Pontinus clemensi*	
Stalkeye scorpion	*Pontinus strigatus*	(E)
Spinyhead scorpion	*Pontinus new sp.*	
Black scorpionfish	*Ectreposebastes imus*	
Devil scorpionfish	*Scorpaenopsis diabolus*	
Sailfin leaffish	*Taenianotus triacanthus*	
Hieroglyphic hawkfish	*Cirrhitus rivulatus*	
Coral hawkfish	*Cirrhitichthys oxycephalus*	
Longnosed hawkfish	*Oxycirrhites typus*	
11/ Goatfishes, searobins, lizardfishes:		
Mexican goatfish	*Mullodichthys dentatus*	
Galápagos searobin, orangethroat searobin	*Prionotus miles*	(E)
White margin searobin	*Prionotus albirostris*	
Sauro lizardfish, banded lizardfish	*Synodus lacertinus*	
California lizardfish	*Synodus lucioceps*	
Spotted lizardfish, shorthead lizardfish	*Synodus scituliceps*	
Lizardfish	*Synodus jenkinsii*	
Marchena lizardfish	*Synodus marchenae*	(E)
Galápagos clingfish	*Arcos poecilophtalmus*	(E)
12/ Anchovies, herrings, remoras, silversides:		
Anchovy	*Anchoa naso*	
Galápagos thread herring	*Opisthonema berlangai*	(E)
Peruvian Pacific sardine	*Sardinops sadax sadax*	
Remora, sharksucker	*Remora remora*	
Silverside	*Eurystole eriarcha*	
Silverside	*Nectarges nesiotes*	(E)
13/ Porgies, bonefishes, tilefishes, dolphins, sunfishes:		
Pacific porgy	*Calamus brachysomus*	
Galápagos porgy	*Calamus taurinus*	
Galápagos seabrim	*Archosargus pourtalesi*	
Bonefish	*Albula vulpes*	
Ocean whitefish	*Caulolatilus princeps*	
Dolphinfish	*Coryphaena hippurus*	
Ocean sunfish	*Mola mola*	
Pacific spadefish	*Chaetodipterus zonatus*	
14/ Jacks, pompanos:		
Gafftopsail pompano	*Trachinotus rhodopus*	
Paloma pompano	*Trachinotus païtensis*	
Steel pompano	*Trachinotus stilbe*	
African pompano	*Alectis ciliaris*	
Pacific moonfish	*Selene peruviana*	
Green jack	*Caranx caballus*	
Pacific crevalle jack	*Caranx caninus*	
Black jack	*Caranx lugubris*	
Gold-spotted jack	*Carangodes orthogrammus*	
Bigeye jack	*Caranx sexfasciatus*	
Horse eye jack	*Caranx latus*	
Blue fin jack	*Caranx melampygus*	
Rainbow runner	*Elagatis bipinnulatus*	

Mackerel jack	*Decapterus pinnulatus*	
Yellowtail scad	*Decapterus santae helenae*	
Shortfin scad	*Seriola peruana*	
Mexican scad	*Decapterus macrosoma*	
Bigeye scad, Chinchard	*Decapterus muroadsi*	
Pacific amberjack	*Selar crumenophtalmus*	
Almaco amberjack	*Seriola colburni*	
Yellowtail	*Seriola rivoliana*	
Fortune jack	*Seriola lalandei*	
Pilot fish	*Naucrates ductor*	
15/ Barracudas, mackerels, tunas, marlins:		
Pelican barracuda	*Sphyraena idiastes*	
Wahoo	*Acanthocybium solanderi*	
Sierra mackerel	*Scomberomorus sierra*	
Striped bonito	*Sarda orientalis*	
Skipjack tuna	*Euthynnus pelamis*	
Black skipjack	*Euthynnus lineatus*	
Yellowfin tuna	*Thunnus albacares*	
Chub mackerel	*Scomber japonicus*	
Striped marlin	*Makaira mitsukurii*	
Black marlin	*Makaira marlina*	
Swordfish	*Xiphias gladius*	
16/ Croakers, drums, mullets, snooks:		
Galápagos rock croaker	*Pareques perissa*	(E)
Yelloweye croaker	*Odontoscion xanthops*	
Bronze croaker	*Odontoscion eurymesops*	(E)
Galápagos croaker	*Umbrina galapagorum*	(E)
Striped mullet	*Mugil cephalus*	
Yellowtail mullet, lisa	*Mugil cephalus rammelsbergii*	
Orange-eyed mullet	*Xenomugil thoburni*	
Galápagos mullet	*Mugil galapagensis*	(E)
Snook	*Centropomus nigrescens*	
17/ Batfishes, frogfishes:		
Galápagos redlips batfish	*Ogcocephalus darwinii*	
Roughjaw frogfish	*Antennarius avalonnis*	
Sanguine frogfish	*Antennarius sanguineus*	
Bandtail frogfish	*Antennarius strigatus*	
18/ Flounders, soles, tonguefishes:		
Pacific sanddab	*Citharichthys sordidus*	
Speckled sanddab	*Citharichthys stigmaeus*	
Blue-eyed flounder	*Bothus mancus*	
Striped sole, spotted fin sole	*Achirus fonsecensis*	
Galápagos sole, reticulated sole	*Asergodes herrei*	
Rainbow tonguefish, spotfin tonguefish	*Symphurus atramentatus*	
Small scale tonguefish	*Symphurus microlepis*	
Freckled tonguefish	*Symphuris varius*	
19/ Morays, snake eels, conger eels:		
Hardtail moray	*Anarchias galapagensis*	
Blackspot moray, hourglass moray	*Muraena clepsydra*	
Panamic green moray, chestnut moray	*Muraena castaneus*	
Magnificent moray, whitespotted moray	*Muraena argus*	
Lentil moray	*Muraena lentiginosa*	

Zebra moray	*Echidna zebra*	
Night moray	*Echidna nocturna*	
Snowflake moray	*Echidna nebulosa*	
Yellowmargin moray	*Gymnothorax flavimarginatus*	
Whitish speckled moray, paintspot moray	*Gymnothorax pictus*	
Black moray, lattice tail moray	*Gymnothorax buroensis*	
Masked moray, Panama moray	*Gymnothorax panamensis*	
Fine-spotted moray	*Gymnothorax dovii*	
Olive moray	*Gymnothorax funebris*	
Whitemouth moray	*Gymnothorax meleagris*	
Slenderjaw moray	*Enchelycore octaviana*	
Mosaic moray, reticulated hookjaw moray	*Enchelycore lichenosa*	
Peppered moray	*Uropterygius polysticus*	
Rusty moray	*Uropterygius necturus*	
Blackeye moray	*Uropterygius versutus*	
Burrowing Galápagos snake eel	*Callechelys galapagensis*	(E)
Snake eel	*Paraletharchus opercularis*	(E)
Snake eel	*Caecula equatorialis*	(E)
Tiger snake eel	*Myrichthys tigrinus (M.maculosus)*	
Pacific snake eel	*Ophichthus triserialis*	
Galápagos cusk eel	*Ophidion species*	(E)
Panama conger eel	*Anosoma gilberti*	
Galápagos garden eel	*Heteroconger klausewitzi*	(E)
20/ **Stingrays, golden rays, eagle rays, mantas:**		
Whiptail stingray	*Dasyatis brevis*	
Longtail stingray	*Dasyatis longus*	
Round stingray	*Urotrygon species*	
Marbled ray, black blotched stingray	*Taeniura meyeri*	
Pacific cownose ray	*Rhinoptera steindachneri*	
Spotted eagle ray	*Aetobatus narinari*	
Witch skate	*Raja velezi*	
Equatorial ray	*Raja equatorialis*	
Southern false skate	*Gurgesiella furvescens*	
Smooth tail mobula	*Mobula munkjana*	
Snouted eagleray	*Myliobatis longirostris*	
Bat eagle ray	*Myliobatis californica*	
Barred eagle ray	*Pteromylaeus asperrimus*	
Giant manta	*Manta birostris*	
Pacific guitarfish	*Rhinobatus planiceps*	
Speckled guitarfish	*Rhinobatus prahli*	
Electric ray	*Torpedo tremens*	
Pacific manta	*Manta hamiltoni*	
21/ **Sharks:** (30 subspecies)		
Whitetip reef shark	*Triaenodon obesus*	
Galápagos requiem shark	*Carcharhinus galapagensis*	
Blacktip shark	*Carcharhinus limbatus*	
Silvertip shark	*Carcharhinus albimarginatus*	
Grey reef shark	*Carcharhinus amblyrhynchos*	
Silky shark	*Carcharhinus falciformis*	
Bignose shark	*Carcharhinus altimus* (deep water)	
Sandbar shark	*Carcharhinus plumbeus*	
Oceanic whitetip	*Carcharhinus longimanus*	
Whitenose shark	*Nasolamia velox*	

Northern phalarope in winter plumage, Rabida 1993

Espanola mockingbird, Gardner Bay 1984

Galápagos dove, Los Gemelos, Santa Cruz Island 1995

Vermillion flycatcher (male), Los Gemelos, Santa Cruz 1993

Vermillion flycatcher (female), Santa Cruz 1993

Large-billed flycatcher, Floreana 1990

Yellow warbler, James Bay 1990

Smooth-billed anis, Santa Cruz 1992

Galapagos hawk feeding on a marine iguana, Fernandina 1992

Galapagos hawk (young), Alcedo 1991

Hawk and mockingbird, Espumilla, Santiago 1990

Short-eared owl, Santa Cruz 1986

Barn owl in Santa Cruz highlands 2006

Small-billed ground finch 1989

Large-billed ground finch, Darwin Station 1988

Cactus finch (male), Santa Cruz 1991

Large cactus finch, Espanola 1991

Small-billed tree finch, Gemelos 1988

Small-billed tree finch (young), Gemelos 1993

Sea lions colony, Gardner Bay, Espanola 1992

Female sea lions, Cristóbal 1989

Sea lion pups, Espanola 1993

Sea lion (male), Gardner Bay, Espanola 1992

Fur sea lion, James Bay, Santiago 1990

Fur sea lion, Santiago 1985

Slipper lobster, Punta Vicente Roca 2001

Red spiny lobster and slipper lobsters, Sombrero Chino 1986

Blue lobster, Elizabeth Bay, Isabela 1986

Sea cucumber or pepino, Isostichopus fuscus, *Santa Fé 1991*

Spotted eagle ray, Bartolomé 1992

Golden cownose rays, Tortuga Negra 1984

Marine turtles mating, Tortuga Negra 1990

Stingrays, Floreana 1990

False killer whales surfacing, Darwin 1993

Common dolphin, Banks Bay, Isabela 1992

Blue shark	*Prionace glauca*
Bigeye thresher	*Alopias superciliosus* (oceanic)
Thresher shark	*Alopias vulpinus* (oceanic)
Pelagic thresher	*Alopias pelagicus* (oceanic)
Speckled smoothhound	*Mustelus mento (Triakidae)* (bottom)
Broadnose smoothhound	*Mustelus sp.* (bottom)
Spotted houndshark	*Triakis maculata*
Pacific angelshark	*Squatina armata*
Galápagos hornshark	*Heterodontus quoyi*
Combtooth dogfish	*Centroscyllium nigrum* (deepwater)
Cookiecutter shark	*Isistius brasiliensis* (deepwater)
Longnose catshark	*Apristurus kampae* (deepwater)
Panama ghost catshark	*Apristurus stenseni* (deepwater)
Tiger shark	*Galeocerdo cuvieri*
Smooth hammerhead	*Sphyrna zygaena*
Scalloped hammerhead	*Sphyrna lewini*
Great hammerhead	*Sphyrna mokarran* (pelagic)
Whale shark	*Rhincodon typus*
Shortfin mako	*Isurus oxyrinchus*
Longfin mako	*Isurus paucus*
Great white shark	*Carcharodon carcharias*
22/ Baleen whales, rorquals:	
Sei whale	*Balaenoptera borealis*
Bryde's whale	*Balaenoptera edeni*
Minke whale	*Balaenoptera acutorostrata*
Blue whale	*Balaenoptera musculus*
Humpback whale	*Megaptera novaeangliae*
23/ Toothed whales, ocean dolphins:	
Sperm whale, cachalot	*Physeter catodon*
Pygmy sperm whale	*Kogia breviceps*
Dwarf sperm whale	*Kogia simus*
Cuvier's beaked whale	*Ziphius cavirostris*
Blainville's beaked whale	*Mesoplodon densirostris*
Lesser beaked whale	*Mesoplodon peruvianus*
Gingkotoothed beaked whale	*Mesoplodon gingkodens*
Melon-headed whale	*Peponocephala electra*
Pygmy killer whale	*Feresa attenuata*
Killer whale, orca	*Orcinus orca*
False killer whale	*Pseudorca crassidens*
Short-finned pilot whale	*Globicephala macrorhyncha*
Long-finned pilot whale	*Globicephala melaena*
Fraser's dolphin	*Lagenodelphis hosei*
Risso's dolphin, grey grampus	*Grampus griseus*
Common dolphin, white bellied	*Delphinus delphis*
Bottle nosed dolphin	*Tursiops truncatus*
Spotted dolphin	*Stenella attenuata*
Spinner dolphin	*Stenella longirostris*
Striped dolphin	*Stenella coeruleoalba*

(List of Cetaceans after David Day, *Noticias de Galápagos,* April 1994)

Total = 357 species (fish = 332; whales and dolphins = 25)

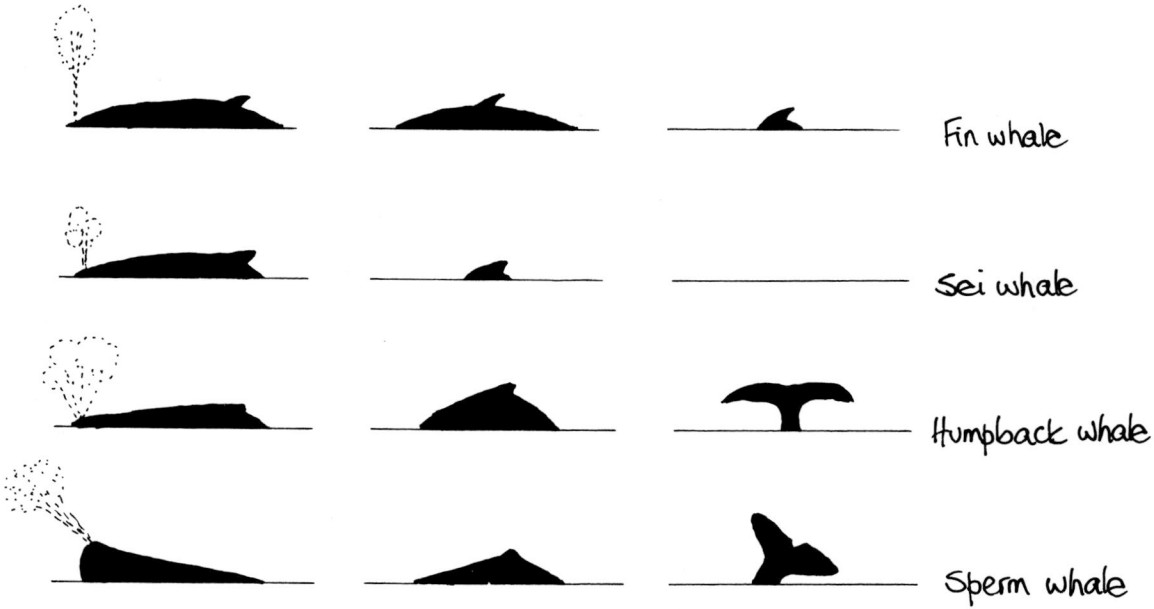

Diving sequence of a few whales
[after Gordon C. Pike, 1956].

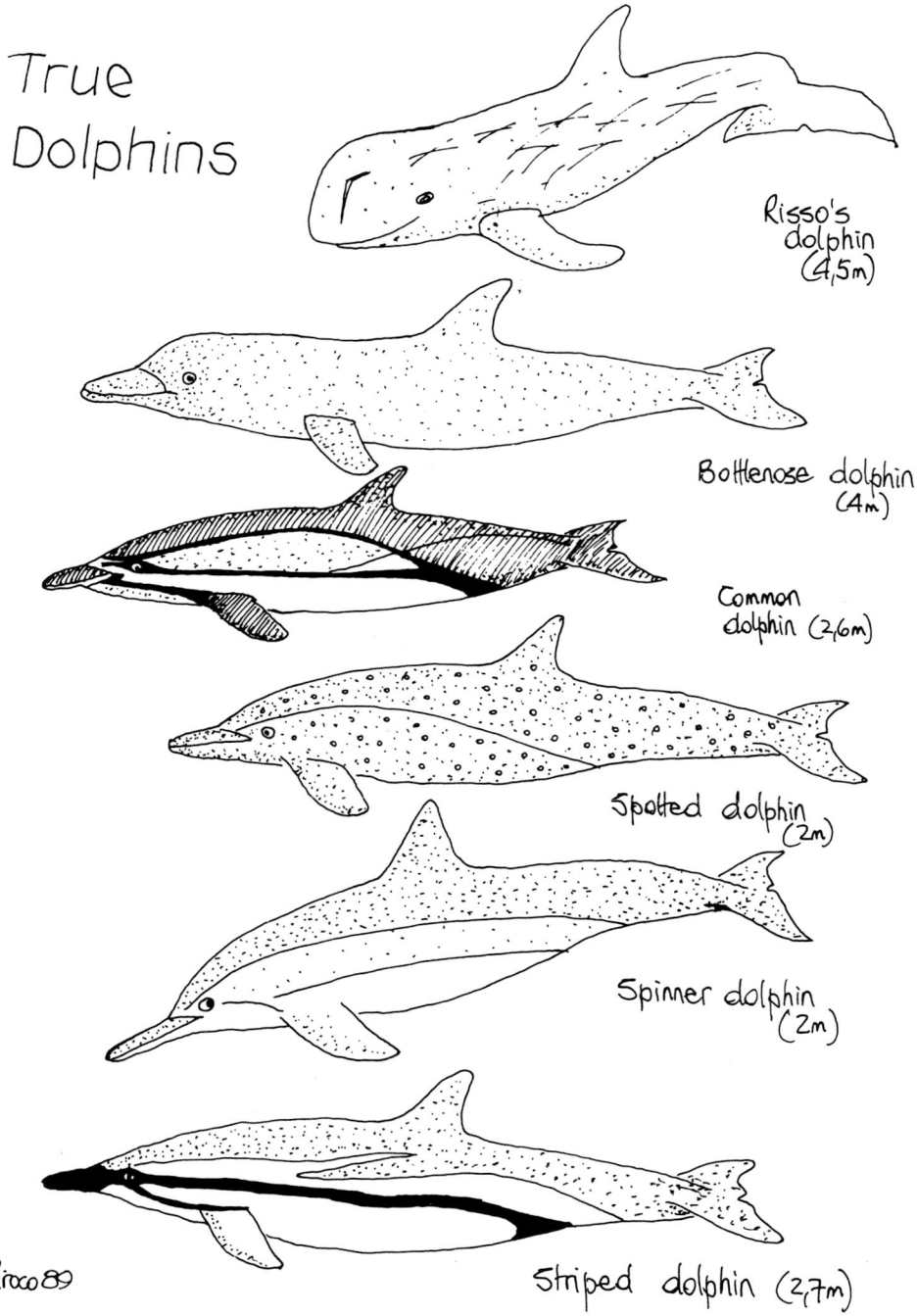
True Dolphins
Risso's dolphin (4,5m)
Bottlenose dolphin (4m)
Common dolphin (2,6m)
Spotted dolphin (2m)
Spinner dolphin (2m)
Striped dolphin (2,7m)
Pirocco 89

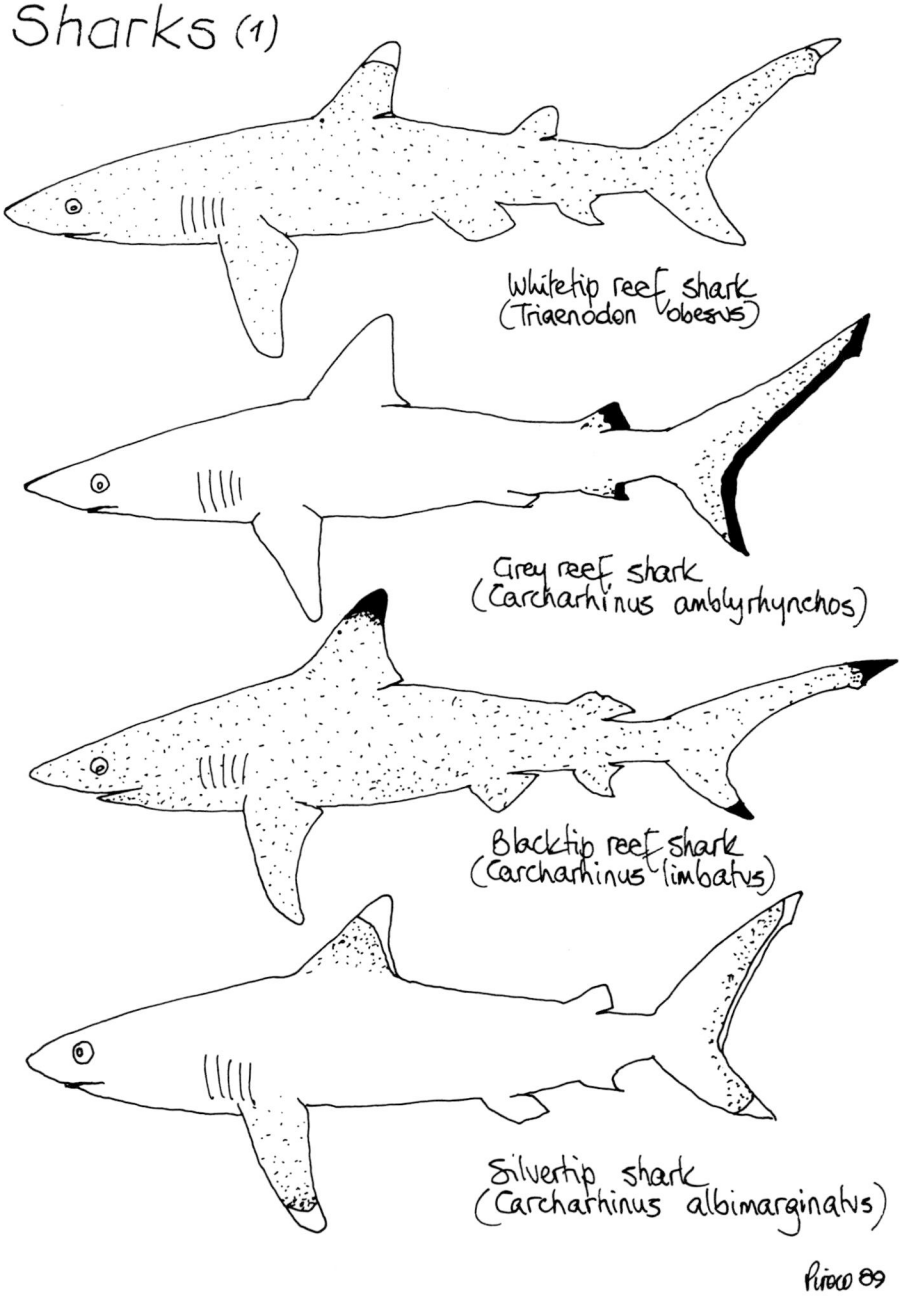
Sharks (1)
Whitetip reef shark
(Triaenodon obesus)
Grey reef shark
(Carcharhinus amblyrhynchos)
Blacktip reef shark
(Carcharhinus limbatus)
Silvertip shark
(Carcharhinus albimarginatus)
Pirco 89

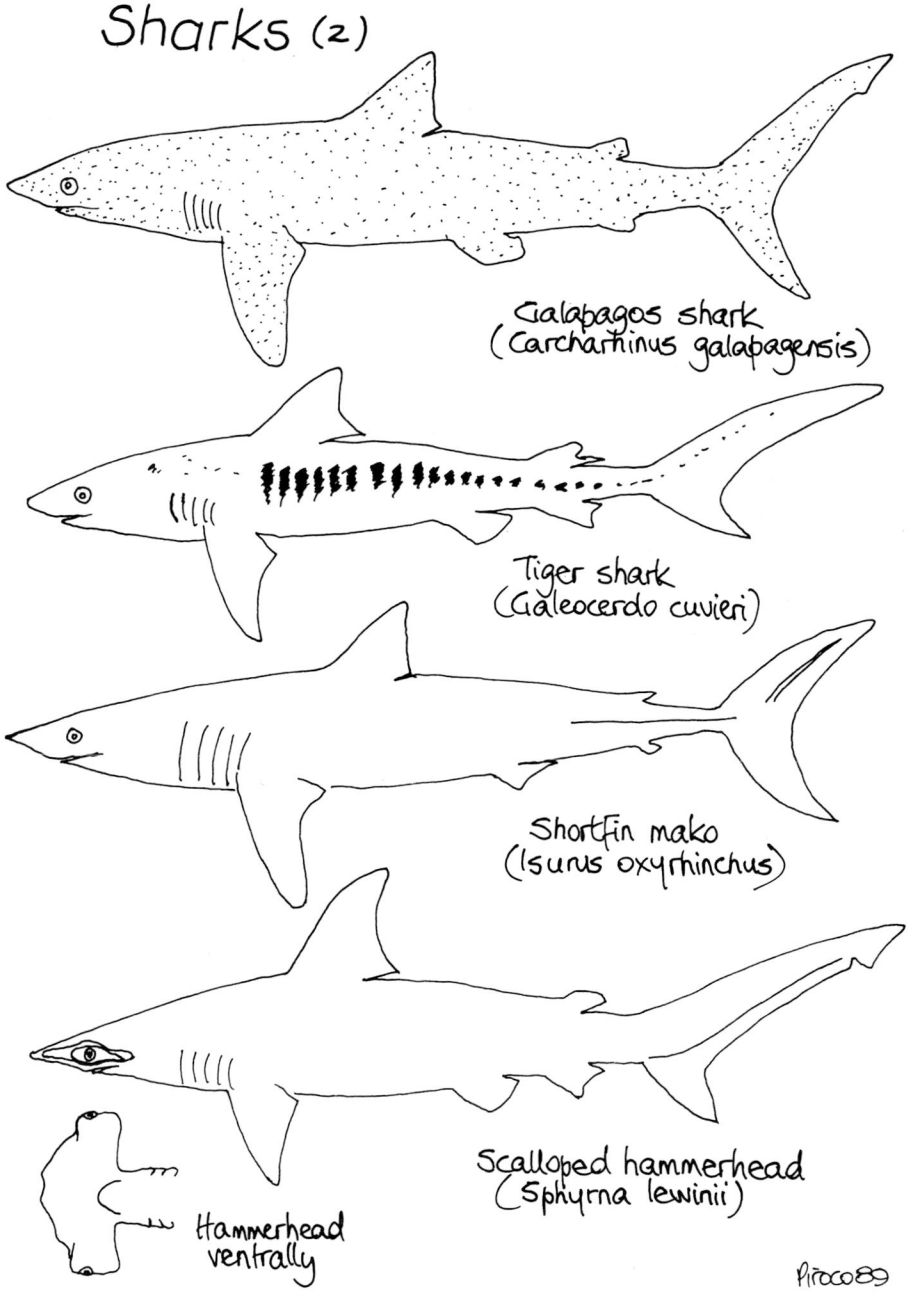
Sharks (2)
Galapagos shark
(Carcharhinus galapagensis)
Tiger shark
(Galeocerdo cuvieri)
Shortfin mako
(Isurus oxyrhinchus)
Scalloped hammerhead
(Sphyrna lewinii)
Hammerhead
ventrally
Pirocoo89

Sharks (3)

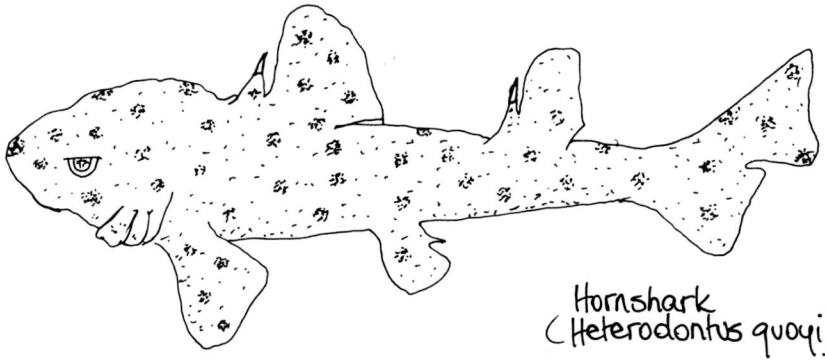

Hornshark
(Heterodontus quoyi)

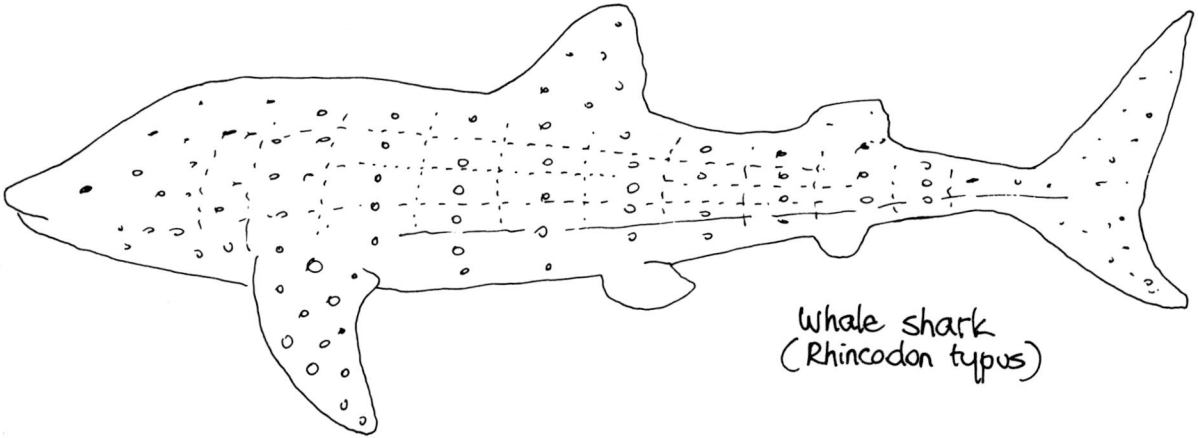

Whale shark
(Rhincodon typus)

Other Marine Animals

Phylum Cnidaria

Class Anthozoa: anemones, corals, gorgonians:

Pacific tube anemone	*Pachycerianthus fimbriatus*
Anemone	*Bunodactis mexicana*
Anemone	*Bunodosoma* sp.
Leopard spotted anemone	*Antiparactis* sp.
Anemone	*Anthopleura* sp.
Zoanthid	*Palythoa* sp.
Zoanthid	*Zoanthus* sp.
Golden sea fan	*Muricea* sp.
Orange cup coral	*Tubastrea coccinea*
Tagus cup coral	*Tubastrea tagusensis*
Pink cup coral	*Tubastrea* sp.
Floreana cup coral	*Tubastrea floreana* (E)
Faulkner's cup coral	*Tubastrea faulkneri*
	Polycyanthus isabela (E)
Yellow polyp black coral	*Antipathes galapagensis*
Panama black coral	*Antipathes panamensis*
	Cycloseris elegans
Pebble coral	*Cycloseris mexicana*
	Gardineroseris planulata
Corals	*Psammocora stellata*
	Psammocora brighami
	Pocillopora damicornis
	Pocillopora elegans
	Pocillopora capitata
	Agaricella sp.
	Porites lobata
	Pavona clavus
	Pavona gigantea
	Pavona varians

Phylum Annelida

Class Polychaeta: segmented worms:

Common fireworm	*Eurythoe complanata*
Ornate fireworm	*Chloeia viridis*

Phylum Mollusca

Class Polyplacophora: chitons

Rippled chiton, Sculptured chiton	*Chiton sulcatus*
Giant Galápagos chiton	*Chiton goodallii* (E)
Galápagos tonicia	*Tonicia arnheimi* (E)
Bristly chiton	*Acanthochitona hirudiniformis*

Class Gastropoda: snails, sea slugs, sea hares, nudibranchs:

Magnificent scallop	*Nodipecten magnificens*
Galápagos abalone	*Haliotis dalli*
Grinning tuna	*Malearingens* (Family Tonnidae)
Chief rocksnail	*Hexaplex princeps*(Family Muricidae)
Panamic horse conch	*Pleuroploca princeps*
Galápagos black sea slug	*Onchidella steindachneri* (E)
Sea hare, Warty seacat	*Dolabrifera dolabrifera*
Purple sea hare	*Aplysia* sp.
Blue ring seahare	*Stylocheilus longicauda* (Aplysiidae)
Walking seahare	*Aplysia cedrosensis* "
Blunted seahare	*Dolabella auricularia* "
Blue aglaja	*Philinopsis cyanea* (Aglajidae)
Panama aglaja	*Navanax aenigmaticus* "
Orange blob, apricot slug	*Berthellina engeli* (Pleurobranchidae)
Warty seaslug	*Pleurobranchus areolatus*
Starred seaslug	*Berthella stellata*
Order Nudibranchia	
White smoothhorn doris	*Conualevia alba* (Conualeviidae)
Dall doris	*Glossodoris dalli* (Chromodorididae)
Red tipped sea goddess	*Glossodoris sedna* "
Baumann doris	*Chromodoris baumanni* "
Ruzafa doris	*Chromodoris ruzafai* "
Sphon doris	*Chromodoris sphoni* "
Starry night nudibranch	*Hypselodoris lapizlauli* "
Carolyn doris	*Platydoris carolinae* (Platydorididae)
Orange doris	*Doriopsylla janaina*(Dendrodorididae)
Mavis doris	*Geitodoris mavis* (Discodorididae)
Galápagos discordis	*Discodoris* sp. (E) "
Blue striped sea slug	*Tambja mullineri* (Polyceridae)
Carnivorous nudibranch	*Roboastra* sp. "
Suborder Aeolidiacea	
Translucent aeolis	*Flabellina telja* (Flabellinidae)
Spanish shawl	*Flabellina* sp. "
Marcus aeolis	*Flabellina marcusorum* "
	Favorinus sp. (Facelinidae)
White aeolis	*Aeolidiella alba* (Aeolidiidae)
India aeolis	*Aeolidiella indica* "
Class Cephalopoda	
Fam. Octopidae	*Octopus oculifer*
Fam. Argonautidae	*Argonauta pacificus*
Fam. Enoploteuthidae	*Abraliopsis affinis*
	Pterygioteuthis giardi
Fam. Ommastrephidae	*Stenoteuthis ovalaniensis*
Fam. Cranchiidae	*Liocranchia reinhardti*

PHYLUM ARTHROPODA

Class Crustacea: crabs, shrimps, lobsters:

Galápagos pebblestone crab	*Mithrax* sp.
Giant hermit crab	*Petrochirus californiensis*
Hairy hermit crab	*Aniculus elegans*
Bar-eyed hermit crab	*Dardanus fucosus*
Swimming crab	*Cronius ruber*
Red crab	*Cancer* sp.
Sally lightfoot crab	*Grapsus grapsus*
Princely fiddler crab	*Uca princeps*
Panamic arrowhead crab	*Stenorhynchus debilis*
Shamed face box crab	*Calappa convexa*
Ghost crab	*Ocypode* sp.
Sea star shrimp	*Periclimenes soror*
Banded coral shrimp	*Stenopus hispidus*
Giant khaki shrimp	*Penaeus californiensis*
Yellowsnout red shrimp	*Rhynchocinetes* sp.
Red spiny lobster	*Panulirus penicillatus*
Blue lobster	*Panulirus gracilis*
Slipper lobster	*Scyllarides astori*

PHYLUM ECHINODERMATA

Class Asteroidea: seastars:

Armored sand star	*Astropecten armatus*
Panamic cushion star	*Pentaceraster cummingi*
(or Gulf star)	*Oreaster occidentalis*
Chocolate chipstar	*Nidorellia armata*
Pyramid sea star	*Pharia pyramidata*
Tan sea star, Blue sea star	*Phataria unifascialis*
Troschel's sea star	*Evasterias troschelii*
Pacific comet star	*Linckia columbiae*
Sunstar	*Heliaster multiradiata*
Red sun star	*Heliaster cumingii* (E)
Bradley sea star	*Mithrodia bradleyi*
Giant sea star	(Punta Vicente Roca, November 2000)

Class Ophiuroidea: brittle stars:

Alexander's spiny brittle star	*Ophiocma alexandri*
Multicolored brittle star	*Ophioderma variegatum*

Class Echinoidea: sea urchins:

Pencil sea urchin	*Eucidaris thouarsii*
Crowned sea urchin	*Centrostephanus coronatus*
Galápagos green sea urchin	*Lytechinus semituberculatus* (E)
Flower sea urchin	*Toxopneustes roseus*

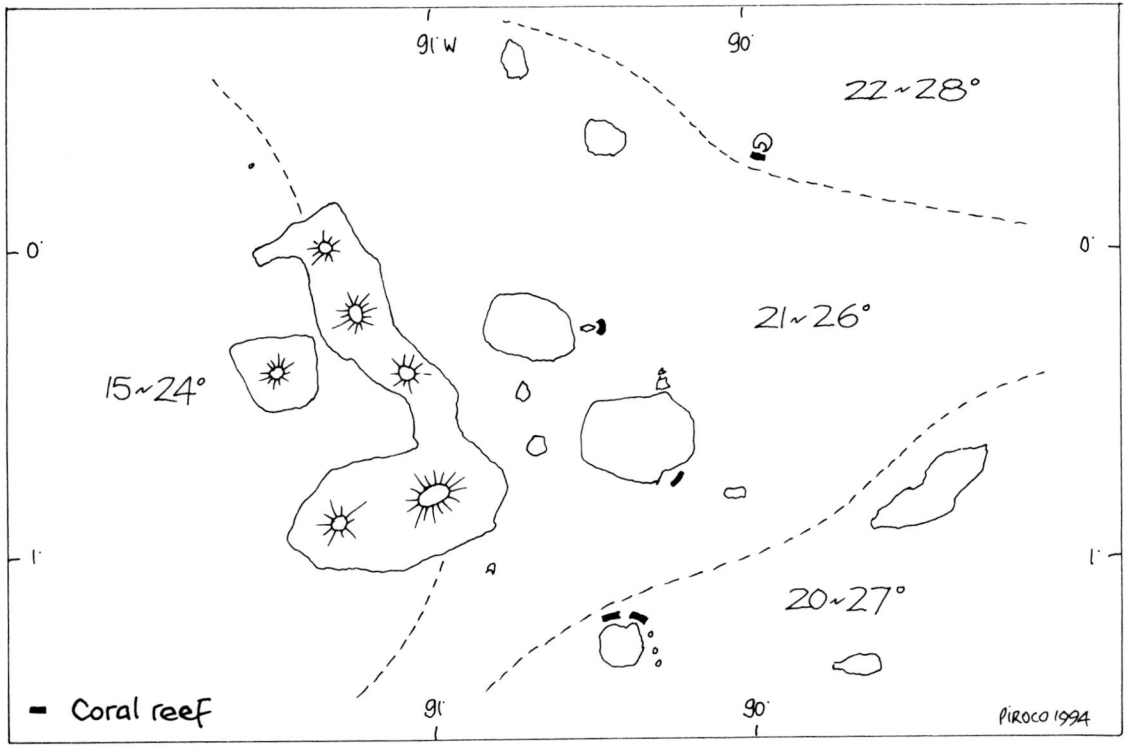

Sea Temperature

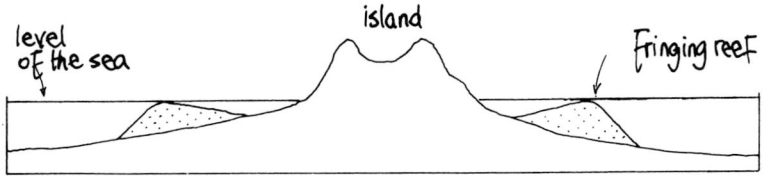

1- Volcanic island. Construction of a coral reef around it.

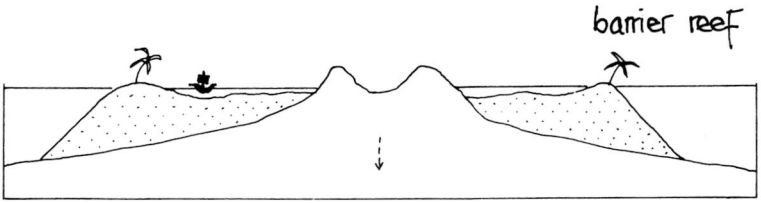

2- The island sinks and is eroded. The reef builds up vertically. e.g. Bora Bora (Society islands).

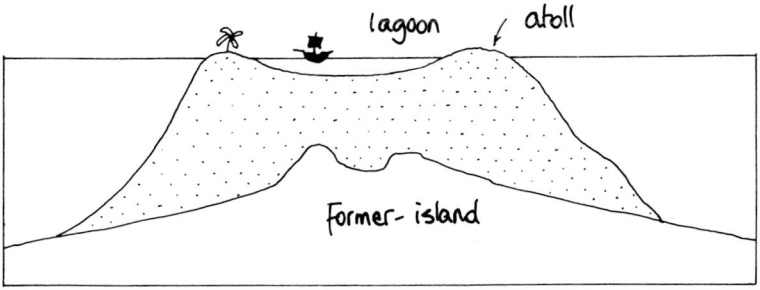

3- The island disappears totally, with the reef building up. The circular reef leaves an atoll.

Evolution of a coral reef

after Darwin

Pidoo 1994

Giant sand dollar	*Clypeaster europacificus*
Heart urchin, sea porcupine	*Lovenia cordiformis*
Grooved heart urchin	*Agassizia scobiculata*
Class Holothuroidea: sea cucumbers:	
Brown spotted sea cucumber	*Holothuria impatiens*
Sulphur sea cucumber	*Holothuria lubrica*
Giant sea cucumber	*Isostichopus fuscus*

REPTILES

Sea snake	*Pelamis platurus*
Marine iguana	*Amblyrhynchus cristatus*
Black turtle	*Chelonia agassizi*

MAMMALS

Sea lion	*Zalophus californianus*
Fur sea lion	*Arctocephalus galapagoensis*

Total: 116 species

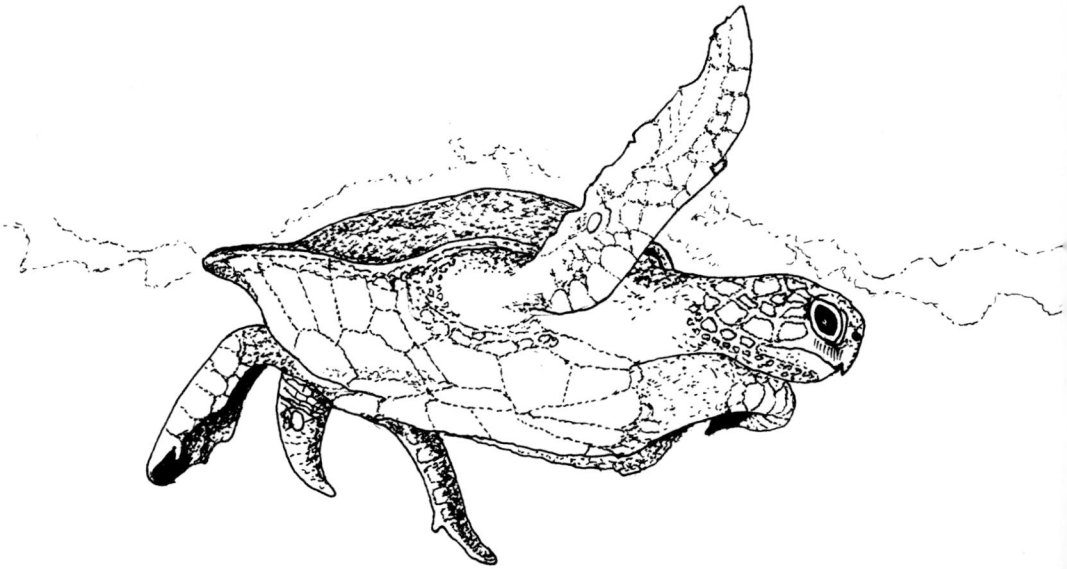

CHAPTER SIX

The Galápagos Marine Reserve; La Pesca Artesanal; Lobsters and Black Coral; Illegal Fishing and the 'Pepinos' affair

La Pesca Artesanal (Artisanal fishing)

In the early days, of the 30 species which were fished in the Galápagos, 90 per cent belonged to the family Serranidae (groupers and seabasses). In the 1950s, mainly *bacalao* (yellow grouper), *lisa* (yellowtail mullet) and lobster were caught. Between the 1930s and 1950s, bacalao were caught on a line (*pinchagua*), then cut in half, salted, dried on the rocks, and exported to the mainland. In the 1980s, bacalao accounted for 50 per cent of industrial fishing, followed by *camotillo* and *mero* (two other groupers). Tuna fishing lagged far behind.

In 1986, annual fishing brought in 150 to 250 tons. Bacalao fishing occurs six months out of the year between October and March, mainly around Isabela Island (until the Marine Reserve was created).

The *norteno* fishing, during the first three months of the year, occurs in the northern islands of Marchena, Darwin and Wolf. The last three months of the year are the season for *camotillo* fishing.

The Galápagos fisheries: 1999–2000 in the RMG (Reserva Marina de Galápagos)

In the 19th century, fishing in the Galápagos was mainly aimed at whales and sea lions. When the original pioneers came, artisanal fishing became a necessity for survival and, later on, turned into a commercial activity. In 1992, a dramatic change occured when the fishing of sea cucumbers was added to the traditional catch of lobsters and fish (Pesca blanca). In 1997, the CDRS initiated the 'Programa de Monitoreo Pesquero' (PMP), a program dedicated to the monitoring of fisheries, in conjunction with the 'Marine Ressources Unit of the Galápagos National Park' (RECMAR) and the fishing cooperatives of the Galápagos.

The number of fishing boats increased more than three times, from 101 boats in 1993 to 341 in year 2000. The number of fishermen, estimated at 150 in 1971, grew by over four times, to reach a figure of 682 fishermen registered officially in year 2000, based on the three main islands of San Cristóbal, Isabela and Santa Cruz (see table of the number of fishermen registered per island, 1997–200). These figures neither include nor reflect illegal fishing activities, of course.

	1997	1999	% increase	2000	% increase
San Cristóbal	203	291	88	342	51
Isabela	130	164	34	177	13
Santa Cruz	124	158	34	163	5

(Number of fishermen registered per island, 1997–2000, Fundacion Natura)

The fishing fleet increased from 128 pangas in 1999 to 226 pangas in 2000, an augmentation of 76 per cent. San Cristóbal is leading far ahead of Isabela and Santa Cruz (table #2, n° and type of embarcations per island 1997–2000).

	San Cristóbal	Santa Cruz	Isabela	Total
Year 1998				
boat	29	24	7	60
panga	50	93	51	194
fibra	1	5	10	16
Total	**80**	**122**	**68**	**270**
Year 1999				
boat	25	17	7	49
panga	51	35	42	128
fibra	1	10	8	19
Total	**77**	**62**	**57**	**196**
Year 2000				
boat	34	23	8	65
panga	105	46	75	226
fibra	14	20	16	50
Total	**153**	**89**	**99**	**341**

(Number and type of embarcations per island, 1997–2000, after Informe Galápagos 1999–2000, Fundacion Natura, Quito)

The fishing activities in 1999 involved three fisheries regulated according to the official calendar. The 'Pesca blanca': various species, all year round; the 'Pepino de mar' or sea cucumber (July–August) and 'langosta', lobster (September–December). The total catch is estimated to be about 626 metric tons, which is 50 per cent more than what the register of fisheries actually states.

Pesca blanca

All year round, it includes pelagic fish, coastal and benthic fishes. More than 70 species are involved. Of the global catch, more than 80 per cent of the total tonnage is concentrated on the first ten species caught. These include: the blacktail mullet (*Mugil cephalus*) 43 per cent, the bacalao (*Mycteroperca olfax*) 15 per cent, the yellowtail mullet (*Mugil rammelsbergii*) nine per cent, the wahoo (*Acanthocybium solandri*) four per cent and the amberjack (*Seriola rivolina*) three per cent. In 1999, the greatest volume was caught by San Cristóbal, followed by Santa Cruz and Isabela.

List of the species exploited by the 'Pesca Artesanal' in the Galápagos Islands (Pesca Blanca), 1999

Family	Scientific name	Common name	Total Weight PMP/ in Kg
Mugilidae	*Mugil cephalus*	Lisa cola negra	96076
Serranidae	*Mycteroperca olfax*	Bacalao	33330
Mugilidae	*Mugil galapagensis*	Lisa rabo amarillo	20250
Scombridae	*Acanthocybium solandri*	Guajo	9847
Carangidae	*Seriola rivoliana*	Palometa, huayaipe	7156
Serranidae	*Paralabrax albomaculatus*	Camotillo	6669
Branchiostegidae	*Caulolatilus princeps*	Blanquillo	5351
Carangidae	*Trachinotus stilbe*	Pampano acerado	4544
Serranidae	*Epinephelus panamensis*	Enjambre	4074
Lutjanidae	*Lutjanus novemfasciatus*	Pargo prieto	4019
Serranidae	*Epinephelus* sp.		3822
Serranidae	*Dermatolepis dermatolepis*	Cagaleche	3458
Scorpaenidae		Pez escorpion	2889
Haemulidae	*Xenichthys agassizi*	Ojon blanco	1973
Scorpaenidae	*Scorpaena plumieri mystes*	Pez escorpion	1889
Serranidae	*Epinephelus cifuentesi*	Norteno	1813
	Hemilutjanus macrophtalmos	Ojo de uva	1794
Labridae	*Semicossyphus darwinii*	Vieja mancha dorada	1418
Serranidae	*Cratinus agassizi*	Plumero	1032
Scombridae	*Thunnus albacares*	Atun aleta amarilla	965
Scombridae	*Thunnus* sp.	Atun	952
Carangidae	*Caranx lugubris*	Jurel negro	908
Scombridae	*Scomberomorus sierra*	Sierra	844
Haemulidae	*Xenichthys xanti*	Ojon	761
Clupeidae	*Opisthonema libertate*	Pinchagua	681
Serranidae	*Epinephelus labriformis*	Cabrilla	602
Scombridae	*Thunnus obesus*	Patudo, ojo grande	292
Carangidae	*Trachinotus stilbe*	Pampano	271
Centropomidae	*Centropomus nigrescens*	Robalo	218
Kyphosidae	*Girella fremenvillei*	Chopa negra	218
Carangidae	*Caranx caballus*	Jurel verde	207
Scorpaenidae	*Pontinus* sp.	Brujo, lechuza	204
Haemulidae	*Anisotremus interruptus*	Burrito, zapatilla	166
Scombridae	*Euthynnus lineatus*	Barrilete negro	159
Lutjanidae	*Pargo* sp.	Pargo	156
Lutjanidae	*Lutjanus argiventris*	Pargo amarillo	152
Carcharhinidae	*Carcharhinus limbatus*	Tiburon punta negra	116

Chanidae	*Chanos chanos*	Lisa diabla	114
Carangidae		Vieja	107
Haemulidae	*Xenocys jessiae*	Jurel	102
Labridae	*Bodianus eclancheri*	Ojon rayado	92
Lutjanidae	*Lutjanus jordani*	Vieja colorada	89
Cacharhinidae		Tiburon	82
Scombridae	*Sarda orientalis*	Bonito	81
Labridae	*Bodianus* sp.	Vieja	80
Clupeidae	*Sardinops sagax*	Sardina	73
Labridae	*Bodianus diplotaenia*	Vieja ribeteada	66
Serranidae	*Alphester afer*	Guaseta del Pacifico	52
Kyphosidae	*Kyphosus elegans*	Chopa de Cortez	51
Carcharhinidae		Cazon	31
Sphyraenidae	*Sphyraena idiastes*	Barracuda	31
Haemulidae	*Haemulon scudderi*	Roncador de Galápagos	29
Oplegnathidae	*Oplegnathus insignis*	Tigris	27
Scaridae	*Nicholsina denticulata*	Lora de diente flojo	26
Gerreidae	*Eucinostomus argenteus*	Mojarra plateada	21
Sparidae	*Archosargus pourtalesi*	Camiseta rayada	21
Gerreidae	*Diapterus peruvianus*	Mojarra	15.23
Haemulidae	*Orthopristis forbesi*	Roncador ojo dorado	14
Coryphaenidae	*Coryphaena hippurus*	Dorado	8.32
Cirrhitidae	*Cirrhitus rivulatus*	Carabali	5.45
Scombridae	*Scomber* sp.	Caballa	5.45
Scombridae	*Scomber japonicus*	Macarela	5
Carangidae	*Alectis ciliaris*	Pampano africano	4.52
Sparidae	*Calamus taurinus*	Plumero de Galápagos	3.50
Scaridae	*Scarus ghobban*	Lora barba azul	2.73
Sciaenidae	*Odontoscion eurymesops*	Bombache ojon	2.73
Scaridae	*Scarus compressus*	Lora verde azul	2.50
		Corvinita	1.36
Xiphiidae	*Makaira* sp.	Pez espada	1.25
Mullidae	*Mulloidichthys dentatus*	Salmonete	0.68
Pomacentridae	*Abudefduf troschelli*	Sargento mayor	0.45
Other species			2,713.14
Total			**223,258.86**

(after Informe Galápagos, 1999–2000 of Fundacion Natura and WWF, Quito, September 2000)

Pepino de mar

In 1999, the fishing of sea cucumbers (*Isostichopus fuscus*) took place between April 1st and May 31st. No quota was established. The 'guias de movilizacion' released by the Galápagos National Park Office registered more than 122 metric tons for the time of the catch, which is about 4.4 million individuals. Puerto Baquerizo Moreno caught 52 per cent of the total, followed by Puerto Villamil and Puerto Ayora.

In 1994, the major catch happened in Fernandina (island of special interest for the fishing sector). The CDRS evaluates that the sea cucumber population has been reduced more than 80 per cent in comparison to the densities of 1993.

Ten years later, in 2004, the scientific investigation by the Darwin Station warned that the sea cucumber resources were not sustainable anymore, and that the fishing of 'pepinos' should be totally banned in 2005. Nevertheless, the Galápagos National Park, under political pressure, allowed a catch of 3 million pepinos for the legal period in July/August. In 2005, no more than 1 million pepinos were fished, bringing forward an economic and social crisis for the fishermen, now pressuring the government for alternative resources, such as the opening of long line fishing in high seas.

The 'Long Line Pilot Study' (2003) recently published by Juan Carlos Daviles (CDRS) showed results (by catch) of an alarming level, mainly shark species. These results will be used in the discussions on local and national levels, regarding the use of the controversial fishing method.

Langosta

Three species of lobster are present in the Galápagos, which are commercially exploited:

Common name	*Scientific name*	*Local name*
Red lobster	*Panulirus penicillatus*	Langosta roja
Blue lobster	*Panulirus gracilis*	Langosta azul
Slipper lobster	*Scyllarides astori*	Langostino

The red lobster, found in the central and northern islands, and northeast of Isabela Island, once made up 60 per cent of the catch. The blue lobster, once 40 per cent of the catch, is larger, and is distributed mostly on the west coast of Isabela (Urvina and Elizabeth Bay) and around the southern coast, as far as Cartago Bay to the east of Isabela Island.

The minimum legal size is 25 centimetres from head to tail. In 1960, the production was 180 tons; in 1965, 65 tons, and in 1983, 94 tons (of which 33 tons consisted of tails). To allow annual reproduction and the survival of the species, a ban on lobster fishing was enforced each year January–February and June–July. Nevertheless, the abusive catch of recent years has brought a dramatic reduction of the resource and, as a result, the Ecuadorian government imposed a total ban for seven years—from January 1, 1993, until the year 2000—in order to restock the lobster species.

Nevertheless, after strikes and protests led by fishermen in 1993–94, the government reopened lobster fishing for three months per year, from July 15 to October 15.

In year 2000, the official period for capture, consumption, transport and commercialization of both the red lobster and the blue lobster extends from September 1 to December 31. The maximum quota was of 35 metric tons; minimum size of tails 15 centimetres or a total length of 26 centimetres. On October 5th, the minimum tail size was brought down to 14 centimetres. The total catch was finally of 54.4 metric tons (Puerto Ayora: 24.9MT, Puerto Baquerizo: 22.9MT, Puerto Villamil: 6.6MT). Of these figures, 52.6 metric tons were exported to the continent, and 1.8 metric tons were kept for local consumption.

Black Coral

Another problem for the Park is the exploitation of the black coral, *Antipathes panamensis*, which is not endemic to the Galápagos, unlike *Antipathes galapagensis* which is endemic. Black coral can reach 70 to 80 years in age and feeds on zooplancton.

Black coral is sought by the craftsmen of Puerta Ayora (Santa Cruz) and Puerto Baquerizo Moreno (San Cristóbal). The coral is carved and polished to make jewellery and other fancy gifts which are then sold in shops as Galápagos souvenirs. At present the Galápagos National Park does not have the power to ban sales or stop this exploitation.

The Galápagos Marine Reserve

'La Reserva Marina de Galápagos' (RMG) is the second largest in the world after the Great Barrier Reef, in Australia. On May 13, 1986, the Ecuadorian government, by presidential decree of Leon Febrès Cordero, established the Reserve of the Galápagos Marine Resources. The 50,000 square kilometres of ocean surface comprises the internal waters of the archipelago. A strip of 15 nautical miles (28 kilometres), extending from the outlying points of the islands, was added. This 'buffer zone' represents another 20,000 square kilometres, bringing the total surface of the Marine Reserve to 70,000 square kilometres.

A committee was created to supervise and control the reserve. Its members are representative of the following departments: agriculture, foreign affairs, defense, industry and commercial fisheries, energy and mining, planning and the INGALA (Instituto Nacional Galápagos).

This biological reserve aims to protect and preserve a number of ecological aspects of the islands, as well as the interaction of the National Park with the Marine Reserve. Industrial fishing is not allowed, but local or artisanal fishing go on as before (see drawing of the Marine Reserve, opposite page). After multiple abuse over the years, a special law was voted in 1998 by the Ecuadorian government to extend the Marine Reserve to 40 nautical miles around the islands. The Marine Reserve Managment Plan was made through a representative multi- sectoral team, called 'Grupo Nucleo', composed of three sectors: fisheries, tourism and conservation, initiated by the Galápagos National Park, CDRS and financed by USAID, GEF and WWF. The Marine Reserve has now a surface of 140,000 sq.km, patrolled by air and by sea: 19 coastal marine patrol trips and 11 patrol flights were made in 1997 ('Guadalupe River' is SPNG's only boat). In March 1999, the master plan for the Marine Reserve was approved for implementation. Legal fishing of 'pepinos' (sea cucumbers) is granted to Galápagos residents for a period of two months (July–August) every year.

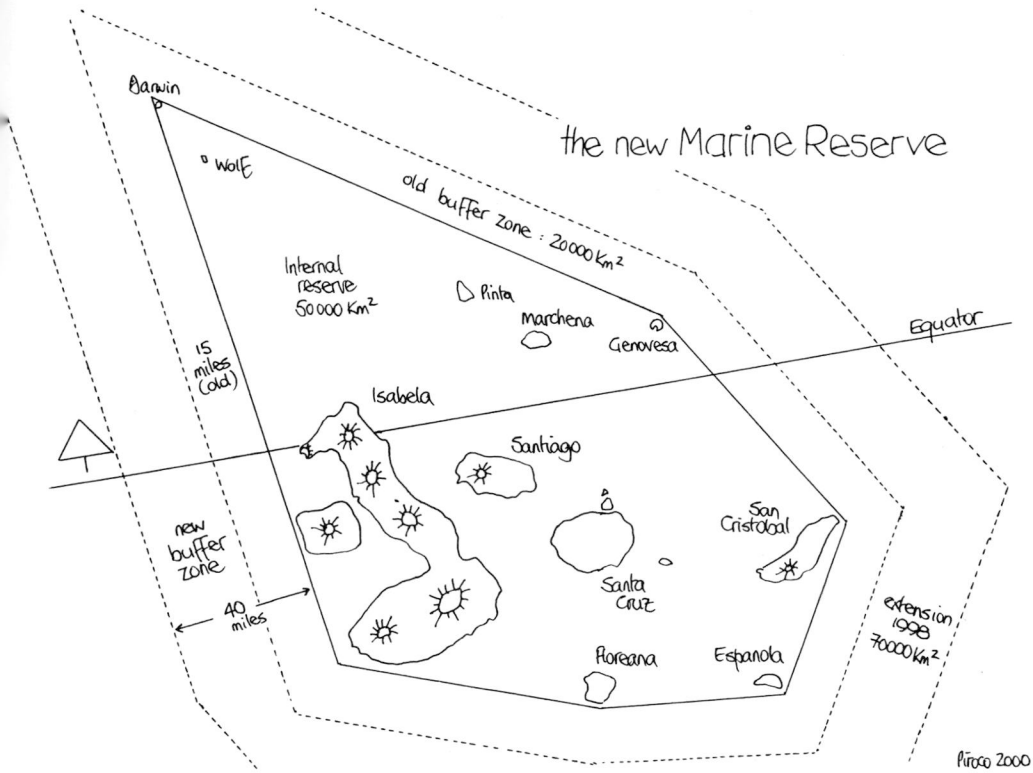

Following the Symposium of Science and Conservation, organized in Brussels in 1998 for the Charles Darwin Foundation, a serious program on the conservation of biodiversity in the Galápagos Marine Reserve, has been developed by the CDRS. In conclusion, the idea is the adoption of a Master Plan with a scientific base: the establishment of the second biggest marine reserve in the world. Ultimately, the goal is to include the Marine Reserve in the list of World Heritage Sites for year 2002.

Conservation of Biodiversity in the RMG

The priorities for future investigation are:

– Investigation and monitoring of the marine and coastal ecosystems of Galápagos.

– Investigation and monitoring of the exploitation of marine ressources

* monitoring of fisheries
* monitoring of populations of sea cucumbers
* investigation and training of the fishermen to minimize the problems of incidental fishing (pesca artesanal)
* to look for experiences in other places, regarding the conservation of sharks (monitoring of populations and collection of data by naturalist guides, loss of sharks by incidental fishing and illegal activities, formulating a conservation plan for sharks within the Master Plan of the Galápagos Marine Reserve.)

(– after R. Bustamente, K. Collins and R. Bensted Smith, CDRS 2000)

Illegal Fishing and The 'Pepinos' Affair

As expected, abuses were not long in surfacing. Striking fishermen came to knock at the government's door to show their anger in 1993. At issue are illegal shark fishing and shark finning (which has caused a furore for some years now), as well as pepino (sea cucumber) fishing. All are pirate fisheries, conducted by sophisticated Japanese fishing boats. The 'pepino war' has gained considerable press attention since 1992.

The shark fishing, stimulated by the Japanese fishing industry, began to cause a stir as far back as 1983. In violation of Ecuadorian law, Japanese boats were penetrating Galápagos waters in the northern islands and around Isabela Island. They were seen on a number of occasions, then escorted away, after paying dubious 'fines'. The Japanese then conceived the following stratagem: They used Ecuadorian boats from Manta (Ecuador), which could be sent into Galápagos waters to fish, while the Japanese mother-ship would safely wait for the catch in international waters. The Japanese ship Choki Maru was nevertheless hailed in 1991, with a shipment of 5,000 shark fins, six kilometres from Cartago Bay, on the east coast of Isabela Island. In 1992, a patrol boat of the Ecuadorian navy captured the Donai, a fishing boat from Manta, near Pinta Island, with a load of 50 hammerhead sharks on board.

The scandal of the sea cucumbers or pepinos blew up in 1992, when pirate camps were discovered on the basaltic coast of Fernandina Island. Local fishermen had settled with their families and were collecting 130,000 to 150,000 pepinos per day. These sea cucumbers, of the species *Isostichopus fuscus,* are marine invertebrates of commercial value in eastern Asian countries. The larvae are an important part of the plankton, which is food for a great number of fish. The sea cucumbers live on rocky bottoms, at a depth of two to 20 metres, and are important for the purification of sea water. The exploitation of the pepinos is a worldwide business which lays waste to an area of the globe for two to four years; the fishermen plunder the resources, then start somewhere else. It started on the coast of Ecuador in 1988, before it spread out to the Galápagos (see photo, page 174). Ten years later, the illegal fishing is still going strong (1998) with shark fins and 'pepinos'. Pirates involved are now equipped with machine guns and other dangerous armaments. On February 20, 1998, fishing boat 'Aleta Amarilla II' from Costa Rica was captured, holding seven bags of shark fin; 10,000 kilograms of tuna, dolphinfish and sharks were found on board.

In May 2000, angry fishermen protested to the Ecuadorian government against the 40 miles Marine Reserve, and the short periods allowed for fishing. The fishing period of the sea cucumbers in 2000 goes from May 22 to July 22. The volume, size of capture and period of fisheries were accepted by the 'Sector Pesquero Artesanal de Galápagos'. These parameters were ignored by the fishermen of Isabela. The installations of SPNG/CDRS were occupied for 48 hours, in Isabela and Cristóbal (without destruction). Tortoises held in Puerto Villamil by demonstrators were returned. The 'Autoridad Interinstitucional de Manejo' (AIM) established that the fishing would close on July 22nd or upon reaching the quota of four and a half million pepinos.

This was followed in November by a general strike of the 'Cooperativas de Pesca', in Isabela, Santa Cruz and San Cristóbal. The SPNG office in Isabela was vandalized and furniture burnt on the street. Juan Chavez, the manager, was almost killed by a mob of 20 fishermen. The 'Ministro del Medio Ambiente' agreed to give one more month of fishing, and an extra fish quota.

In 2004, one of the activities of the CDRS Department of Communication is to increase the capacity of the local community to manage Galápagos natural resources sustainably. In other words, to encourage fishermen, users of the Marine Reserve, to produce proposals for management, based on scientific information (Galápagos Research, No.63, June 2005). A survey of knowledge, attitude and practices of the fishermen was carried out during 2004, most of them having secondary education, and in the 25–54 age group. 60 per cent of the fishermen did not know about 'participatory monitoring', 30 per cent did not wish to participate in the sea cucumber monitoring, but 60 per cent agreed to participate in the lobster monitoring. Half had no confidence in the results, one third believed it was prejudicial to them, 60 per cent believed that the results were manipulated. Most agreed that the fisheries cooperatives should carry out and pay for the monitoring of sea cucumbers, but half believed the fishing sector did not use the results of lobster monitoring.

PART THREE

DESCRIPTION OF THE ISLANDS

Description of the Islands

Baltra—North Seymour Santa Cruz South Plaza Santa Fé Daphné Rábida Pinzón	CENTRAL ISLANDS
Floreana Española San Cristóbal	SOUTHERN ISLANDS
Genovesa Marchena Pinta Wolf Darwin	NORTHERN ISLANDS
Santiago Bartolomé Sombrero Chino Isabela Fernandina	WESTERN ISLANDS

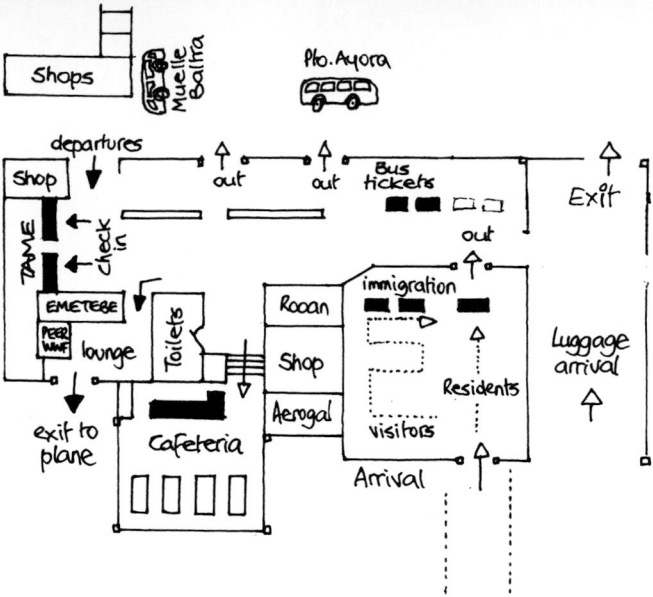
Shops
Muelle Baltra
Pto. Ayora
departures
Shop
out
out
Bus tickets
Exit
TAME
check in
out
immigration
EMETEBE
PEER WAVE
lounge
Toilets
Rocan
Shop
Aerogal
Residents
Luggage arrival
exit to plane
Cafeteria
visitors
Arrival

Baltra airport
North Seymour
Mosquera
north channel
Capitania
Aeolean cove
Baltra
Airport
Itabaca channel
Ferry
Santa Cruz
buses
to Puerto Ayora - 40 Km
Piroco 2004

CHAPTER ONE

The Central Islands

Baltra

The plane leaves Quito at 9:30 am and stops over at Guayaquil. It takes off again at around 11 am. After an hour and a quarter of cloudless flight, you'll be in sight of San Cristóbal Island, which will appear on the port side, bedecked with a layer of cotton-shaped clouds. The black-indented shoreline is fringed with waves of white foam. A few minutes later, you may view the Gordon Rocks, then the Plaza Islands in the distant haze. Finally, you will fly over the luminous sandbar of Mosquera Island. The plane will tilt to port before landing on the island of Baltra. The B-737 of TAME airlines, inaugurated on October 22, 1980, stops in the heart of the arid zone, a land covered with cacti. On October 7, 2003 TAME inaugurated a new service from Quito to Baltra, with two Airbus A320s, bringing a new touch of luxury to air travel in Ecuador. This in turn, was a reaction to Aerogal's new competition.

In 2009, four planes, from both TAME and AEROGAL airlines, are landing everyday in Baltra. A US$10 visitor tax was introduced by INGALA in 2008, and is charged upon arrival.

At Baltra Island, the Galápagos National Park customs will ask you to pay an entry fee of US$100 (since 1998), and you will be given a leaflet of visitor's rules. The bus Baltra–Muelle or Baltra–Canal is now free, included in the cost of the TAME ticket. The ferry boat and the bus Canal–Puerto Ayora cost about US$3.

A small island north of Santa Cruz, Baltra is a basaltic plateau—which belongs geologically to Santa Cruz—faulted in an east–west direction. In the distant past, the island was once connected to Santa Cruz and North Seymour. Some fossiliferous tuff beds, between lava flows, are the proof of an ancient tectonic uplift. Sheer cliffs rise to the north, to the east and south. The entire island leans towards the west.

On the west coast, Aeolean Cove offers smooth sand beaches. This port is used by the Ecuadorian navy and is also the site of an air force base. Departures and arrivals of numerous tourist boats are made from there. A few cargo ships which visit the archipelago also call in. Baltra Airport was built by the Americans during World War II. The army base was intended to defend the Panama Canal against Japanese air raids, but the attack never came. Rumour has it that the Americans were partly responsible for the eradication of land iguanas on the island, aided by the presence of feral goats, which ate all the vegetation edible to iguanas. The Ecuadorian air force received the base at the end of the war; today it's a civil and military airport, as well as a naval base.

After a 40-year absence, land iguanas were reintroduced to Baltra by the Galápagos National Park. On June 19, 1991, 35 iguanas (five years old) from the breeding centre in Santa Cruz were freed on the island. The following year, in April 1992, 12 land iguanas (eight to ten years old) were released. The first year of the project showed a survival rate of at least 40 per cent. An eradication of cats was carried out in 2002–03.

Baltra is connected to the island of Santa Cruz by a ferry that daily crosses the Itabaca Channel. From the landing site it is 40 kilometres to the town of Puerto Ayora, or one and a half hours by the minibus of CITTEG, the local transport company (see map of Baltra, page 200). Baltra Airport was closed from May 15 to September 15, 2005 for renovation of the airstrip. San Cristóbal was used as the main airport in the Galápagos Islands.

North Seymour

North of Baltra, Seymour is a small flat island with a land surface of two square kilometres, very similar to Baltra and typical of the arid zone. Palo santos are endemic to the island. Opuntia, the local prickly pear cactus, is the food of the land iguanas.

A trail, about two kilometres long, makes a loop to the southwest, inland and along the rocky coast, crossing the colony of blue-footed boobies then the colony of magnificent frigates. The nesting area of the frigatebirds mixes with that of the boobies. Two species of frigates share the same habitat in harmony. Their nests of twigs are made on the palo santos, as well as on the salt bushes bordering the beach. A few marine iguanas walk across the white coral sand, leaving tracks of their tail and claws. Sea lions bask on the black lava rocks, and the surf crashes on the rocky shore of the west coast at sunset. In the background, the eroded tuff cones of Daphné Mayor and Daphné Minor rise above the ocean surface.

At Seymour, the dry landing on rocks is sometimes difficult, depending on the tide and the season. Rocks may be slippery, and shoes should be worn. A short distance away, Mosquera Islet is an ideal place for a walk when the sun goes down. White sands host a colony of sea lions. Beware of the territorial males, which are known to be aggressive, even in the water. A cautious swim is highly recommended (see map, page 203).

Santa Cruz

land surface: 986 square km
elevation: 864 m; main town: Puerto Ayora

The most populous of the islands, Santa Cruz possesses a radio which transmits at 1410 KHz (since 1974). Of the five inhabited islands of the Galápagos, Santa Cruz and particularly Puerto Ayora, the touristic capital, have for the last 15 years had the highest immigration rate in the archipelago. The population of Santa Cruz Island was estimated to be about 10,000 people in 2005.

All the vegetation zones are represented on Santa Cruz, stretching from the littoral zone up to the fern zone at the top of Mount Crocker. The windward side is more humid and diversified than the leeward side, which is very dry. This is especially understandable when one considers that the dominant winds are the southeast tradewinds, and that the precipitation of garua falls on that side of the island.

Geologically, Santa Cruz is well eroded, and the oldest formations are found to the northeast. Facing the Plazas Islands is Cerro Colorado (the Red Rock), a tectonically uplifted hill in which basaltic lava and fossiliferous tuff are layered with volcanic tuffs of Miocene geological times. The human history started in the 20th century, when European

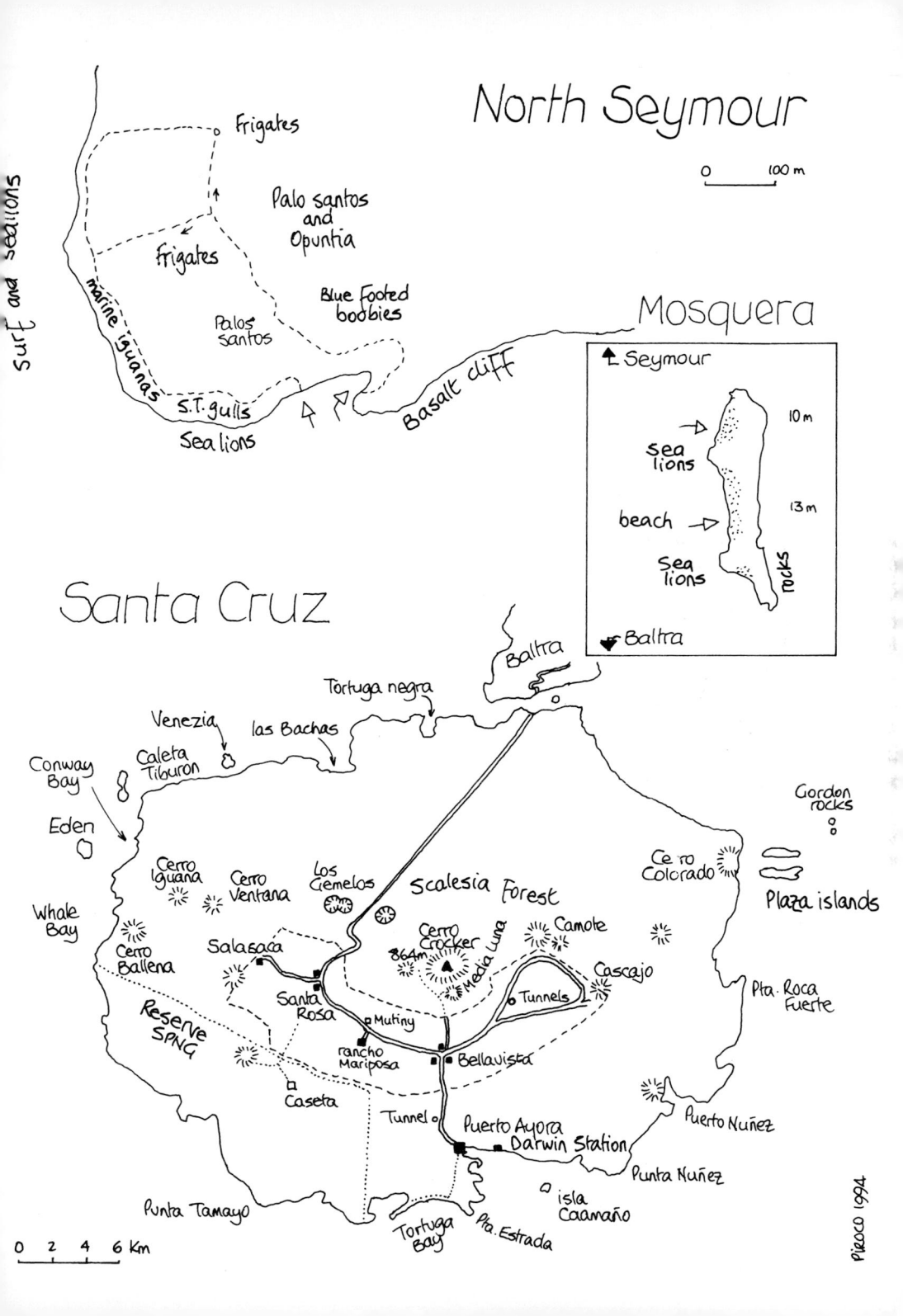
North Seymour
0 100 m
Frigates
Palo santos and Opuntia
Frigates
Blue Footed boobies
Palos santos
marine iguanas
S.T. gulls
Sea lions
Basalt cliff
Surf and sea lions
Mosquera
Seymour
10 m
sea lions
13 m
beach
sea lions
rocks
Baltra
Santa Cruz
Baltra
Tortuga negra
Venezia
las Bachas
Caleta Tiburon
Conway Bay
Eden
Gordon rocks
Cerro Iguana
Cerro Ventana
Los Gemelos
Scalesia Forest
Cerro Colorado
Plaza islands
Whale Bay
Cerro Ballena
Salasaca
Cerro Crocker
864m
Media Luna
Camote
Cascajo
Tunnels
Pta. Roca Fuerte
Santa Rosa
Reserve SPNG
Mutiny
rancho Mariposa
Bellavista
Caseta
Tunnel
Puerto Ayora
Darwin Station
Puerto Nuñez
Punta Nuñez
isla Caamaño
Punta Tamayo
Tortuga Bay
Pta. Estrada
0 2 4 6 Km
PIROCO 1994

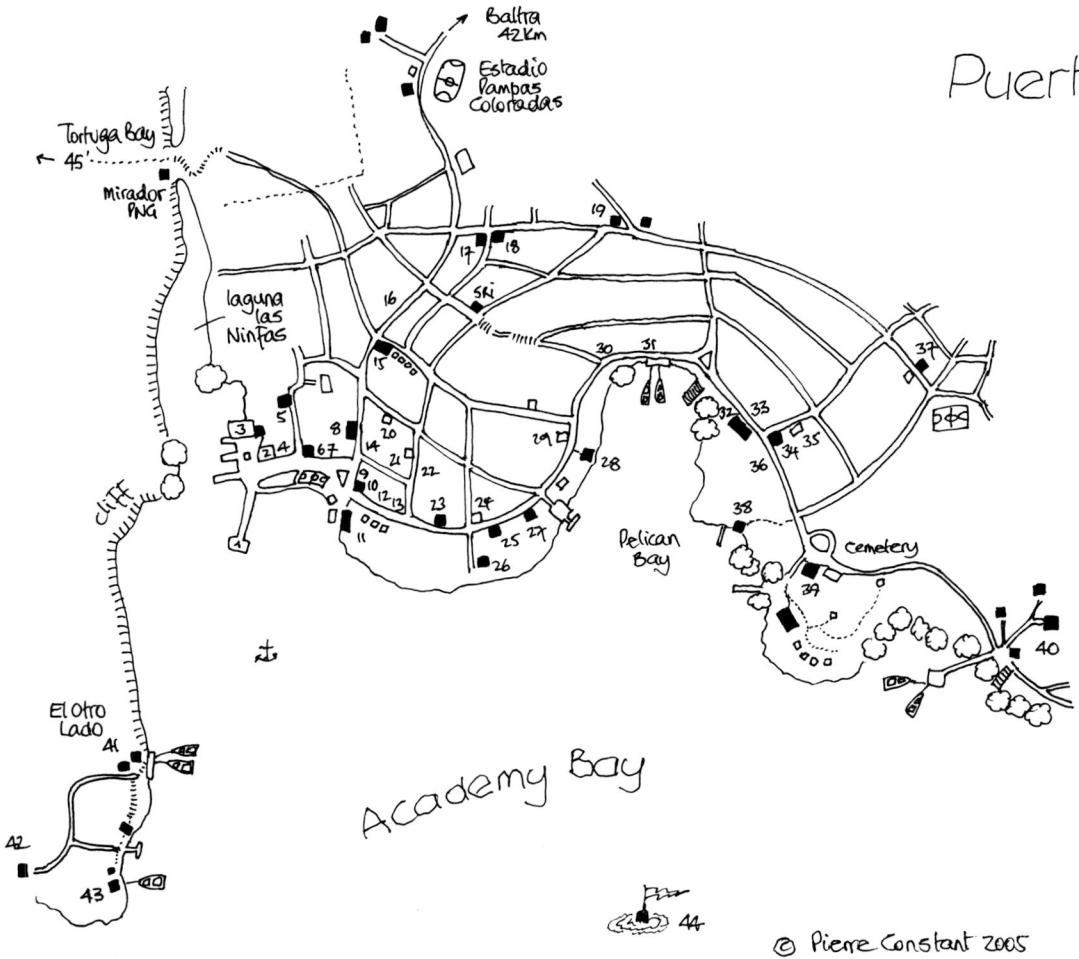
Puerto Ayora
Baltra 42Km
Estadio Pampas Coloradas
Tortuga Bay
45'
Mirador PNG
laguna las Ninfas
cliff
El Otro Lado
Academy Bay
Pelican Bay
cemetery
1 Main jetty
2 Proinsular supermarket
3 Restaurant Salvavidas
4 Post office + EMETEBE
5 Hotel Castro
6 El Descanso del guia restaurant
7 Nauticiving + CITTEG bus tickets
8 Hospital
9 Hernan pizzeria
10 PEER Boutique + Internet
11 Capitania del Puerto - Navy base
12 Frutas de Mar resto. + Five Fingers
13 Rincon del alma restaurant
14 La Choza internet
15 Colegio nacional + Hawker's street
16 Pacifictel + Panaderia la Selecta
17 Moneygram
18 Protesub decompression chamber
19 Mecanica Galdrado
20 Hotel Palmeras
21 Hotel Lirio de Mar
22 Hotel Salinas
23 Municipio Santa Cruz
24 Limon y Café - Residencial Amigos
25 TAME
26 Police station - Immigration
27 la Garrapata - la Panga - El Bongo
28 Banco del Pacifico
29 Moonrise travel agency
30 Peregrina bed + breakfast
31 Muelle Pescadores - Sol y Mar diving
32 Quagar Nautica
33 Pension Gloria
34 Hotel Silberstein + restaurant
35 Bodega Blanca
36 BHL
37 Hotel Fernandina
38 Hotel Red Mangrove Inn
39 Scuba Iguana + ex Galapagos Hotel
40 Galapagos National Park
41 ETICA
42 Hotel Finch
43 Angermeyer Point restaurant
44 M/N Iguana wreck 1988
© Pierre Constant 2005

Galápagos National Park + Charles Darwin Station

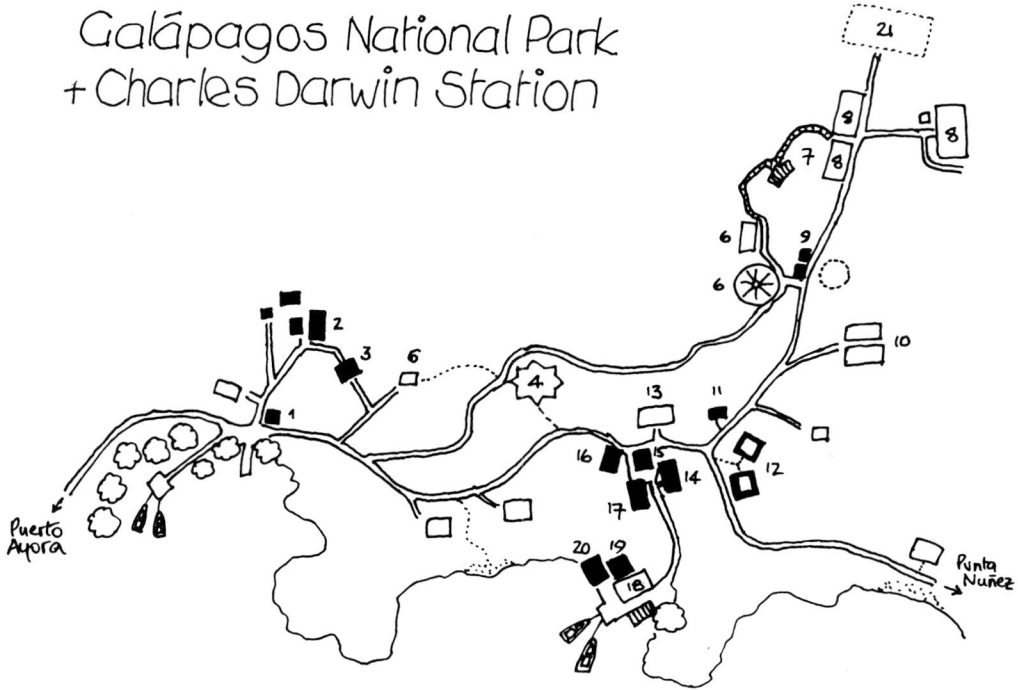

1 National Park Information
2 SPNG - National Park Offices
3 SPNG - Recursos Marinos
4 Van Straelen Exhibition Hall
5 Auditorio
6 Tortoises breeding center
7 Lonesome George corral
8 Giant tortoises corrals
9 Kiosk + Bar - Darwin Station
10 CDRS - Dormitories
11 Insect containment Facility
12 Tomas Fisher Science building
13 CDRS - workshops
14 CDRS - library
15 CDRS - Administration
16 Education - computing
17 Laboratories
18 Workshops
19 BIOMAR - Marine lab.
20 CDRS dining hall
21 land iguanas breeding pens

Piroco 2001

and American settlers arrived between the two world wars. The soil being fertile, the villages of Bellavista and Santa Rosa were founded in the tropical humid zone of the highlands. A great number of exotic plants were introduced: sugarcane, coffee, bananas, oranges, lemon trees and avocado trees. Domestic animals were also introduced. Most of them turned feral, creating a serious and disastrous impact on the native species of the island. But this will be explained later. The eradication of pigeons was done in 2002.

A colony of land iguanas may be observed at Conway Bay, on the northwest coast. Facing the bay, on Eden Island, is a small colony of sea lions. Marine iguanas are well represented on the shores all around Santa Cruz, but a colony is established on Isla Coamaño (facing Puerto Ayora), as well as in Punta Nunez, on the southern coast. Eight species of finch are found on the island, and the Hawaiian petrel nests in the highlands. Almost all the species of birds found in the Galápagos have been observed on Santa Cruz.

Punta Ayora is the commercial and tourist centre of the archipelago. From here, cattle and coffee are exported to the mainland. The southwestern part of the port is inhabited by a small colony of European immigrants, who arrived in the 1920s and 30s (see Appendix 3, Human Population of the Galápagos).

From Puerto Ayora, it is possible to make day trips or tours around the islands by chartering a small boat (with cook, captain and guide) among five to eight people. The cost involved is about $50–100 per person per day. The cruise usually lasts up to one week, and the itinerary is decided by the passengers.

HOTELS (2009 prices in US$, listed according to price)

Hotel Finch, high class, $200 and above.

Hotel Sol y Mar, single $175, double $195 includes BF. E: info@hotelsolymar.com; www.hotelsolymar.com.ec

Red Mangrove Inn, single $173, double $214, triple $255 + Red Sushi restaurant. E: info@redmangrove.com; www.redmangrove.com

Hotel Silberstein, single $113, double $165, includes BF + IVA. E: info@galextur.com

Hotel Lobo de Mar, single $93.70, double $96.80, triple $116.60 includes BF + IVA

Hotel Fernandina, single 90, double $120, triple $140 includes buffet BF. E: hotelfernandina@islasantacruz.com

Hotel Castro, single $60, double $80, triple $100, quadruple $110, includes BF + IVA. E: hotel_castro@hotmail.com

Hotel Las Ninfas, single $49, double $65.

Hotel Palmeras, single $35, double $55, includes BF.

Hotel Salinas, single $20, double $25.

Hotel Flamingo, single $15, double $20.

Hotel Elizabeth, single $16.80, double $33–$40.

Hotel Lirio del Mar, single $15, double $30 with bathroom and fan.

Hotel Gardner, single $25, double $30 includes BF. E: hotelgardner@yahoo.com; www.hotelgardnergalapagos.com

Bed & Breakfast Peregrina, singles and doubles, $20 per person.
Pension Gloria, singles and doubles, $10 per person.
Residencial Los Amigos, only 4 bed– and 5 bed– rooms.

RESTAURANTS (listed alphabetically)
Angermeyer Point, fancy restaurant on the other side of the harbour, with waterfront terrace. Access by taxi boat, $0.50.
Cafeteria del Mar, seafood grill next to Pension Gloria.
El Chocolate, in Pelican Bay, good 'almuerzos', breakfast, sandwiches, pizzas, spaghetti.
El descanso del guia (de Irlanda) a favourite for breakfast, facing the harbour park.
El Encanto, breakfast, facing the hospital.
El Rincon del Alma, facing the 'Capitania de puerto', traditional food.
Frutas de Mar, cevicheria, small place but delicious.
Hawker's street, food stalls near 'Colegio Nacional Galápagos', encocados, cheap 'almuerzos'. and 'meriendas'. Check 'William' or 'Las Delicias de Ludmila'.
Hernan Restaurant & Pizzeria, on the main square, a popular place for 'gringos'.
La Dolce Vita, Italian restaurant, parrilladas.
La Garrapata, a classic for dining out, **El Bongo** bar, **La Panga** discoteca.
La Trattoria de Pipo, Italian (Pelican Bay).
Limon y Café Bar, facing TAME office, music bar and dancing place.
Proinsular supermarket, at the harbour, food, drinks, wines, alcohol, books.
Red Sushi, Japanese food at the Red Mangrove Inn.
Salvavidas Restaurant, nice location on the harbour, typical.
The Rock, bar, snacks, pool table, international food, fancy setting with plasma TV, music.

OTHER (listed alphabetically)
Banco del Pacifico (Pelican Bay), bank, near Hotel Sol y Mar.
EMETEBE office in Puerto Ayora, above the 'Proinsular' supermarket. Two flights a day from Baltra to San Cristóbal or Isabela from one-way $79 (colono ie resident of the islands) or $120 return in 2007; $99 or $158 return (Ecuadorian national); $158 or $198 return (foreigners) (from Baltra to Isabela or Cristóbal); $91 (Isabela to Cristóbal). From Monday to Saturday. E: emetebe@ecua.net.ec. Tel. in Santa Cruz: (05)2526 177; in Baltra (05)2529 193; in Guayaquil (04)2292 492; in Isabela (05)2529 155; in San Cristóbal (05)2520 615 or 2521 427.
Fibras (speedboats) to Puerto Villamil (Isabela), leave daily at 2pm in front of Restaurant Salvavidas in the harbour, and return at 6am the next day.
Macarron Diving Academy, in Pelican Bay, facing the 'muelle de los Pescadores'; new dive centre, ex-dive master and instructor of Scuba Iguana, a charismatic character.
Nautidiving, of Vicente Berdonces, dive centre in Pelican Bay. Catamaran 'Pilotin II', dive boat for 10 passengers and 2 guides. Two dives in Academy Bay; North Seymour, Mosquera,

Daphné $140. Intro dive $80; night dive $80; PADI courses in open water $400; advanced $250. Cruises to Wolf and Darwin, 8 days/7 nights $1799 (3 dives per day). Tel. (05) 2526 096.
Scuba Iguana, of Mathias Espinosa and Jack Nelson, at Hotel Galápagos (since 1995), two dives in Academy Bay; also Santa Fé, Seymour and Gordon; Floreana (9 sites) for $150 (Gordon, Santa Fe), $155 (other sites) including equipment, lunch, towels, snacks. Prices on internet go up to $175; intro dive: $150; open water: $350 to $600; advanced: $450 to $650; rescue $350 to $500; Nitrox: $200 to $395; dive master: $800; instructor, $1500. Tel: (05) 2526 497. Dive boat: *Iguana*, two x 85HP outboard motors, 10 passengers.

PACIFICTEL telephone office. Connections with the mainland since 1993. International calls available since 1994. Originally Bellsouth phone booths appeared in Puerto Ayora in year 2000, but they were changed to Movistar 'Telefonica' telephone booths in 2005. Cards available for $5–10–20.

Taxi Service
$1 in town. To Bellavista, $2 (7 kilometres); Media Luna (10 kilometres) $4 return; Santa Rosa or El Chato (19 kilometres) $7 return; Salasaca (21 kilometres) $10 return; Garrapatero (25 kilometres) $15; Itabaca channel (41 kilometres) $18.

Boat Taxi
$0.50 in the harbour, from pier to boats.

Surfing
'Afficionados' of surf have their surf club in Pelican Bay, and practise their sport in Tortuga Bay (surf boards for rent) or even in Baltra. However, the best spots are in Puerto Baquerizo Moreno, on San Cristóbal Island (check page 233).

Sightseeing
The Charles Darwin Research Station, open from 7 am to 5 pm, Monday to Friday; library open 7 am to 12 pm; and Saturday 8 am to 12 pm.
Van Straelen Exhibition Hall (museum on Galápagos Natural History).
Breeding centre for young tortoises, with elevated walkways and tortoise corrals, including that of Lonesome George, the survivor of Pinta Island.
A few **sandy beaches** can be found beyond the Darwin Station, when you head towards the cliff of Punta Nunez. The dirt road leading to the Darwin Station is 1.5 kilometres long, bordered with red, black and white mangroves; giant cacti (*Opuntia* and *Jasminocereus*); spiny shrubs such as *Scutia pauciflora,* and other shrubs such as *Maytenus octogona.* The administrative building of the Galápagos National Park is on the way to the Darwin Station, at the first road crossing to the left (see maps of Puerto Ayora and of the Darwin Station, pages 204–205).

Bottlenose dolphins, Banks Bay, Isabela 1988

Surfing sea lions, Seymour 1991

Cushion star and black coral, Cousin's Rock 2000

Yellowtail surgeonfishes, Marchena 1992

Sea lion in the black coral, Cousin's Rock 1990

Diver with marble ray, Cousin's 2004

Orange cup coral, Bartolomé 2005

Bluechin parrotfish, Rabida 2004

Whitetip reef shark, Wolf Island

Scalloped hammerhead shark, Darwin 1993

Mexican hogfish (male), Gordon Rocks 2002

Hammerhead shark, Darwin Arch 2004

School of blue and gold snappers, Albany 2004

Freshwater spring of El Estero, Isabela 2006

Red lipped batfish, Bartolomé 2008

Starry flatworm, Piedra Blanca 2005

Mexican hogfish and school of black striped salemas, Enderby 2008

Bigeye jacks, Darwin 1993

School of Galápagos grunts

Fine spotted moray, Gymnothorax dovii, Marchena 1993

Excursions from Puerto Ayora

Tortuga Bay (Turtle Bay)

To reach this white sand beach, less than one hour away from Puerto Ayora, first take the road to Baltra, in town, then turn left about 150 metres after leaving the main square on the port. A paved road climbs to the top of the *barranco* (canyon) along a stairway before changing to a decent trail. The easy graveled way, opened in 1982, has been paved in 1998 and replaces the old track on the lava rocks, crossing the arid zone of the palo santos and cacti (sports shoes are advised). Don't forget your hat, sun protection and drinking water, for the equatorial sun is fierce.

In Tortuga Bay, you may see nesting pelicans in the mangroves (warm season), and maybe flamingos in the lagoon. If you go for a swim, do not venture beyond the last wave, for the currents are dangerous at low tide, and sharks could be waiting. Return before sunset (6 pm). The excursion is worth it (see map, page 218).

Los Gemelos (the Twins)

On the road to Baltra, beyond the village of Santa Rosa, in the humid tropical zone of the scalesia (*Scalesia pedunculata*) forest. The Gemelos are two pit-craters over 30 metres deep located on either side of the road. They may be explosion craters, or they may have been created by the collapse of the roof of some magma chamber, following circumferencial fissures. A few trails wander around the craters. Many land birds may be seen, such as the vermilion flycatcher, the large-bill flycatcher, the short-eared owl, the Galápagos dove, and a great number of Darwin's finches, including the carpenter finch, which uses a stick as a tool to help extract larvae from old stumps.

It is advisable to go to Los Gemelos in the early morning, around 8 am, with the minibus of CITTEG heading to Baltra. (There is no chance of finding a bus during the daytime; transport is by hire only.) The village of Santa Rosa is about two kilometres downhill.

The Tortoise Reserve (Caseta and El Chato)

In the humid zone, this is the ideal place to observe giant tortoises in the wild. From Santa Rosa, a trail—five kilometres long and sometimes very muddy—leads to Caseta and to El Chato. It takes two to three hours on foot. The vegetation is composed of high scalesia, guayabillo (*Psidium galapageium*) and pega pega (*Pisonia floribunda*) grasses. Darwin's finches are plentiful, as are flycatchers. There is a camping site at Caseta, and it is possible to hire horses at Santa Rosa (see map of Santa Cruz, page 203).

Alternatively, one may see tortoises in private farms, such as Poza Pamela or, even better, at Rancho Mariposa, run by Steve and Jenny Divine, who have a cozy little country restaurant (expect to pay about US$14 for a meal) with great scenery, and a pond where tortoises come to drink freely. An entry fee is charged ($3).

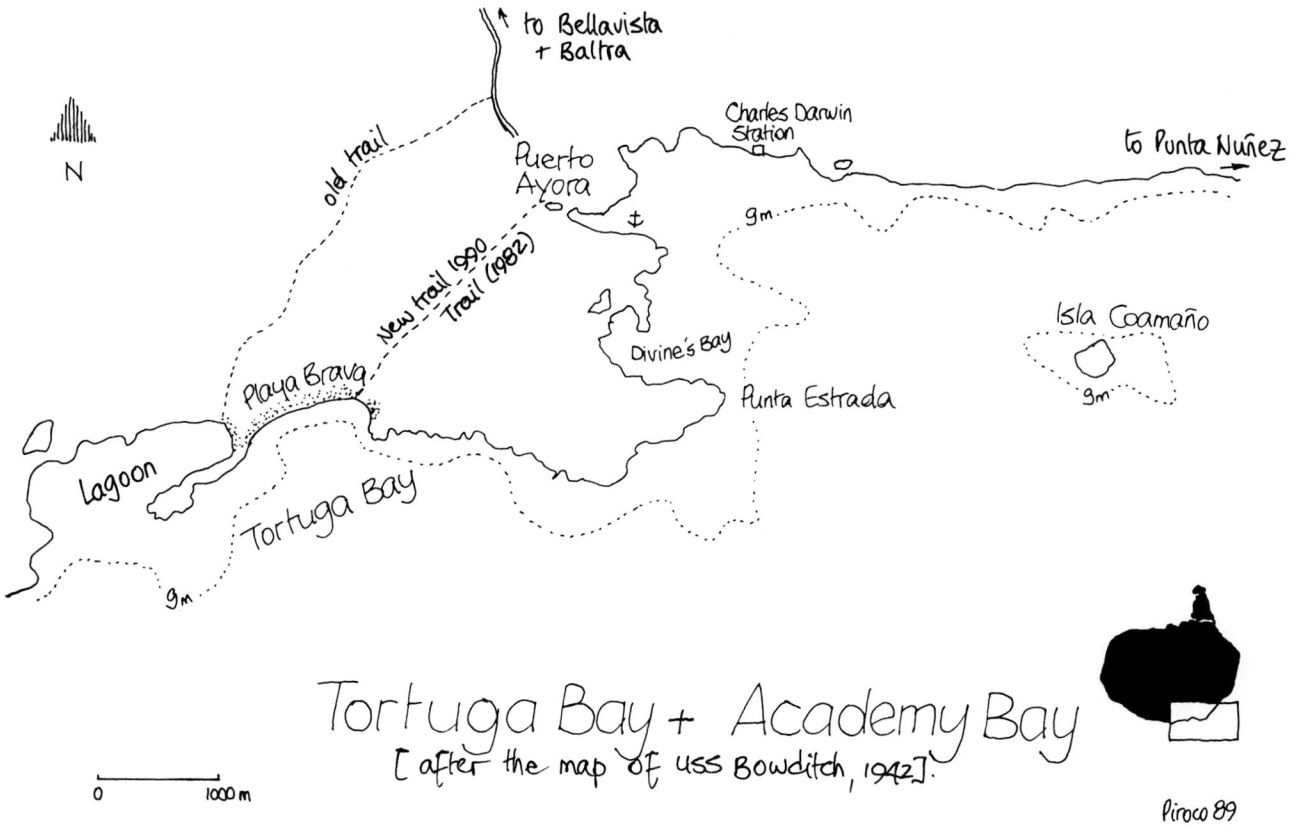

Tortuga Bay + Academy Bay
[after the map of USS Bowditch, 1942].

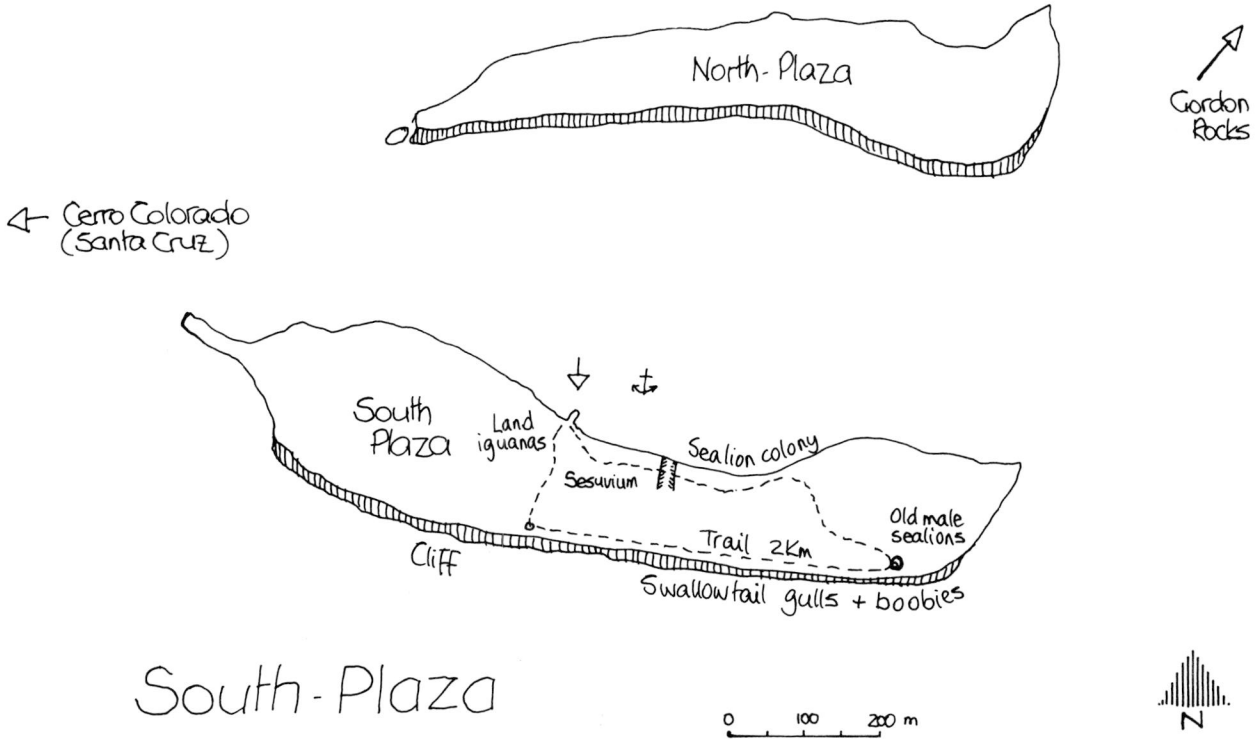
North-Plaza
Gordon Rocks
Cerro Colorado (Santa Cruz)
South Plaza
Land iguanas
Sealion colony
Sesuvium
Old male sealions
Trail 2Km
Cliff
Swallowtail gulls + boobies
South-Plaza
0 100 200 m
N

Los Tunneles (the lava tunnels)

Lava tubes, a few hundred metres to a few kilometres long, are one of the curiosities of Santa Cruz. There is a small one, three kilometres away from Puerto Ayora on the left side of the road. With a diameter of about 10 metres, it is large enough for a subway train to go through. Another tunnel, two kilometres long, is found east of Bellavista on private land. There is another in Salasaca, west of Santa Rosa, and a third on the land of Furio—an Italian man who has a ranch and a restaurant named Mutiny ($14.80 + 20% tax, tunnel fee: $4)—facing the access road to Steve Divine, not far from Santa Rosa. Furio Valbonesi has recently opened a new luxury hotel on his land (mid-2000). Futuristic and impressive, expect to pay $150 to $1,200 for a room or a suite.

Media Luna and Mount Crocker

The trail which leads to the *zona alta* or highlands starts from Bellavista and crosses the agricultural zone (with coffee and avocado plantations) before it gets to the pampa of the miconias (see chapter on flora). It takes an hour to an hour and a half to see Media Luna, a half-moon volcanic cone covered with miconia bushes. A new gravel road accessible to taxis leads up almost to Media Luna. In this garua-swept area, the trail is muddy and slippery so expect to get your feet wet. The garua may be so thick that nothing can be seen once the miconia zone is reached. Do not venture further or you may get lost. This walk is very good for observing the vegetation zones and the trees introduced by the settlers, including *Psidium guayaba*, with yellow fruit, or *goyava*, bordering the trail. Cows graze in the fields, in the company of cattle egrets (*Bubulcus ibis*), often sitting on their backs.

On a clear day you may walk farther up to Puntudo, a small volcano at the top of the island, with a conspicuous conical shape. Mount Crocker, the highest summit of Santa Cruz at 864 metres is two hours from Bellavista and three kilometres beyond Media Luna. The site is extraordinary, with a 360-degree panorama, taking in Baltra and Seymour to the north and the two Daphnés to the northwest. This lunar landscape is utterly spectacular, with a chain of tuff cones, broken lava tubes (where volcanic water holes are numerous) and the scalesia forest sliding up the slopes like a wave up the beach (see map of Santa Cruz, page 203).

South Plaza

land surface: 13 square km
elevation: 25 m

The Plazas Islands (North and South) are east of Santa Cruz, a few hundred metres from the coast. There, Cerro Colorado (the Red Rock) rises up with its fossiliferous tuff beds. The two islands were uplifted by tectonic action at the same time as Cerro Colorado, and are both tilted towards the north.

Only South Plaza Island is open to visitors, the other island being closed and reserved for scientific research (see drawing, page 219).

The vegetation belongs to the arid zone and is represented by annual plants such as sesuvium, and by opuntia cacti. *Sesuvium edmonstonei* (endemic) is a plant of the succulent family, with red or green almond-shaped leaves, depending on the dry or the wet season. The island wears a red carpet during the months of May to December.

A colony of about 1,000 sea lions inhabits the island. A great number of these marine mammals gather around the disembarking site, playing or porpoising out of the water like dolphins. Do not get close to the male named Charlie, who is known to be aggressive and even bites on occasion.

South Plaza is a good place for observing yellow-brown land iguanas. It is prohibited to feed the reptiles. Years back, when the rules of the Galápagos National Park were not so strict, visitors used to bring oranges and hand them over to the iguanas, who loved the fruit. They became conditioned to such an extent that when a group of tourists arrived at the landing site, land iguanas would run to meet the newcomers, and climb on the visitors' knees to eat the precious fruit. The food balance of the reptiles was seriously affected, and the Galápagos National Park had to bring an end to these illicit practices.

A dangerous cliff borders the south of the island, where many sea lions rest. You may observe swallowtail gulls, tropicbirds, frigates, blue-footed boobies, and Nazca boobies, Audubon shearwaters, pelicans gliding in the sky. From the top of the cliff (watch out: two guides fell over and ended up at the hospital or died. Pepe Salcedo fell there in March 1998), you may see turtles, rays, yellowtail mullets and sharks. The feral goats were eradicated from the island in 1961. South Plaza is an easy day trip from Puerto Ayora. Gordon Rocks, a short distance away, is a good diving site.

Santa Fé

land surface: 24 square kilometres
elevation: 259 metres

Another island uplifted by tectonic action, where some of the oldest basaltic rocks of the archipelago have been dated at 2.7 million years. Santa Fé is to the southeast of Santa Cruz, and can be easily seen from Puerto Ayora (see map, page 222).

In the middle of a sunny day, the lagoon of Santa Fé turns into an eye-catching turquoise blue. The white sandy bottom is only a few metres below the surface. On the beach, sea lions bask lazily in the sun. A trail leads inland to the top of a cliff, from where the view is breathtaking. Two species of land iguanas inhabit the archipelago, but one of these, the endemic *Conolophus pallidus,* dwells only on Santa Fé; it is bigger, with a whitish colour, sometimes chocolate brown when moulting. It sports a prominent dorsal crest, and the eyes are often blood shot.

The vegetation is of the arid type. The forest of the giant prickly pear cacti, *Opuntia echios* var. *barringtonensis,* is striking for the size of the trunks. On the cliff, *Scalesia affinis* plants or Radiate headed scalesia, is an attractive bush with white flowers and exquisite fragrance.

The Galápagos hawk often overlooks the beach from the top of a salt bush or a palo santo. A species of endemic rice rat is also known to inhabit the island.

Sea lions, sea turtles, small white-tip reef sharks, spotted eagle rays and round stingrays are common to the small bay. Feral goats were eradicated in 1971. Watch out for stingrays in shallow water.

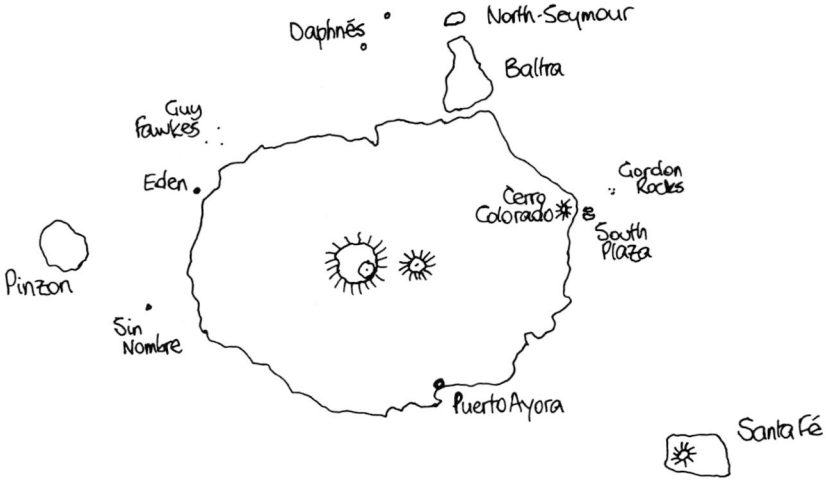

Santa Fe ~ north east bay

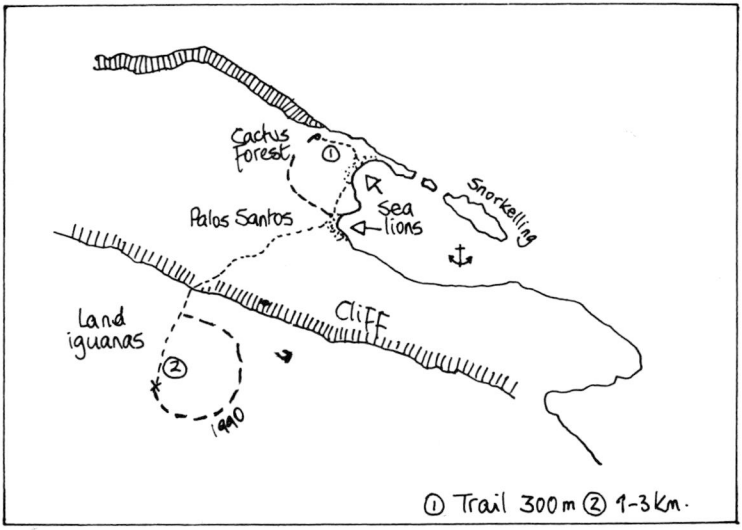

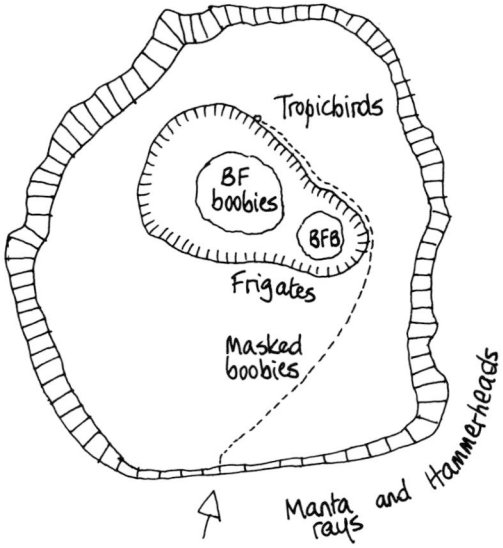

Daphné mayor

Rabida

DAPHNÉ

land surface: 32 ha
elevation: 120 m

North of Santa Cruz and west of Baltra Island, Daphné is a tuff cone above the surface of the ocean, which can be observed from the airport. In fact there are two islands: Daphné Mayor and Daphné Minor. The latter is the older, and erosion has reduced the original cone to a cylinder-shaped island with sheer cliffs. Daphné Mayor has kept its full cone, with a main crater and a second lateral crater, on the south rim.

Vegetation is poor and mainly represented by croton, palo santos, opuntia cacti and sesuvium. The curiosity of Daphné is the colony of blue-footed boobies, dwelling on the floor of the crater, where the birds nest between April and December.

Magnificent frigatebirds are found on the slopes and on the rim, as well as Nazca boobies, finches and short-eared owls. Tropicbirds nest in the cliff of Daphné Minor, but fly over Daphné Mayor, too. The landscape is splendid in the early morning after sunrise. The palo santo of Daphné is endemic (see map, page 223).

RÁBIDA (JERVIS)

land surface: 5 square km
elevation: 367 m

Jervis, the English name of Rábida Island, is located near the geographic centre of the archipelago. The island is made of eroded hills and lava ejected from spatter cones. Rábida is more volcanically diversified than any other island of the Galápagos.

Vegetation is composed of palo santos, opuntias and spiny shrubs. Behind the red sand beach at the north of the island, a brackish lagoon shelters a population of flamingos, Bahama pintail ducks and common stilts. Pelicans nest by the beach in the salt bushes (*Cryptocarpus pyriformis*), locally known as *monte salado*. Blue-footed boobies and Nazca boobies are found in the cliffs.

A new trail leads to the top of a small hill, on the left of the beach. Downhill, on the the right side, portions of the purple-red cliff frequently crumble into the sea. Feral goats were exterminated in 1970 and 1975. (see map, page 223).

PINZÓN

land surface: 12 square km
max. elevation: 450 m

West of Santa Cruz, Pinzón is a small island of no apparent interest except, like Rábida, for its geological diversity. The west and southwest parts of the volcano collapsed due to marine erosion and volcanic fractures. On the west coast, the cliffs rise up to 150 metres. Disembarking on the island is therefore difficult.

The vegetation is represented by croton and by spiny shrubs. Inland, near the old crater, lives a population of giant tortoises. Finches are tame, and Galápagos hawks are plentiful. Lava lizards and snakes are also present. One of the great problems of Pinzón was until recently the proliferation of *Rattus rattus*, the black rat, which feeds on eggs and young reptiles. The SPNG, the Galápagos National Park Service, eradicated the rats by traps and poison in September–November 1989.

CHAPTER TWO

THE SOUTHERN ISLANDS

FLOREANA

land surface: 24 square km
elevation: 864 m

The southernmost island of the archipelago, along with Española, Floreana is of volcanic origin, very old, and its numerous volcanoes have reached an advanced stage of erosion. No volcanic activity was reported for a long time. South of Post Office Bay, Cerro Paja, the summit of the island, seems to be lost in its eternal sleep. Puerto Velasco Ibarra, the capital, is a mere village under the sun, and its population was just 65 inhabitants in 1986.

In the highlands, the vegetation is diversified and luxurious. Since Floreana was the first colonized island in the 19th century, it contains many species of plants introduced by the settlers. The visitor sites are Punta Cormorant, Corona del Diablo (or Devil's Crown), Post Office Bay and Black Beach on the west coast.

Punta Cormorant

North of Floreana, this is a beautiful green sand beach. The colour is due to the abundance of green olivine crystals in the volcanic tuff. The beach is fringed by white and black mangroves, behind which is a flamingo lagoon. These waders are easily frightened; be as quiet as possible when observing. Adults are pink and juveniles whitish. Flamingos feed on an aquatic insect, *Trichocorixia,* and a small lagoon shrimp *Artemia.* The site is also favorable for observing common stilts, Bahama pintails, whimbrels and ruddy turnstones.

A great number of plants are endemic to Punta Cormorant, such as *Lecocarpus pinnatifidus* and *Scalesia villosa,* with arrow-shaped leaves covered with white hair. On the top of the dune of the white sand beach grows *Nolana galapageia,* a dense shrub with fat yellow almond-shaped leaves.

Corona del Diablo

Also known as Onslow or Devil's Crown, the marine site is a short distance from Punta Cormorant, 250 metres offshore. It used to be good for skin or scuba diving.

The submarine life—Pocillopora, Pavona and Porites corals, pencil sea urchins, parrotfish, wrasses, king angelfishes, yellowtail surgeonfish, Mexican hogfish—is the main attraction here, but it was much visited in the last ten years. Other creatures to be seen include amberjacks, blue and gold snappers, white-tip sharks, hammerhead sharks (sometimes), rays and turtles. On the outside of the crown (to the north), the current is strong from east to west (see drawing, page 226).

Floreana

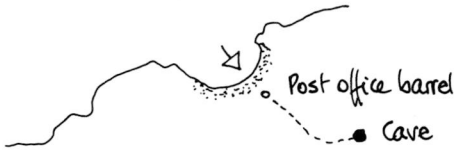

Post Office Bay

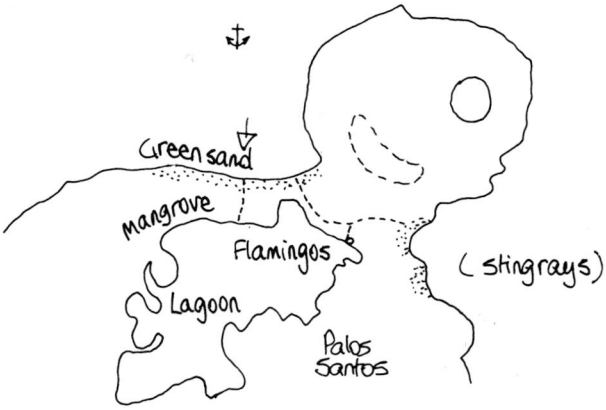

Punta Cormorant + Devil's crown

Post Office Bay
At this historic site a man named Hathaway erected a wooden barrel in 1793. It was used as a post office for passing ships, first by whalers and later by visiting yachts and tourists. A trail behind the barrel leads to a cave (lava tube) not far inland (see map, page 226).

In 1926, Norwegians settled on Floreana to start a fish-canning factory. Unfortunately, the experience ended two years later. Loberia Islet, near Post Office Bay, has a colony of sea lions.

Black Beach and Puerto Velasco Ibarra
In the early 20th century, Floreana was the theatre where tragic and mysterious events were played out which drew the attention of Europe to this faraway island in the eastern Pacific. One day in 1929, Dr. Friedrich Ritter, a German dentist by profession and a philosopher by nature, arrived on the deserted island with his assistant and mistress Dore Strauch, and asked to disembark at Black Beach, as if it were the most natural thing to do. Both of them lived as Robinson Crusoes for the next three years, before the arrival of the Wittmers in 1932, a German family of farmers from Bayern, with a poliomyelitic son.

This little world managed on its own until the arrival later that year of Baroness von Wagner de Bousquet, a German diva, with her two lovers, Lorenz and Philipson. She had it in mind to construct a hotel for 'millionaires', but built nothing more than a shack of planks and corrugated iron, which she proudly named Hacienda Paraïso. Soon, she claimed the island for her own and declared herself 'Empress of Floreana', intending to impose her rule by the whip and the revolver. Things rapidly turned bitter.

To make a long story short, the baroness and Philipson disappeared without a trace in 1935. Lorenz escaped with a Norwegian fisherman from San Cristóbal and a few months later was found dead and mummified on a deserted beach of Marchena Island, after having capsized. Four days later, on November 21, Dr Ritter, learning about the drama, died on Floreana. It is suspected that he was poisoned by Dore Strauch with a rotten chicken, though he was known to be a strict vegetarian. The woman returned to Germany, where she published a book entitled *Satan Came to Eden*. Nobody knows the truth of the story, nor will ever know. But in the end, it seems that Lorenz killed the baroness and Philipson, with the help of Wittmer and Dr Ritter. Margret Wittmer denies the fact, claiming that the cursed couple left the island for Tahiti on a private yacht (see *The Galápagos Affair,* by John Treherne, London 1983).

Margret Wittmer, the last survivor, knew more than she wanted to say. She lived at Black Beach with her daughters, where she owned a small hotel, a restaurant, a souvenir shop and ran the local *correos,* the Ecuadorian post office. She did not make orange wine anymore. She had opened an eight-room hotel with toilet and showers ($30 per day, full board). Margret Wittmer died in March 2000, at the age of 95 years.

Española

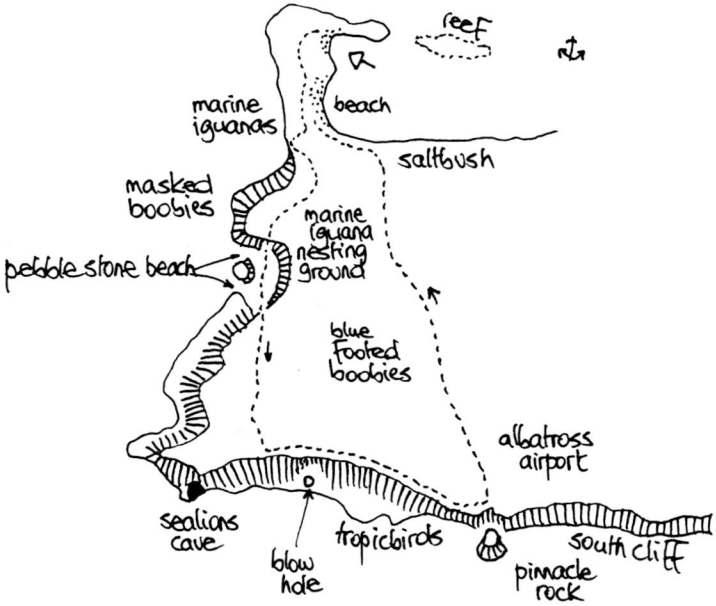

Punta Suarez

Piroco 2000

It is possible to hire a pickup for $16 round-trip to visit the highlands of Floreana, as well as the freshwater spring used by pirates in the 17th century and the caves carved in the volcanic tuff where they found a refuge well before the arrival of the Wittmers.

ESPAÑOLA

land surface: 61 square km; max. elevation: 206 m

Known in English as Hood, this volcanic island has a central volcano. Another island was discovered recently, east of Española, submerged a few metres under the ocean surface. This proves that the archipelago is older than once thought, and that it has long been in subduction under the South American mainland.

Bordered by steep cliffs, the southern coast is washed by surf and spray. The vegetation is typical of the arid and transition zones, with a number of spiny shrubs. Feral goats were eradicated from Española in 1978. Under the programme started in 1970, the SPNG has reintroduced 369 small giant tortoises on Española over the course of 20 years. In March 2000, the number of tortoises returned to the island reached 1,000.

The richness of the fauna is not only evidenced in the colonies of seabirds, such as the blue-footed and Nazca boobies, but also in the presence of the endemic albatross, *Diomedea irrorata*. Despite its inhospitable look, Punta Suarez hosts a great variety of seabirds and land birds. Albatrosses nest on the island between mid-March and mid-December. Boobies are inland or on the cliffs all year-round. swallowtail gulls, oystercatchers, lava herons, night herons, Galápagos doves, the small ground finches, warbler finches, large cactus finches, Española mockingbirds (endemic to Española), Galápagos hawks, marine iguanas, lava lizards and Galápagos snakes are also found on Hood, as well as the saddleback tortoise (which you will not see!).

There is a blowhole on the basaltic shore, at the end of the trail in Punta Suarez. The seawater rushes violently under the lava bedrock, then is ejected upward through cracks in a vaporous plume to a height of 25 metres. Some 20 to 25 pilot whales, with bottlenose dolphins were seen at Punta Suarez in June 2000 (Lynn Fowler).

To the northeast of Española, Gardner Bay has a very long sandy beach facing an island of the same name. Sea lions bask lazily in the sun and the Española mockingbirds swarm on the beach, eminently curious about all visitors (see drawing, page 228).

SAN CRISTÓBAL

land surface: 558 square km; elevation: 730 m

The administrative centre of the archipelago, with Puerto Baquerizo Moreno as capital, San Cristóbal is also the islands' second Ecuadorian naval base. The population was nearly 8,000 people in 1993 (versus 2,752 in 1986). Curiously, in 2005, the population of San Cristóbal was officially 5633 people (info. Municipio). The radio 'Voz de Galápagos' has broadcast since 1969.

The geography of the island is composed of two distinct parts. The west part has a central volcano culminating at about 700 metres (San Joaquin), with a few parasitic cones. The eastern part of the island, made of spatter cones and lava flows, does not rise above 160 metres. It was once thought that San Cristóbal was the oldest island because it is the easternmost of the Galápagos, but there is no proof of this. The slopes exposed to the north are arid and desolated, while those oriented to the south are more humid, being exposed to the southeast tradewinds.

Wreck Bay, the southwest tip of San Cristóbal, shelters the village of Puerto Baquerizo Moreno. The old wooden houses that faced the sea in the past, separated by lava flows and yellow sand beaches, has given way gradually to concrete buildings and houses made of volcanic rocks. Over the last 15 years the provincial town has gained some kind of charm and is definitely attached to its image of progress. It is now a booming town.

In the highlands, eight kilometres away, the village of Progreso was once the site of the penal colony founded by Manuel Cobos in 1888. Cobos created a sugarcane factory, where the convicts were put to hard labour. A notorious tyrant, Manuel Cobos abused the women of his men, and he was eventually killed by a Colombian convict with a machete in 1904.

The humid zone of San Cristóbal does not produce sugarcane any longer, but bananas, oranges, grapefruits, lemons, guavas, avocados and coffee are grown. The settlers introduced animals such as goats, rats, cats, dogs, and a species of salamander. Pigeons were eradicated from San Cristóbal in 2002.

The visitor's sites are Cerro de Las Tijeretas (Frigatebird Hill), La Galápaguera (tortoise reserve), the freshwater lake of El Junco. Kicker Rock (Leon Dormido) and Stephens Bay, the Loberia and Isla Lobos.

Taxi service: from Puerto Baquerizo to Loberia (1.5 km) $6 R/T, El Junco (17 km) $18 R/T, Galapaguera (25 km) $24 R/T, Puerto Chino (28 km) $30 R/T, La Soledad $5. Circuit: El Junco–Galapaguera–Soledad–Loberia, $40.

HOTELS (2005 prices in US$)

Cabanas Miconia, on the waterfront; single $42, double $84 with IVA
Suites Bellavista, $20 per person, with fridge, cosy with A/C, facing the 'muelle de turismo'.
Hotel Orca, Playa de Oro, single $25, double $35 + 22% tax, includes BF. 4 rooms with seaview at $60
Hotel Northia, single $25, double $40, with fan, TV, balcony, include IVA
Hostal Los Cactus, in front of Pacifictel (barrio Algarrobo), single $15, double $24, includes BF.
Hotel Mar Azul, singles $15–20, doubles $25–30–50 with TV, fridge, A/C
Hotel Chatham, on Airport road, single $15, double $25
Residencial San Francisco, on the waterfront, single $10, double $12
Hostel Galápagos, next to Hotel Orca, Playa de Oro
Cabanas Don Jorge, out of town on a hill above Playa Mann, $15 per person with fridge and kitchenette, garden

RESTAURANTS

La Playa, near the navy base, á la carte
Miconia, overlooking the 'muelle', terrace upstairs, good views
Restaurant Rosita, surf information, tours
Albacora, near school, a la carte

(see map of Puerto Baquerizo Moreno, opposite)

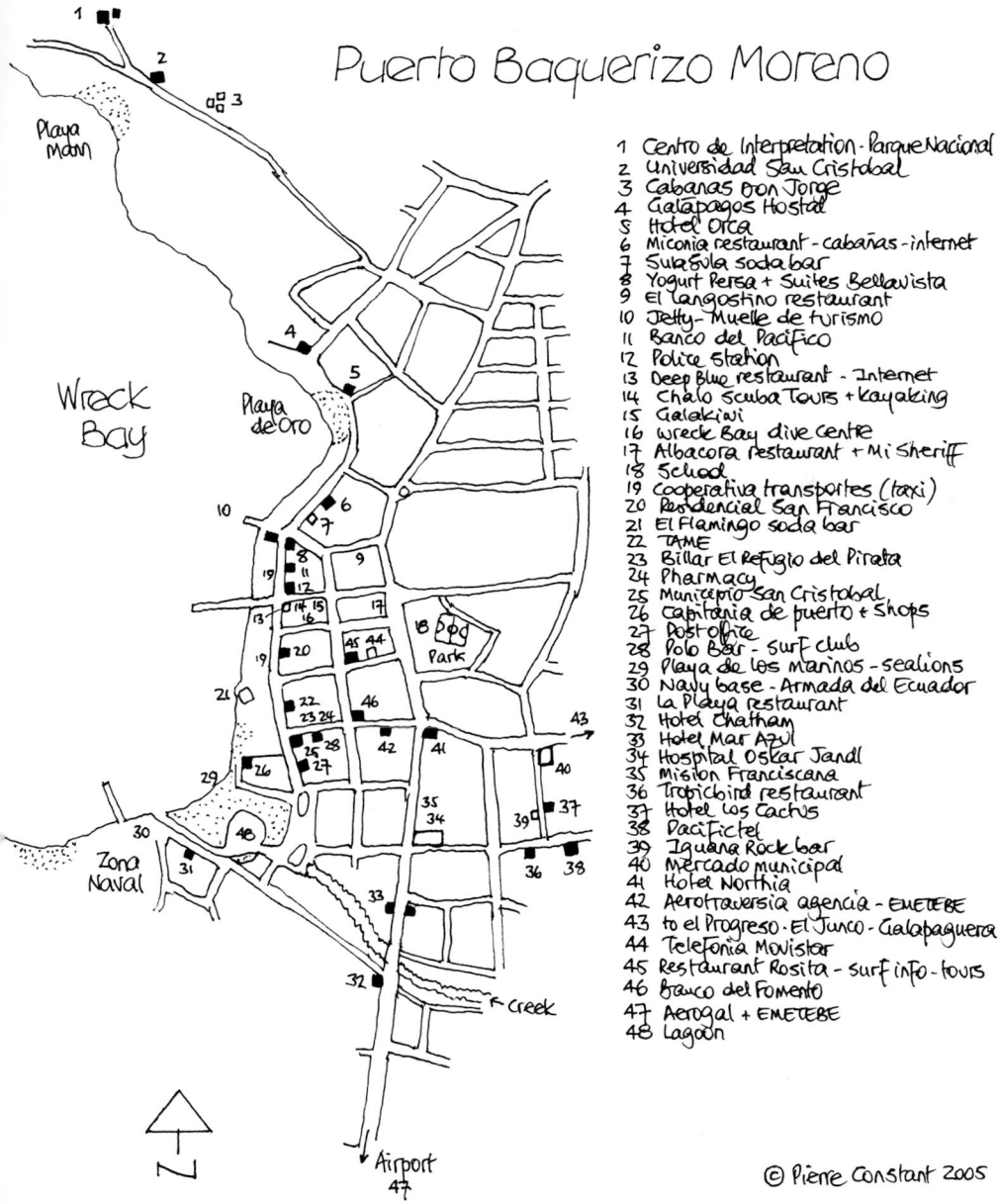
Puerto Baquerizo Moreno
Playa Mann
Wreck Bay
Playa de Oro
Park
Zona Naval
creek
Airport
47
N
1 Centro de Interpretation - Parque Nacional
2 Universidad San Cristobal
3 Cabanas Don Jorge
4 Galapagos Hostal
5 Hotel Orca
6 Miconia restaurant - cabañas - internet
7 Sula Sula soda bar
8 Yogurt Persa + Suites Bellavista
9 El Langostino restaurant
10 Jetty - Muelle de turismo
11 Banco del Pacifico
12 Police station
13 Deep Blue restaurant - Internet
14 Chalo Scuba Tours + kayaking
15 Galakiwi
16 wreck Bay dive centre
17 Albacora restaurant + Mi Sheriff
18 School
19 Cooperativa transportes (taxi)
20 Residencial San Francisco
21 El Flamingo soda bar
22 TAME
23 Billar El Refugio del Pirata
24 Pharmacy
25 Municipio San Cristobal
26 Capitania de puerto + Shops
27 Post office
28 Polo Bar - surf club
29 Playa de los Marinos - sealions
30 Navy base - Armada del Ecuador
31 La Playa restaurant
32 Hotel Chatham
33 Hotel Mar Azul
34 Hospital Oskar Jandl
35 Mision Franciscana
36 Tropicbird restaurant
37 Hotel Los Cactus
38 Pacifictel
39 Iguana Rock bar
40 Mercado municipal
41 Hotel Northia
42 Aerotraversia agencia - EMETEBE
43 to el Progreso - El Junco - Galapaguera
44 Telefonia Movistar
45 Restaurant Rosita - surf info - tours
46 Banco del Fomento
47 Aerogal + EMETEBE
48 Lagoon
© Pierre Constant 2005

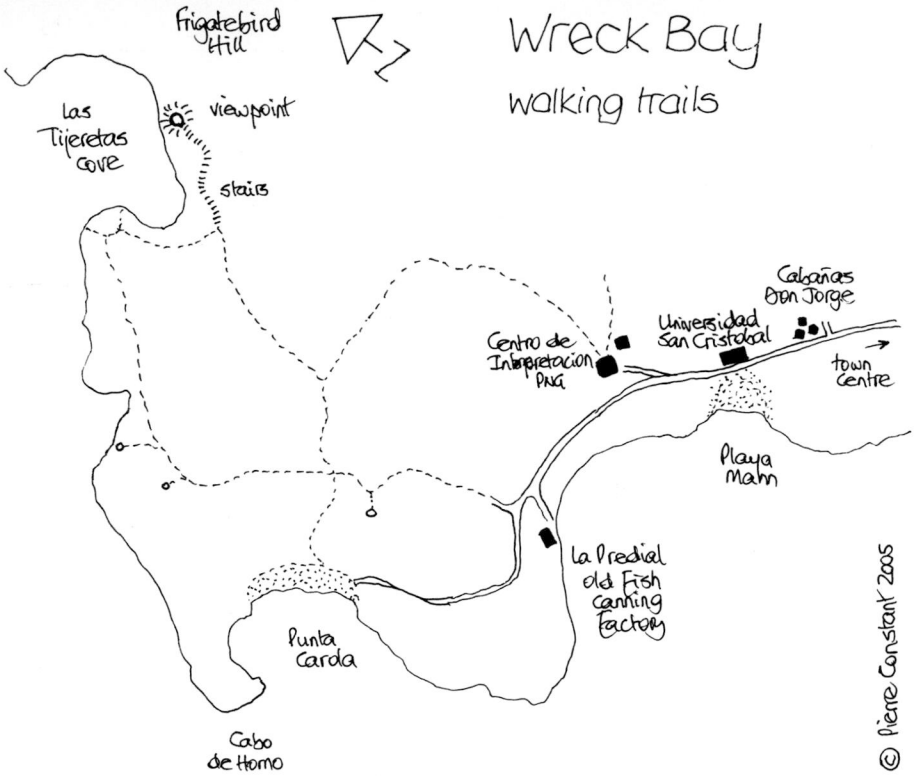

Mi Sheriff, near school. Try the roasted chicken (pollo a la brasa)
Tropic bird, almuerzos, meriendas, á la carte meals
Deep Blue Bar, with restaurant, on the waterfront
Zanzibar, on the waterfront
Yogurt Persa, on the waterfront, facing 'muelle de turismo'

Puerto Baquerizo has developed a lot since the opening of the new airport in 1986 and the influx of tourism. The latest (2005) schedules provide three flights a week from Quito. For details see pages 284–5.

To see

Centro de Interpretacion (SPNG + Fundacion Charles Darwin), since 1998. A new information center on human and natural history, inaugurated by Prince Philip de Asturias of Spain and President Yamil Mahuad of Ecuador. A US$4 millions project with the help of Agencia Espanola de Cooperacion Internacional. Must be seen.

Museo de San Cristóbal (opened in 1990), open Monday–Saturday 8:30–12:00 pm, and 3:30–5:30 pm. Little museum of natural history. Relocated in Colegio Humboldt in 2003.

La Loberia, half an hour's walk beyond the airport, has a small colony of sea lions, on a white sandbeach.

Port Captain (Capitania del Puerto), for visiting sail boats, the right to drop anchor is 20 days in each port. Port fees: the arrival tax: $0.01 x TRB (Tonnelaje de Regreso Bruto= Gross Tonnage), access channel: $0.15 x TRB, anchoring: $1.50 x TRB, Format (Faros y Boyas):

$0.16, lighting: $3 x TRB, format (arribo/salida): $0.16, zarpe: $0.16 x TRB. Mooring fees (*Faros y boyas*): $3 per ton, mooring: $0.1/ton/day. The Galápagos National Park tax is not required, but if the crew plans to visit the islands of the National Park, that would be on a local boat only (fee: US$100 to the National Park). For foreign vessels a longer anchoring time in port will only be allowed in case of damage to the boat, which has rendered it unsailable. A fumigation certificate of the last port is required, otherwise the boat must be fumigated on arrival in the Galápagos.

INTERNET

In front of the police station or at Miconia restaurant, $2/hour.

SURFING

San Cristóbal has been the Galápagos surfers' paradise since 1998, attracting crowds from Brazil, Venezuela, Peru, Panama, Australia, USA. Renowned spots are Punta Carola, El Canon, Tongo Reef, La Loberia. The best months are January–March and October. 'Temporada del norte': Dec–April, northeast tradewinds (Pta Carola, El Canon, Manglecito). 'Temporada del sur': August–November southeast tradewinds (Loberia, Tongo Reef, AD reef, El Canon). Information at Restaurant Rosita, called Jose Villamil y Ignacio de Hernan (ask for Umberto Hernandez) or at the 'Club de Surf' at the Polo's Bar.

Among the new activities offered in San Cristóbal, surfing is attracting a new breed of sports-loving visitors, who can now enjoy the waves at Punta Carola, Pta. Basoa, Punta Finger, Caleta Tortuga, Hobbs Bay and Roca Ballena. See San Cristóbal map locations (page 235).

DIVING

Chalo Scuba Tours (since 1997, of Gonzalo Quiroga and Victor Carrion) with a 9.5m boat. $100 for two dives at Leon Dormido, $80 in the Bahia (steamboat Caragua or Tijeretas), $120 to Punta Pitt, minimum 6 persons or Roca Estate; $140 to Espanola Island and Gardner Island. Diving courses: open water $300 (5 days); advanced $250; rescue $350; dive master $800. Kayaking and snorkelling.

Wreck Bay Dive Centre (since 2004, Ivan Lopez), 2 dives with boat, picnic, dive guide and equipment: US$100, to Leon Dormido, Isla Lobos, 5 Fingers or US$80 in Wreck Bay (2 wrecks): Caragua wreck, Tijeretas cove.

Galakiwi (since December 2004, of New Zealander Tim Cooney) $100 for 2 dives at Leon Dormido and Isla Lobos. Kayaking available.

EXCURSIONS AROUND SAN CRISTÓBAL

CERRO DE LAS TIJERETAS (FRIGATEBIRD HILL)

A short distance from the port of San Cristóbal, beyond Playa Mann, is a hill covered with palo santos, overlooking an almost circular cove. The trail passes by an abandoned fish-canning factory and goes on to another beach. From there, turn right uphill. The track may be covered by vegetation in the hot season. Nevertheless, you may observe frigates having their courtship display in March–April. Birds are few, however, in the dry season. There's a beautiful panoramic view of the surrounding coastline, heading to the northeast. A new trail with wooden stairway was built up Cerro de las Tijeretas in 1998, with 'miradors' on the hilltop.

Laguna El Junco

This natural lagoon is located in the highlands at an elevation of 700 metres, 19 kilometres from Puerto Baquerizo Moreno. The only freshwater pool on the island, this crater lake has a diameter of 270 metres, a surface of 360,000 square metres and a depth of 6 metres. It is supplied by rain water only.

The sedimentary deposits of this lagoon were studied by the American geologist Paul Colinvaux (1966), who concluded that the age of El Junco was 48,000 years. The name 'Junco' comes from the sedges that invade the banks of the lake. In 1978, the lake even overflowed after the hard rains, and a small creek occasionally flows towards the south of the island. The best period to visit El Junco is from December to May during the hot season. A daily local bus links Puerto Baquerizo and Progreso, from where it is a two-hour walk to the lake. On a clear day, the view from the summit is excellent. A few resident birds live at the lake, including the Bahama pintail, the moorhen, the whimbrel and the semipalmated plover.

La Galápaguera de Cerro Colorado

This road to the highlands leads to this new tortoise reserve, with trails and an interpretation centre.

La Soledad

Small village of the highlands, with views to the north coast, a nice church and the 'Café del Mirador' open on week ends.

Leon Dormido

Also known as Kicker's Rock, this cathedral of tuff rises in the middle of the ocean, off Stephens Bay, to the northeast of Puerto Baquerizo. It is a three-hour trip by local boat. The 'Sleeping Lion' has vertiginous cliffs and hosts a number of seabirds, such as Nazca boobies, blue-footed boobies, great frigates and tropic birds. Some sea lions rest on the rocks at the base of the cliff. A narrow channel allows a panga to go through Leon Dormido, between the sheer tuff walls, cutting through from east to west. Sharks are present in the troubled waters.

Facing Kicker's Rock on the coast, Cerro Brujo (the 'Sorcerer's Mountain') stands at the end of a long white sand beach. A sea lion colony, shorebirds, pelicans and boobies are seen. A beautiful place for a swim or for a stroll at sunset.

Isla Lobos

One hour by boat on the way to Leon Dormido. This insignificant island of basaltic rocks is separated from San Cristóbal by a narrow arm of seawater. Sea lions inhabit the site, and blue-footed boobies nest on the white sand. A relaxing atmosphere in a landscape of primitive beauty. A 300-metre trail crosses the island from east to west.

San Cristobal

surfing waves scuba diving

Punta Pitt

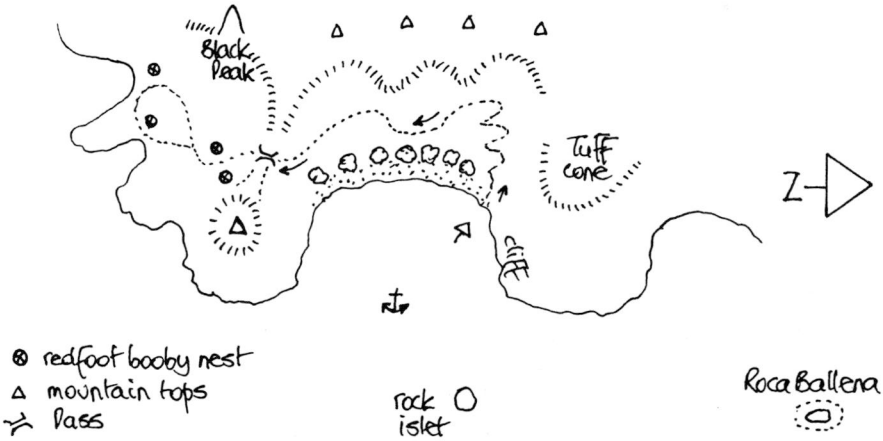

Piroco 2004

Punta Pitt

This site was opened by the Galápagos National Park in the beginning of 1989. It is the eastern tip of the Galápagos archipelago. The mountainous landscape is carved from the tuff formations of an ancient eroded volcano. The green sand cove where one disembarks is guarded by two tuff cones, furrowed by erosion. Behind the beach, where a few old sea lion males lie at times, the vegetation of saltbushes and spiny shrubs (*Scutia pauciflora*) gives way to a mini-canyon which climbs up a hill. The panorama from the viewpoint is magnificent. The trail draws a half moon around the site, goes over a pass, and climbs downhill and south to a vegetation of palo santos (where some frigates nest). *Muyuyos* (or *Cordea lutea*) trees and big yellow-green shrubs (*Nolana galapageia*) are often nesting sites for red-footed boobies. One may observe the 'morpho blanco' variety of red-footed boobies. Blue-footed boobies nest on the ground in the middle of the trail, marking their nesting site with a corona of their excrement. The trail climbs slightly, with good views on the sea, where at times dolphins porpoise along the coast. All around you the succulent plant sesuvium covers the ground with a red carpet in the dry season. The track makes a loop before returning to the starting point (see drawing, page 235).

A small rocky islet facing Punta Pitt is a fine spot for skin diving. The water is often crystal clear, but also chilly.

La Galápaguera

Not far from Punta Pitt and to the west, la Galápaguera is a site where you may meet giant tortoises. But one may walk a lot and get lost, since the trail is not clear and is covered with vegetation in the hot season. Not all guides know about the site, and many dare not venture there.

Oil Spill in Paradise

If the Marine Reserve of the Galápagos has been already the occasion for the spilling of a lot of ink in writing, nobody ever suspected that such a horrible thing could happen to the islands. On the 20th of January 2001, the oil tanker *Jessica*, apparently a very old boat, on its way from Guayaquil to Puerto Baquerizo Moreno, crashed on the rocks at 2am during the night, on some rocky islet off the south coast of San Cristóbal. In no time, the boat started sinking and a disastrous oil spill (bunker and diesel) spread over a surface area of 1,250 square kilometres, drifting across the archipelago, to Santa Fé and Isabela. Fortunately, the South Equatorial current diverted the flow quickly away from the islands and the damage was, after all, minor.

Of course, some birds (boobies and pelicans) and marine life (sea lions) were affected and stained with oil, a heartbreaking image in the eyes of public opinion. The media coverage was fast to feed on the information, to tarnish the face of both the Galápagos Islands and the National Park, which was not fair. Yes, someone was to blame, the captain, the crew, the merchant marine for allowing rusty old floating wrecks to a sacred place like a World Heritage Site, and the carelessness of the relevant authorities.

However, let us just take this as a serious warning: the pollution factor, that could be repeated in the future if drastic measures are not enforced straightaway.

The psychological shock was strong for the Galápagos National Park Office. Suddenly, human differences arising between various factions and groups of different interests and motivation, were forgotten for a time. The urgent crisis proved to be a unifying factor. An emergency plan was elaborated, following a meeting of the Ministro del Medio Ambiente, the governor of Galápagos, the Commandant of the II Zona Naval, a technician of Petroecuador and the director of the Galápagos National Park.

Everybody helped to clean up, to do something to save the animals that could be saved, and to react responsibly towards a situation that was clearly affecting everybody, equally. At work on day two were the SPNG personnel, the fishermen, the personnel of the 2nda Zona Naval, anti-contamination technicians of DIGMER (Merchant Marine) and technicians of Petroecuador. The difficulty was to control the spill in areas between 'Cerro de las Tijeretas' and Isla Lobos (San Cristóbal) and on Santa Fé Island, 20 miles away. Detergent was used profusely to split the sheet of oil. In the afternoon of that Sunday, a C-130 aircraft from the US coastguards arrived, to deal with that sort of emergency. The boat *Cirius* came over from Guayaquil and helped suck the fuel out of the sinking *Jessica*.

On day three, the works had managed to control with relative success the main area of contamination in Bahia Naufragio, in San Cristóbal. The US coastguards managed to take out all the fuel that was on port side of the *Jessica*. On Santa Fé Island various sealions were polluted, among which 15 juveniles that were attended to by the veterinaries of SPNG. In conclusion, the spill did not affect Santa Cruz, nor any other island, with the exception of Santa Fé. (After a report from Eliecer Cruz, director of SPNG, January 22, 2001)

The tanker *Jessica* hit the rocks on Schinromi Reef, at the entrance of Wreck Bay, on the western tip of San Cristóbal Island, in front of Puerto Baquerizo Moreno. The oil spill spread towards Santa Fe, the east coast of Santa Cruz and Tortuga Bay, the southern part of Isabela near Puerto Villamil and the east coast of Floreana.

In an article published in *Ocean Realm* magazine in Spring 2001, famous environmentalist and founder of the "Sea Sheperd Conservation Society", Captain Paul Watson, was there with his ship the *Sirenian*, a 95ft former United States Coast Guard cutter, arriving a few hours later on the site of the *Jesssica*. He claims that the tanker was uninsured, captain and crew unqualified, with no proper charts, but the tanks still intact, although sea water was gushing into the engine room. "A rust encrusted calamity waiting to happen, mechanically and electronically unseaworthy." Originally en route for Baltra, the *Jessica* was re-routed to Puerto Baquerizo on San Cristóbal Island, in order to refuel the Galápagos Explorer, a large ecotourism boat and the only one to use bunker C fuel oil in the Galápagos. Despite objections from the Galápagos National Park, she had been granted an operating permit by the government. Captain Watson reports that the oil spill could have been avoided if not for a 'four day debate over a US$600,000 bill', asked by the US government from the Ecuadorian government, to send an oil spill strike team from the gulf coast. The US coast guards finally arrived, but too late; the spill was estimated at over five million dollars to clean up.

CHAPTER THREE

THE NORTHERN ISLANDS

GENOVESA

land surface: 14 square km; elevation: 75 m

This rather flat island to the northwest of the archipelago looks like a huge parrot beak, opened towards the rest of the Galápagos. The central volcano is now a big caldera filled with seawater to a depth of 65 metres. Darwin Bay, open to the ocean, is also a huge collapsed caldera submerged by seawater, 180 metres deep in the centre. A narrow and shallow passage allows sailboats and other ships to enter the bay by following an alignment of beacons. Cliffs rise up to 20 or 30 metres all around the bay. A sperm whale was seen at the entrance of the bay in April 2000.

Darwin Bay

One disembarks on a small white coral beach, under the indifferent eye of the swallowtail gulls. Salt bushes (*Cryptocarpus pyriformis*) border the beach, where red-footed boobies, Nazca boobies and great frigates nest throughout the year. The species do not always get along too well; frigates tend to steal the nests of the boobies, while boobies destroy the eggs of the frigates.

Some tide pools are hidden behind a lava ridge bordering the bay. Night and lava herons, looking for small fry, are common. Sea lions come to have a swim there at times. The trail climbs onto the cliff. Swallowtail gulls make a nest of white coral pieces and black volcanic gravel, where they lay a big white egg speckled brownish black (camouflaging it against the background). Opuntia cacti and *Croton scouleri* shrubs are everywhere. Red-footed boobies (juveniles), gulls and frigates hover above the cliff overlooking the bay, taking advantage of the rising winds.

Prince Philip's Steps

The name was given after the visit of Prince Philip of the United Kingdom some years ago. The site (see map, page 240), south of Darwin Bay, is on the top of a cliff. After a dry landing on rocks, one climbs up 25 metres through a *barranco* and reaches the arid zone of palo santos, where great frigates nest in the trees and Nazca boobies on the ground. The trail heads inland to the east coast, an old *pahoehoe* lava flow, reddish brown because of oxidation and erosion. One will notice a big crack, which was created when the lava was still hot and fluid and flowed back into the fracture, like icing on a chocolate cake. Storm petrels swarm the sky by hundreds. A colony of hundreds of thousands is believed to inhabit the area. Short-eared owls hide in the crack of the lava flow and prey on the storm petrels.

MARCHENA

land surface: 115 square km; elevation: 343 m

Desolated in its external aspect, Marchena is located 50 kilometres west of Genovesa. The island is the top of a large shield volcano, with numerous small volcanic cones in the caldera and on the slopes of the volcano. The first recorded eruption occurred on September 25, 1991, with incandescent clouds during the night and lava flows to the southwest.

Marchena is not officially open to visitors, even though it is possible to disembark on the black sand beach on the southwest of the island. The Playa de los Muertos is the place where Lorenz was found dead in 1934, after being shipwrecked with a Norwegian fisherman.

Pinta

Northwest of Marchena, Pinta rises to an elevation of 750 metres. Two geological areas are distinguished. The oldest is a narrow band on the west coast, the remains of an old volcano that collapsed into the ocean. Cliffs rise up to 90 metres. A crack separates this old cliff from a younger volcano (765 metres in elevation). No eruption has been recorded on Pinta.

It is possible to drop anchor at Cape Ibbetson, to the south of the island. The vegetation is dry on the coast, humid in the highlands. For a long time, Pinta was the home of Lonesome George, last survivor of the giant tortoises. He is now a resident of the Darwin Station. Scientists and filmmakers aboard the boat *Quest*, flew above Pinta with an helicopter in the year 2000, looking for any survivor of the giant tortoises, without any success.

Darwin and Wolf

Isolated like two black sheep to the northwest of the archipelago, Darwin and Wolf, also known as Culpepper and Wenman, seem to be outcasts. These islands are the eroded summits of two large calderas, which rise 1,800 metres from the bottom of the ocean (see drawings, page 241).

Darwin

A flat island, 165 metres in elevation, surrounded on all sides by vertical cliffs, where the surf breaks. A helicopter landed on the high plateau of Darwin in 1964. Two hundred metres off the eastern shore of the island, a monumental arch is formed on a shallow platform. Like an Arc de Triomphe facing east, this symbolic gate reminds people of the first navigators, who came from that direction. Nazca boobies and red-footed boobies dwell on Darwin Arch, while hammerhead sharks and whale sharks silently roam in the blue depths. False killer whales have been seen surfacing along the northeast coast of Darwin (author's own observation, December 1993). Royal terns and sooty terns are also frequent residents on Darwin.

Wolf

Very similar to its neighbour, Wolf rises up to 250 metres, with high cliffs, 225 metres in elevation. Even though it is not a visitor's site, it is possible to disembark on the island, but climbing to the top is risky. An old abandoned lighthouse has stood there for years.

Like Darwin, Wolf is a haven for seabirds, such as great frigatebirds, red-footed boobies, Nazca boobies, tropicbirds and swallowtail gulls, which nest in the cliff. Fur sea lions have a small colony in the north of the island, and also on a pile of rocks on the east coast. Hammerhead sharks cruise back and forth offshore. Dolphins often accompany boats approaching Wolf as far as the anchorage on the west coast.

The common vegetation is the croton shrub and the opuntia cactus. The sharpbill ground finch, known as the 'vampire finch', lives on Wolf and drinks the blood of Nazca boobies from the base of the wing feathers. Both Darwin and Wolf are excellent diving sites.

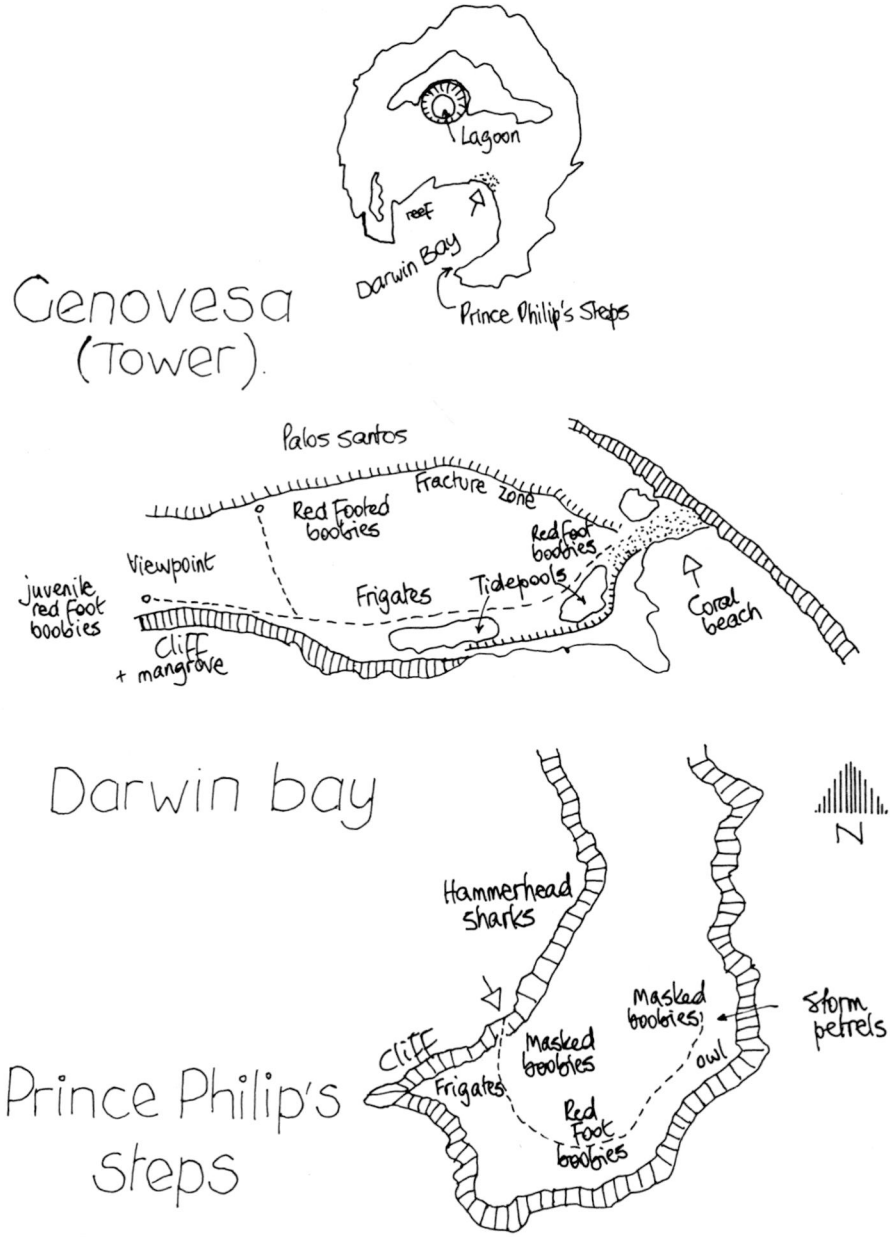
Lagoon
reef
Darwin Bay
Prince Philip's Steps
Genovesa (Tower).
Palos santos
Fracture zone
Red Footed boobies
Red foot boobies
Viewpoint
juvenile red foot boobies
Frigates
Tidepools
Coral beach
Cliff + mangrove
Darwin bay
N
Hammerhead sharks
Masked boobies
Storm petrels
Cliff
Masked boobies
owl
Frigates
Red Foot boobies
Prince Philip's steps

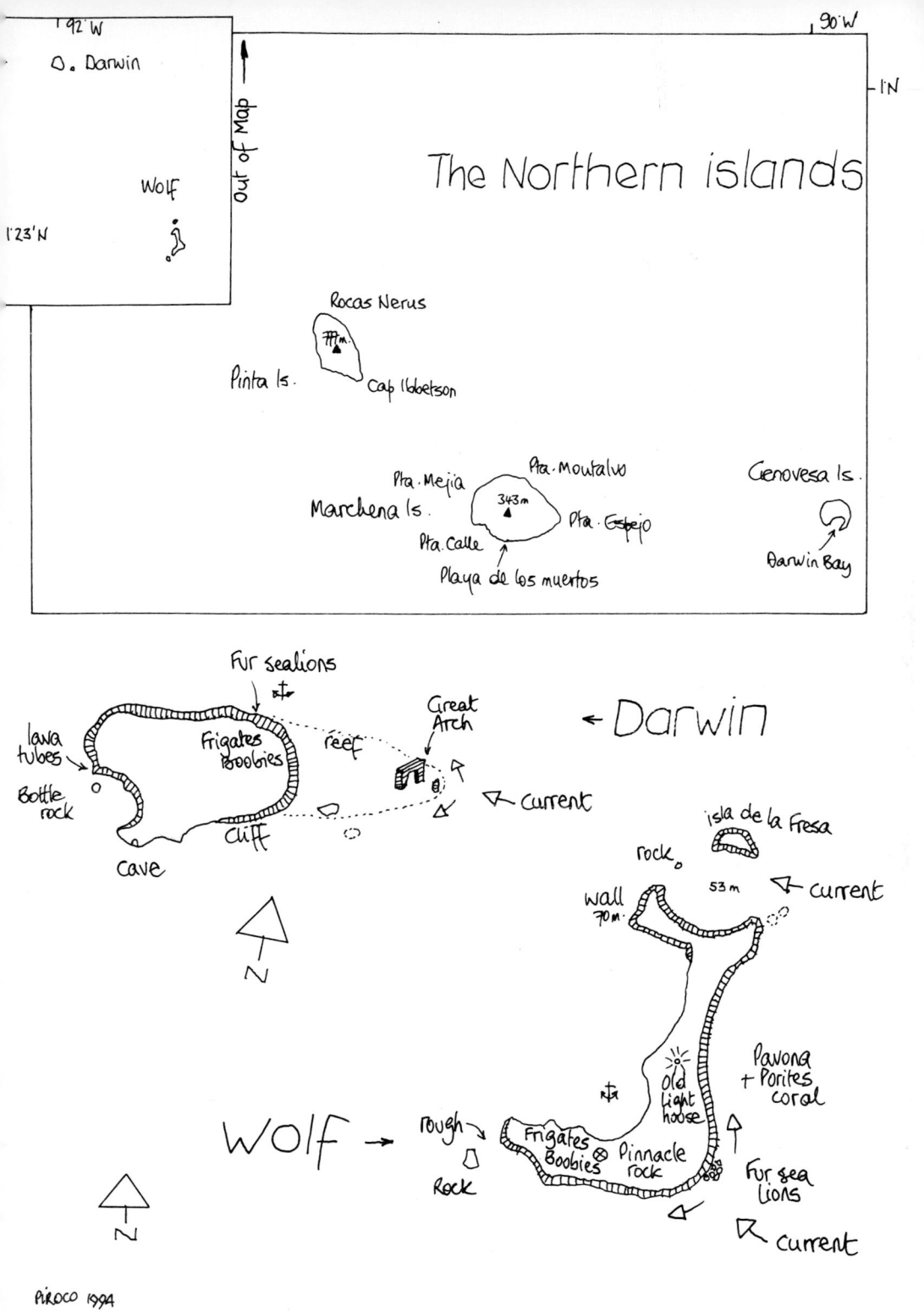
92°W
90°W
1°N
1°23'N
Darwin
Wolf
Out of Map
The Northern islands
Rocas Nerus
Pinta Is.
Cap Hobetson
Pta. Mejia
Pta. Moutalvo
Marchena Is.
343m
Pta. Espejo
Pta. Calle
Playa de los muertos
Genovesa Is.
Darwin Bay
Fur sealions
Great Arch
Darwin
lava tubes
Frigates
Boobies
reef
Bottle rock
current
cliff
cave
N
isla de la Fresa
rock
53m
current
wall
70m
Pavona + Porites coral
Old Light house
Wolf
rough
Frigates
Boobies
Pinnacle rock
Fur sea lions
Rock
N
current

PIROCO 1994

CHAPTER FOUR

THE WESTERN ISLANDS

SANTIAGO

Also known as James or San Salvador, the island, located west of Santa Cruz, is composed of a number of tuff cones and a central volcano bedecked with vegetation (see map, page 244). Many volcanic eruptions were recorded in the last century. The vegetation is dense in the highlands, and a scalesia forest covers the northwest side of the central volcano. The southern coast, and a five-kilometres band inland, are only lava flows with arid vegetation.

Many animals were introduced by man in the time of the pirates, such as goats, pigs, donkeys and rats. The visitor's sites are James Bay (Puerto Egas), Espumilla Beach, Buccaneer's Cove and Sullivan Bay. James Bay, or Puerto Egas, on the west coast of Santiago, with a black sand beach and small cliffs of tuff formations, was once upon a time colonized by man. In the 1920s and again in the 1960s, salt was extracted from the crater of a tuff cone, a 45-minute walk away (three kilometres). The remains of some buildings still stand on the cliff. The vegetation around is poor and was destroyed by the population of feral goats that inhabit the area, except for the shrub *Castela galapageia*—with little oval-shaped leaves and round red fruits—which are poisonous to the goats.

A 'Sugar Loaf' rises above James Bay. It's hard to climb, but you'll be rewarded with a spectacular view of two craters of tuff cones and the panorama of the bay. An easier walk would be to 'the grottos', basaltic marine caves with open roof, on the littoral. These natural pools are an enchanting place, where sea lions and fur sea lions come to play.

Shorebirds are numerous, and include as lava herons, oystercatchers, whimbrels, semipalmated plovers and wandering tattlers. *Zayapas,* red and turquoise blue crabs, are everywhere. Galápagos doves and Galápagos hawks are also common in the area .

Since 1988, the Galápagos National Park Service and the Charles Darwin Research Station have joined forces to eradicate feral pigs on Santiago, with the sponsorship of Lindblad Expeditions Inc. of New York. The results of the "Proyecto Isabela" programme were successful in 1999 and 2000 and now feral pigs are practically extinct on Santiago.

In 2004, 32 field trips to Santiago were accomplished. 122 Judas goats were deployed with helicopter support, then another 90. The goat population has now been reduced to extremely low levels. Donkeys have been eradicated.

Playa Espumilla

North of James Bay, Espumilla (which means 'foam' in Spanish) is a beautiful golden sand beach, fringed with mangroves. Two brackish lagoons lie behind, with a few resident birds: flamingos, common stilts, Bahama pintail ducks, semipalmated plovers. Many turtle nests may be found in the sand dunes under the mangrove trees. Sometimes turtles get lost in the lagoon, and die if they cannot find their way back to the sea. A trail to the right climbs over the hill, where land birds such as vermilion flycatchers and large-bill flycatchers can be seen.

Buccaneer's Cove

Farther north is beautiful Buccaneer's Cove, with red-purple sand. Pirates used to come here to refit their boats and search for water and tortoises. Ceramic jars were found at the bottom of the bay; some had wine, others marmalade.

Sea lions bask on the beach. One should be aware of the dangerous surf that crashes on the beach when disembarking or embarking. Cliffs of tuff formations surround the cove, the natural statue of 'the Monk' guarding this magic site, and the small islet in the centre of the bay are all part of the fabulous landscape that is created in the warm light of sunset (see map of Santiago, page 244).

Sullivan Bay

Facing Bartolomé Island, on the east coast of Santiago. Two imposing tuff cones rise in the middle of an enormous lava field, of a *pahoehoe* surface type. The landscape of ropey lava, the intestinal figures created by the lava flow and the *hornitos* (pockets of gas and water trapped under a crust of lava, and later exploded) are among the curiosities of Sullivan Bay. The loop trail, marked with small black and white posts, can be walked in an hour and 15 minutes. Oystercatchers often wander along the shoreline.

BARTOLOMÉ

land surface: 1.2 square km
max. elevation: 114 m

A very impressive little island in front of Sullivan Bay, with a landscape of real volcanic desolation: tuff cones, spatter cones, scoria formations and black volcanic sand. A trail leads to the summit of the central volcano; a stairway made of *cedrela* wood was constructed by the Galápagos National Park to stop the island's quick erosion caused by daily visitors. From the top of the volcano, the view is extraordinary. Towards the east, a field of spatter cones punctuates the island. Towards the west, one is amazed by the isthmus of Bartolomé, covered by mangroves and bordered by two small coves of golden sand in the shape of half moons. On the north beach, the Pinnacle Rock stands like a finger pointed to the sky. This volcanic needle is the last remaining piece of a tuff cone, eroded and partially bombed by American pilots during the World War II. Today it is the most photographed part of the island (see drawing, page 245).

The only vegetation on the slopes of the volcano is *Tiquilia,* a little white plant which grows in the volcanic sand, and *Chamaesyca* (an Euphorbiaceae), which forms a small tuft of green or red with tiny white flowers. The lava cactus, *Brachycereus,* an endemic genus, grows on the old lava flow uphill of the first stairway. One may notice some broken lava tubes which climb down the slope of the volcano. It is possible to swim and skin dive at the north cove, under Pinnacle Rock, where the underwater life is attractive. Maybe you will be lucky enough to meet some Galápagos penguins swimming about, porpoising at the surface, or speeding like torpedoes behind a school of fish. There is a small colony in a sheltered cove behind Pinnacle Rock. In March 2000, hundreds of blue nudibranchs were seen floating near Pinnacle Rock. Some samples were taken to the CDRS. Only one survived: they were cannibals!

Bucaneer's cove
Punta Cordova
Albany
Espumilla beach
James bay
Puerto Egas
Cousin's rock
Sullivan bay
Bartolomé
Cape Nepean
Bainbridge rocks
Sombrero chino
Rabida
Beagle rocks
Santiago (James).
Palos Santos
Lagoon (Flamingos)
Mangrove beach
Old waterfall
Lagoon
Espumilla beach
James Bay
Black sand beach
Old salt mine
Hawks
45'
Ruins
15'
1H15
Wild goats
Fur sealions
Grottos
Pan de Azucar
James Bay

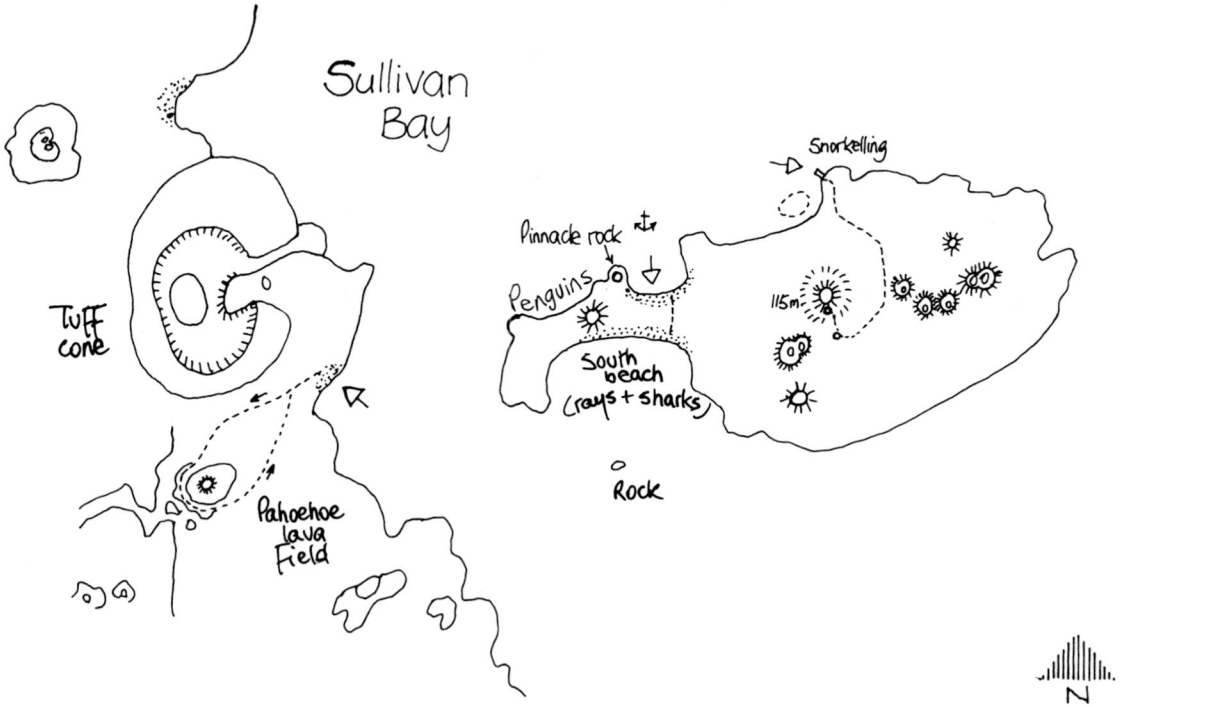

Sullivan bay + Bartolomé

[after an aerial photograph by the US AirForce, 1946].

The south beach is unsuitable for swimming due to stingrays, small whitetip and blacktip sharks. Spotted eagle rays can be observed at the surface, and black turtles are plentiful during the months of November and December, when they come to lay eggs on the beach. Herons prey on baby turtles running down the beach after they hatch.

Sombrero Chino

Only a hundred metres from the southeastern coast of Santiago island, Sombrero Chino ('Chinese Hat') is separated from the big island by a marvellous turquoise-blue lagoon. The island is made of a few adjacent craters and very old, fragile *pahoehoe* lava flows. The vegetation is meager, but some very colourful sesuvium plants are scattered around.

The trail, 350 metres long, runs from the northern white sand beach, where sea lions and penguins are common, to the western part of the island. There, the lava bedrock hosts a colony of marine iguanas, which often wallow in tide pools. The waves crash against the nearby cliffs, spraying the whole area with mist. Some Galápagos hawks overlook their kingdom from the top of the island. Sombrero Chino is an ideal place for snorkelling or skin diving in the lagoon.

Isabela

land surface: 4,588 square kilometres
elevation: 1,707 metres

By far the biggest island of the archipelago, Isabela's land surface accounts for half of the archipelago's total. It measures 132 kilometres from north to south and 84 kilometres at its greatest width. The island is composed of six main volcanoes, five of which evolved in calderas, the old stage of a shield volcano. The largest caldera is ten kilometres in diameter. From the oldest to the youngest these volcanoes are: Sierra Negra, Alcedo, Darwin, Wolf, Cerro Azul. The sixth is Ecuador volcano, at the northwestern tip of the island (the seahorse nose of Isabela), has been destroyed by erosion and wave action. It is estimated that more than 2,500 cones are present on Isabela. Wolf volcano, which culminates at 1707 metres is the highest summit. However, the latest map of the Instituto Geografico Militar del Ecuador (June 2005) shows Wolf's highest point at 1646 metres. Cerro Azul volcano in southern Isabela is now the second highest summit in the Galápagos Islands, at an elevation of 1689 metres. A rare population of the endemic moth *Epiplema becki* (Lepidoptera of the Uraniidae family) was discovered in 2004 on both Wolf and Sierra Negra volcanoes, on their host plant *Duranta dombeyana*, a bush of the Scalesia forest. The equator passes through both Ecuador and Wolf volcanoes. All these volcanoes are considered very active. The most recent eruptions occurred on Cerro Azul and Sierra Negra in 1979, on Wolf in 1982. Some earthquakes shook Alcedo in March 1991. An eruption on Cerro Azul, in September 1998, created a spatter cone on the west slope. Cerro Azul erupted for one and a half months in 1998. Fernandina erupted in 1995, 2001 and in May 2005.

In 2004, a base camp for helicopter operations was constructed in northern Isabela. Aerial hunting of feral goats has been carried out over 90 per cent of the land, resulting in very low densities of goats. 187 Judas goats were deployed on Ecuador and Wolf volcanoes.

Alcedo Volcano

The trail to Alcedo starts from the small black cove of Alcedo Beach (volcanic gravel), on the east coast of the island. It follows an *aa* lava flow and a canyon dug by rain water. The track crosses the arid zone of palo santos and croton. The climb should be made early, before sunrise, because the heat becomes torrid during the day. Fortunately, some big trees provide shade along the way at two possible stops. Expect it to take three to five hours to reach the rim of the crater, depending on the individual. After a slow ascent for most of the hike, the last climb is very strenuous before you get to the top, and volcanic gravel slips under your feet. You may meet some female tortoises on the trail in the hot season, as they walk down to the lowlands to nest in June.

The caldera of Alcedo is seven kilometres wide; the crater floor, 200 metres below the rim, is an immense lava field bedecked with palo santos and spiny shrubs. The rim is covered with shrubs and small trees, such as cat's claws, *Zanthoxylum fagara* (local name *una de gato*), and *Tournefortia pubescens*. There are also some endemic tree ferns of the species *Cyathea weatherbyana*.

Fumaroles can be observed on the southern slope of the caldera (another two or three hours' walk). The 'geyser' is no more than a hot waterhole spewing vaporous fumes. Sulphur deposits are also seen farther away. On the rim and inside the caldera, thousands of tortoises gather during the wet season to wallow happily in muddy rain pools, which rehydrates them and protects them from ticks. With a population estimated at 5,000 individuals, the Alcedo tortoise is the most flourishing in the Galápagos. In the dry season, tortoises hide in the bushes, on the rim of the crater, or dig a sort of burrow to hide from the fierce sun.

The Galápagos hawk is very common in the hot season, and the inquisitive juveniles often hover over your head. Goats, donkeys and cats live on the slopes of the volcano, causing minor damage to the vegetation and to land birds.

It is possible to camp on Alcedo, but fires are prohibited. Bring your stove, enough water (two litres per day) and a flashlight if you spend the night (see map, page 249).

In year 2000, Alcedo is still closed to visitors for the last five years, due to presence of a serious goat population. The National Park plans to eradicate goats with helicopters and hunters, also using radiotelemetry to localize groups of goats, with 'Chivo judas'.

Punta Garcia

This site used to be accessible by *panga* only. The landscape was once a breeding site of flightless cormorants, just above the waterline, but the birds seem to have deserted the place. This rare seabird of the Galápagos breeds from March to September. Brown pelicans are sometimes present. The lagoon is not very safe for swimming, due to troubled water and sharks.

Punta Albemarle

At the northern tip of Isabela Island, this site was an American radar base during World War II. Disembarking is not easy because of the surf. The largest form of marine iguana in the Galápagos is found at Punta Albemarle. There are quite a few nests of flightless cormorants, and a little colony of fur sea lions.

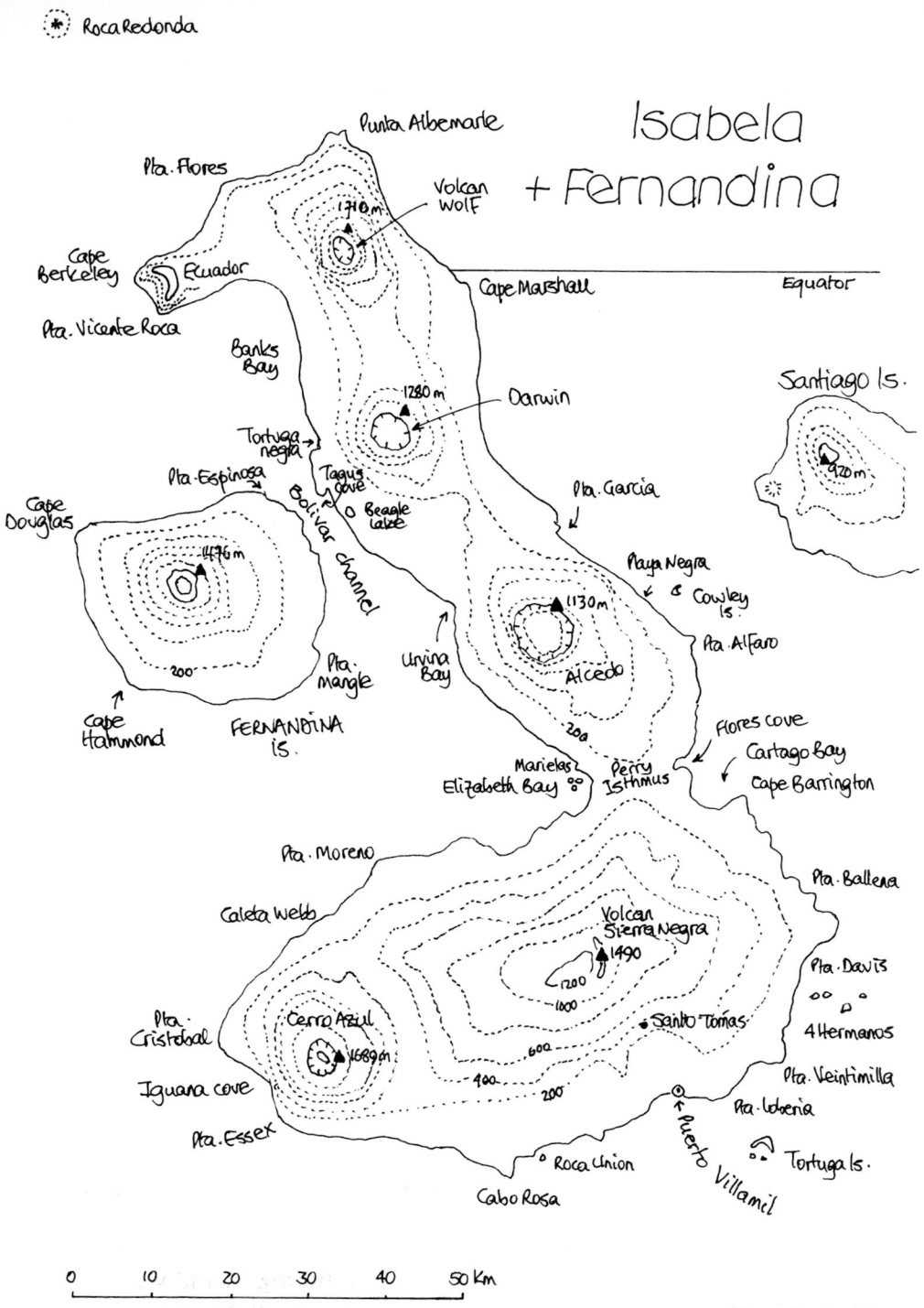
Roca Redonda
Isabela + Fernandina
Punta Albemarle
Pta. Flores
Volcan Wolf
1710 m
Cape Berkeley
Ecuador
Pta. Vicente Roca
Cape Marshall
Equator
Banks Bay
1280 m
Darwin
Santiago Is.
920 m
Tortuga negra
Pta. Espinosa
Tagus cove
Beagle lake
Bolivar channel
Pta. Garcia
Cape Douglas
1476 m
200
Playa Negra
Cowley Is.
1130 m
Pta. Alfaro
Urvina Bay
Alcedo
Pta. Mangle
Cape Hammond
FERNANDINA IS.
200
Flores cove
Cartago Bay
Cape Barrington
Marielas
Elizabeth Bay
Perry Isthmus
Pta. Moreno
Pta. Ballena
Caleta Webb
Volcan Sierra Negra
1490
1200
1000
Pta. Davis
Pta. Cristobal
Cerro Azul
1689 m
Santo Tomas
4 Hermanos
600
400
200
Iguana cove
Pta. Veintimilla
Pta. Loberia
Pta. Essex
Roca Union
Puerto Villamil
Tortuga Is.
Cabo Rosa
0 10 20 30 40 50 Km
© Pierre Constant 2005

Alcedo beach
3 to 5 HR walk
big tree
canyon
"Aa" lava flow
1097m
big tree
Viewpoint
camp
Sulphur deposits
Caldera
Tortoises
camp
Tortoise ponds
Fumaroles [2 to 3 HR walk from the viewpoint].
Alcedo volcano
mangroves
lagoon
Islas Marielas
penguins
channel
lava field
Piraco 2001
0
500 m
Elizabeth bay

Punta Vicente Roca

This is the southern tip of Volcan Ecuador, the 'nose' of Isabela Island, shaped like a seahorse. The sheltered cove is a good anchorage for boats. Inland, a saltwater lagoon is trapped by some lava flow and tuff formations. A small colony of blue footed boobies nests on the ridge overlooking the lagoon. At sea level, a marine cave called 'Oreja del Burro' is conspicuous and has a submarine connection with the lagoon, where sealions come in to bask in the sun. Marine iguanas were seen nesting in February 2000, then, nine Galápagos penguins with seven juveniles (Paula Tagle). A group of five to six sunfishes was seen at Punta Vicente Roca in April 2000. A young orca was reported in June, by Lynn Fowler and the "Polaris guides".

Punta Tortuga

On the west coast, slightly north of Tagus Cove, Punta Tortuga is a beach of dark sand, behind which is a mangrove swamp. One may observe the mangrove finch, similar to the carpenter finch but with a shorter and sharper bill.

The area was tectonically uplifted in 1975. In 1825, the American ship *Tartar,* anchored in Banks Bay, north of the site, and witnessed a volcanic eruption on Fernandina, 15 kilometres to the south. The air temperature rose to 50°C, and the sea temperature reached 40°C, so warm that the tar on the riggings began to melt. The eruption lasted for two weeks.

Tagus Cove

This small, U-shaped cove was a refuge of pirates and whalers. It is still a historical site, if one considers all the graffiti on the surrounding cliffs. Today, any kind of painting is forbidden and punishable. The name 'Tagus' was given in 1814 by a British navy ship of the same name, which came to look for tortoises and found some.

The landing site is awkward and rather slippery on the rocks. Behind the tuff formations bordering the cove, a wooden stairway, constructed by the Galápagos National Park in 1990, climbs up to a viewpoint. From there one discovers Darwin Lake down below. The brackish lagoon is perfectly circular, and is elevated above sea level by tectonic uplift. The white palo santos are everywhere around Darwin Lake, and turn happily green during the wet season. Darwin's finches are found in swarms, to the benefit of the feral cats that inhabit the area. The cats were studied by Mike Konecny in 1980; this American scientist partially lost his vision due to a viral disease as he attached radio collars around the cats' necks.

The trail goes halfway around the lake, then heads inland up to a ridge with a few spatter cones. From the viewpoint, one may appreciate the impressive landscape of Darwin volcano's lava flow (*aa* surface type) and, on a clear day, the wide silhouette of Ecuador and Wolf volcanoes to the north. A man with solid ranger shoes, would lose the sole of his boots after four kilometres of hard walking on the lava of this convict's country. The feral dogs that live in the area have developed the ability to cross the basaltic surface, thanks to horny pads under their feet, which protect them against cuts—a remarkable example of adaptation to the environment. The most extraordinary fact is that these dogs can drink seawater without any ill effect. A giant tortoise of about 20 years old and a land iguana, were discovered in Tagus Cove, by Fausto Arellana (March 2000).

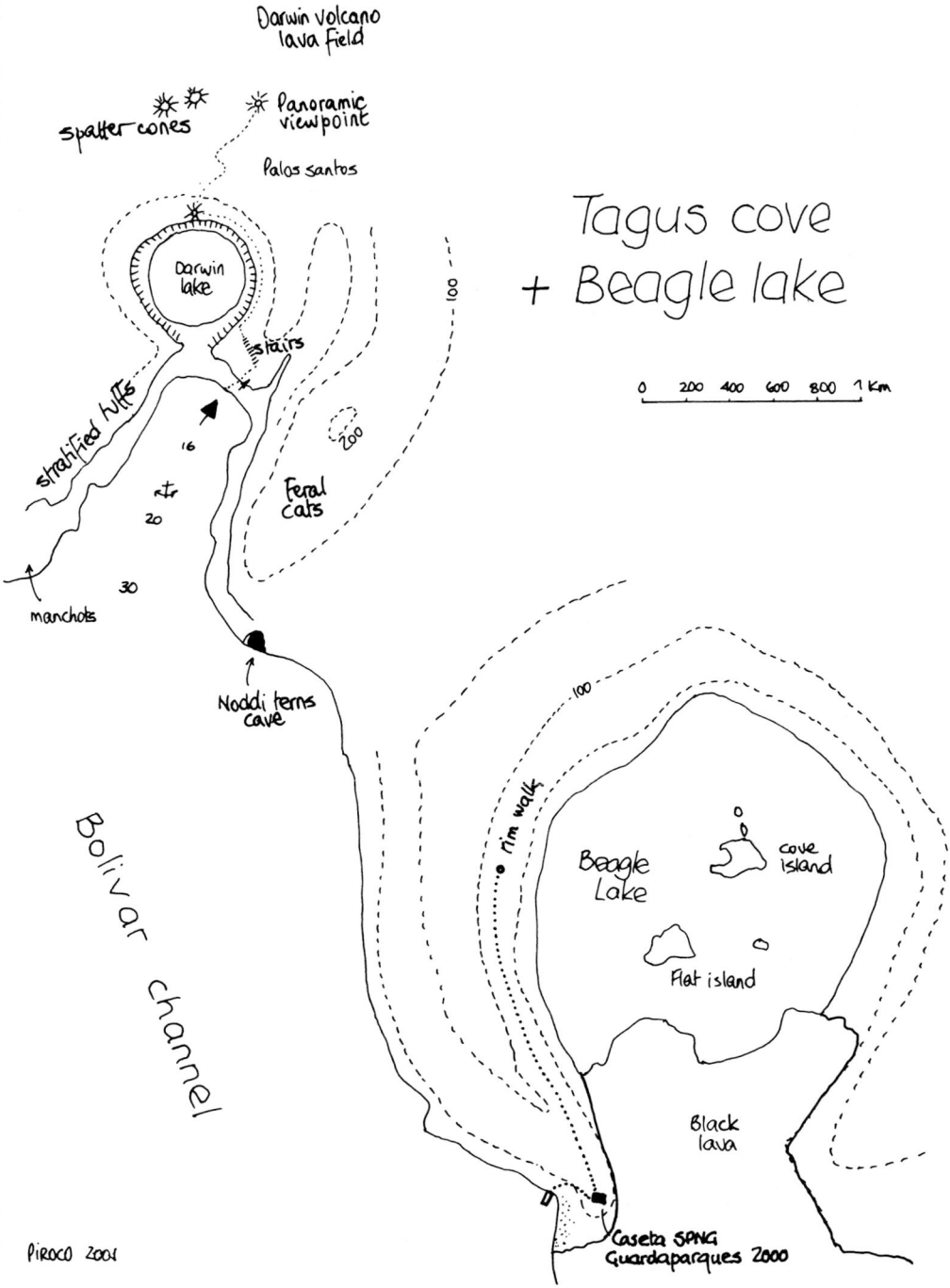
Darwin volcano lava field
spatter cones
Panoramic viewpoint
Palos santos
Tagus cove + Beagle lake
Darwin lake
stairs
100
0 200 400 600 800 1 Km
stratified tuffs
16
200
Feral cats
20
30
manchots
Noddi terns cave
100
rim walk
Beagle Lake
cove island
Flat island
Bolivar channel
Black lava
Caseta SPNG Guardaparques 2000
PIROCO 2001

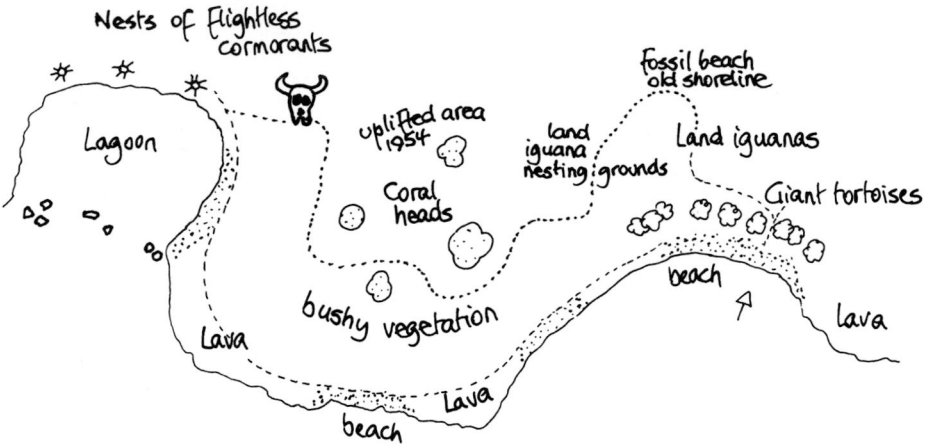

Urvina bay

Punta Espinosa

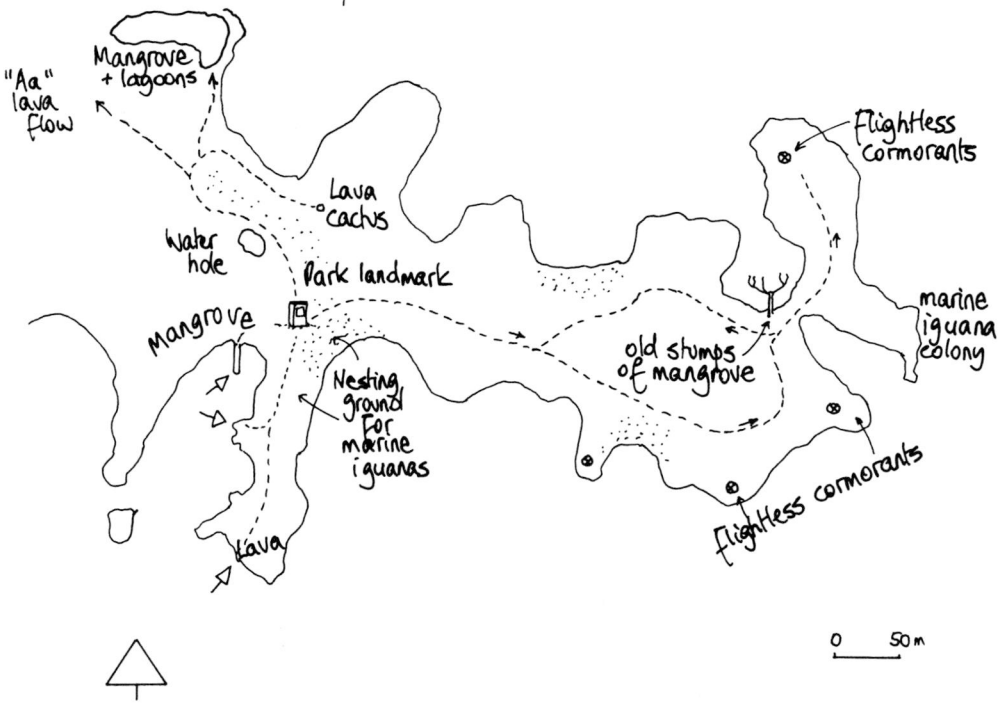

PIROCO 1994

It is possible to take a *panga* ride along the cliffs of Tagus Cove to observe pelican nests, blue-footed boobies, noddy terns in a marine cave, Galápagos penguins standing peacefully on a rock by the water, marine iguanas basking in the sun and lazy sea lions. Snorkelling and skin diving in Tagus Cove are interesting, especially at night, when one may see hornsharks on the volcanic gravel bottom and redlip batfishes (at greater depth). The new 'Caseta' of SPNG was built in 2000, south of Tagus, near Beagle Lake, for 'guardaparques' to control the Bolivar Channel and illegal fishing activities. (See drawing, page 252.)

Urvina Bay

West of Alcedo volcano, Urvina Bay was tectonically uplifted in 1954. Coral heads (nowadays white) were thrust five metres above sea level, as were six kilometres of coastline. A lateral eruption of volcan Alcedo occurred a few months later.

After a wet landing on a white sand beach, Urvina is a good site for seeing giant tortoises, big land iguanas and marine iguanas. Half an hour away from the beach along the shore, one may discover a few nests of flightless cormorants around a sheltered lagoon, where common egrets and great blue herons are also present (see drawing, page 254). A trail goes inland, from the land iguanas nesting grounds to the lagoon of the flightless cormorants. A male sealion was observed eating a whitetip shark, in February 2000 (Jason Hermann, Ernest Vaca and Roberto Plaza).

Elizabeth Bay

South of Urvina Bay and west of the Perry Isthmus, Elizabeth Bay is a marine site where landing is not allowed. As you pass by the small islets in the middle of the bay, you may sight Galápagos penguins, but they are as rare as flightless cormorants. A narrow channel penetrates farther inland, in a dense mangrove area with unusually tall trees, and opens up on a big lagoon with many arms. It is a haven for green turtles, golden rays and spotted eagle rays, small white-tip sharks. Marine turtle mate in the lagoon in November–December. You may snorkel down the entrance channel, with the outgoing tide, to see turtles and stingrays (see drawing, page 249).

Punta Moreno

This is a typical *pahoehoe* lava flow, southwest of Elizabeth Bay, with numerous cracks and water holes, formed when the roof of gas pockets under the lava surface broke in. A rich life has developed in and around these natural pools. One may see flamingos, Bahama pintails, great blue herons. Pelicans nest in the mangroves. Feral dogs roam the region and attack marine iguanas and sea lions. A fishing eagle was observed by guide Luis Rodriguez (February 2000). A pair of mangrove finches was also seen in a courtship display.

Puerto Villamil

Principal centre of Isabela district, on the south coast of the island. It is one of the least inhabited islands, with a population of about 1,700 people (1999), and an 'end-of-the world' feeling. The fishermen's village was founded in 1897 by Don Antonio Gil, an honorable citizen from Guayaquil. This is one of the most beautiful sites of the archipelago, with marvelous white sand beaches that stretch for kilometres. The historical past of Isabela is rich in fabulous and terrible stories. In fact, Turtle Bay (Bahia de la Tortuga) was used by pirates;

buried treasure was hidden there, and some was discovered in 1974. Behind Villamil and along the coast, brackish lagoons are a refuge for flamingos, whimbrels, white-cheeked pintails, common stilts and gallinules. Frogs, recently introduced, make their home there.

Following the beach to the west, one passes by the cemetery of Puerto Villamil (one kilometre), with old graves and rotten crosses. A new dirt road replaces the old trail and heads inland at the end of the beach. The taxi cost is $5 one way or $10 return. A number of visitors' sites are found along the way, making the excursion an interesting day out. At the end of the long white beach you shall find a trail to La Playita (107 metres), further on to 'Pozas Verdes' (80 metres) and 'Los Tunos' viewpoint, two brackish water lookouts with candelabra cacti. One reaches a roundabout with two trails leading to 'Playa del amor' (50 metres) and to 'Tunel del Estero' (75 metres), a lava tube going underground. Later on, you pass by 'Poza Redonda' and 'Poza Escondida' to the right, and over 'Puente Merengue' with a nice view of the ocean and the rolling waves. Take a left to follow 'El Estero' trail (226 metres), leading to a fresh water spring. Shortly before coming in view of the penitentiary, 'Cerro Orchilla', a hilltop and viewpoint, is worth a climb for the magnificent panorama of Bahia Tortuga in the afternoon sun. The 'Muro de las Lagrimas', the Wall of Tears' was erected from big lava blocks by convicts of the penal colony. The penitentiary of Isabela was opened in 1944 at a foot of a desolated hill, in the arid zone, two to three hours' walk from Villamil. Following a mutiny that was mentioned in the press at the time, it was definitively closed down and blown up in 1959. More than 200 convicts had been forced to hard labour. Life was horrible there and the cruelty of the guards was legendary. This period will remain forever in the memory of Isabela. Of the penitentiary itself, the only ruins are a standing cylinder of rusted iron, and a huge wall of basalt, 50 metres long, five metres wide and eight metres tall. Behind the Wall of Tears, a trail climbs up the hill, from where you may best contemplate the desolation and perhaps feel a chill run up your spine. In the far distance, the bay of Villamil shines from the timeless surf that crashes on the beach, and the magnificent turquoise-blue waters in the midday sun are an exotic image that help dispel the unhappy past.

Beyond the Muro de las Lagrimas, a trail leads to Playa Barahona through the arid zone (2 hours return). A beautiful beach frequented by feral cats and wild pigs at sunset, looking for turtle nests, on which they feed.

On the way back, notice the solitary coconut tree on the right. A pirate's treasure was discovered there 30 years ago by a mysterious Frenchman who left no trace of his passage but for a big hole with some rusted pieces of iron. Long considered the black sheep of the Galápagos, due to its obscure past and a population of 85 per cent fishermen, the small paradise lost of Puerto Villamil is slowly opening to a new wave of 'ecotourism'. The current mayor Pablo Gordillo has remodelled the main pier of the village with romantic lamp posts, volcanic stones and a creative wooden railing. A 'mirador', erected on the lava flow bordering the beach, overlooks the vast expanse of the Pacific ocean, giving you the thrilling sensation of the penitentiary days. There, facing the sea breeze, you can act Leonardo di Caprio, arms stretched out on the bow of the Titanic, and impress your loved one with a stance to remember.

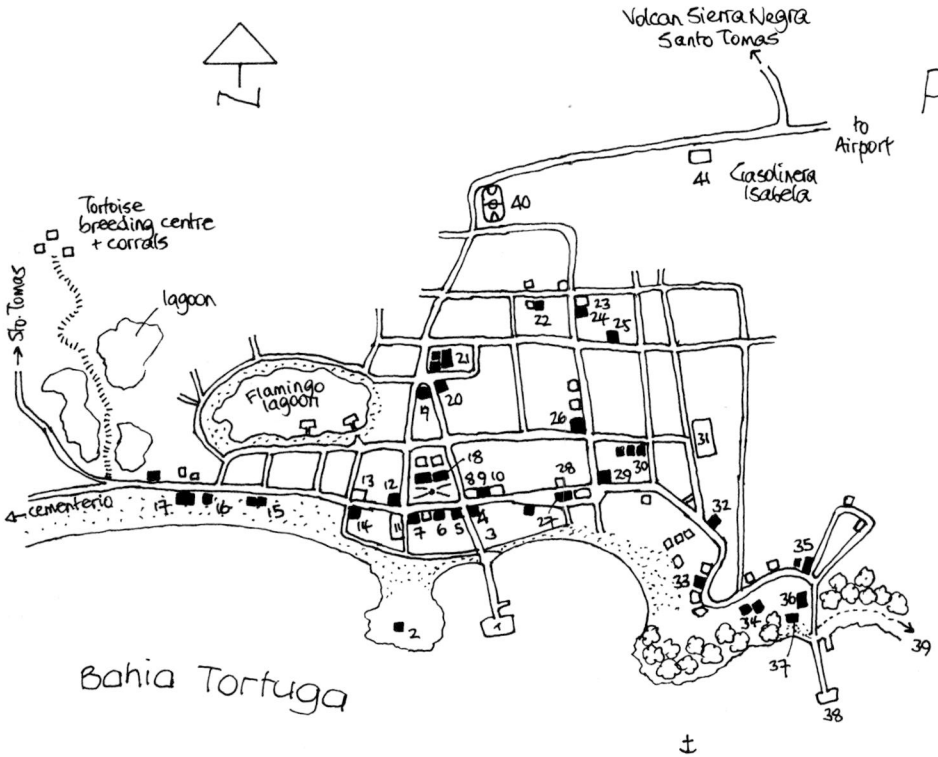

Puerto Villamil

1 Old jetty
2 Mirador
3 Capitania del puerto - Navy base
4 Police station
5 Restaurant Costa Azul + La Choza
6 Restaurant El Encanto de la Pepa
7 Porta - National + international calls
8 EMETEBE
9 Pacifictel
10 Moneygram
11 Dispensary
12 Comercial Noboa
13 Galápagos National Park office
14 Centro educacion ambiental Fundacion Darwin
15 Cormorant beach house
16 Beto's beach bar + Hostal
17 Pink house
18 Municipio
19 Comercial la Isla
20 Albatros internet
21 mercado municipal
22 Panadena la Delicia - bakery
23 Pacifictel - phone + fax
24 Easynet cybercafe
25 Hotel San Vicente + Sierra Negra tours
26 Residencial las Gardenias
27 Comercial Jordan
28 CDE - Post office
29 Ferreteria Ana Karolina
30 Hostal Tero Real
31 Colegio Fray Augustin Azkunaga
32 Hotel Ballena Azul + Isabela del Mar
33 Hotel Casa de Marita
34 INGALA
35 Scubadragon dive centre
36 SICGAL quarantine control
37 Club Nautico - beach bar
38 Embarcadero - jetty
39 Concha y Perla trail to lagoon
40 Stadium

© Pierre Constant - 2005

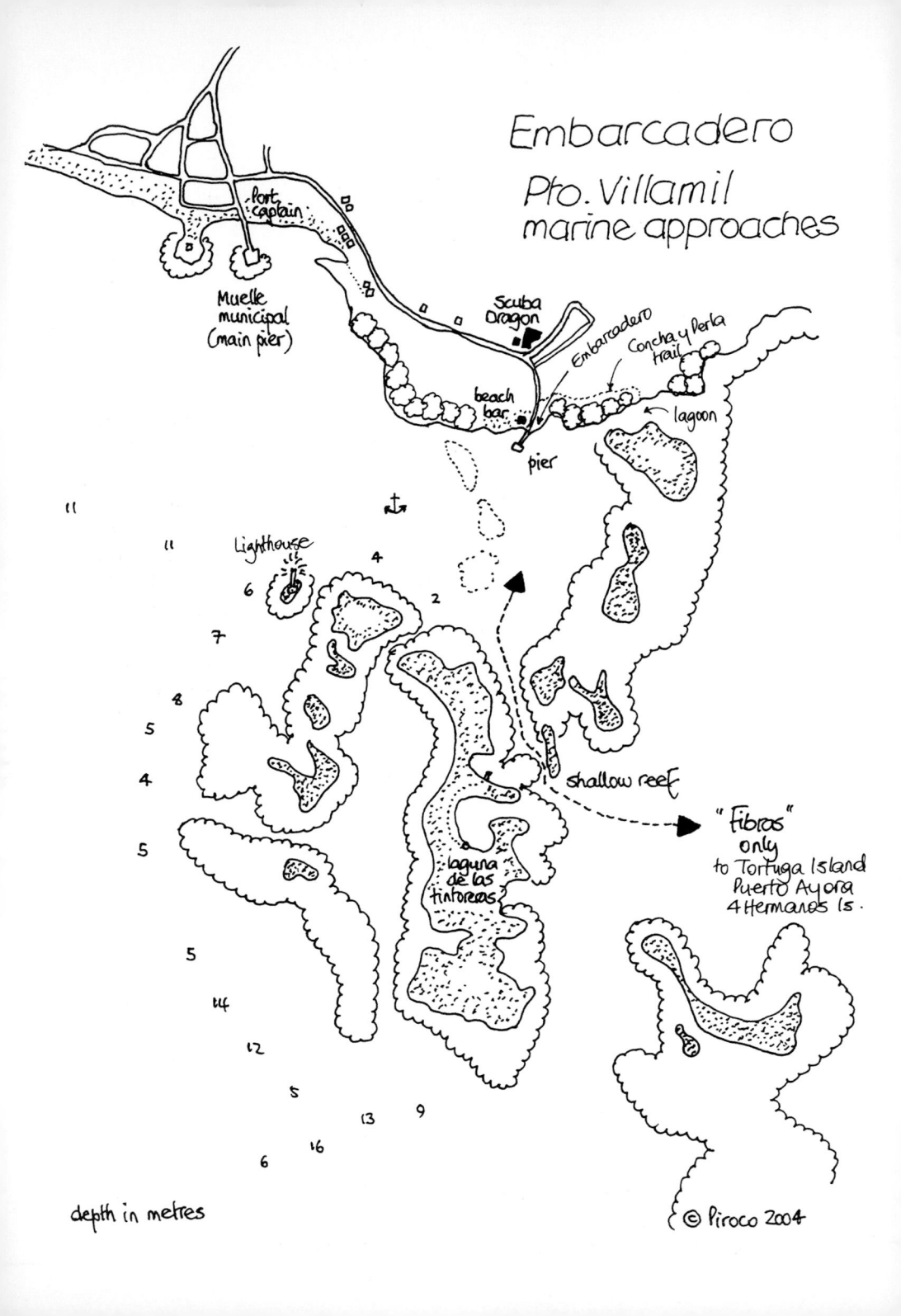
Embarcadero
Pto. Villamil
marine approaches
Port Captain
Muelle municipal (main pier)
Scuba Dragon
Embarcadero
Concha y Perla trail
beach bar
lagoon
pier
Lighthouse
shallow reef
"Fibras" only to Tortuga Island Puerto Ayora 4 Hermanos Is.
laguna de las tintoreras
11
11
4
6
2
7
8
5
4
5
5
14
12
5
13
9
16
6
depth in metres
© Piroco 2004

The new 'Malecon' or waterfront promenade is an attractive playground for kids and adults alike, with a volleyball ground and beach games. It extends all the way through town, past the Fundacion Darwin and the National Park offices, to the 'Poza de los flamingos', where at night you can watch the flamingoes sleep in a group, standing on one foot. Some observation ramps make access to the brackish water much easier now. Definitely a 'must do' experience to enjoy Puerto Villamil's night life. Another one is to watch the 'Bingo' at Comercial Jordan: "Chocolateamos, chocolateamos!... atencion!... 17... marque el 17!...", worth a look anytime after dark, you'll feel part of an old movie, with dim lights and characters of another time.

An airport was built more than ten years ago with a landing strip of white coral, but it was found later on that it was not practical because it was wrongly oriented in respect to the southeast tradewinds, and the site was abandoned.

On the beach at the end of the village, a deserted-looking pink house is swept by the ocean wind. The last time it was used, two Japanese men changed the main hall into a sea cucumber depot for eight months before they disappeared with their smuggled goods. There are some *comedors* and food places in town (see map, page 255). To get to Isabela on your own, ask for *'la Lancha Estrella de Mar'* (Oficina Galaven, $17.25 (colono), $34.50 (foreigners and nationals) in Puerto Ayora, Santa Cruz Island), a ferryboat that goes to the inhabited islands once or twice a week, and which also transports mail and cargo (see page 207). Three 'fibras' (fisherman's speedboat) travel daily at 2pm between Puerto Villamil and Puerto Ayora, returning at 6am the following day. Ask for 'Darwin Explorer' Tel: (05) 2529 401 or Henry Segovia Tel: (05) 2529 249, alternatively at the 'Capitania del puerto'. Cost is $30. Another boat 'Lancha INGALA', is supposed to operate between Villamil and Puerto Ayora on Sundays, but never does. Maybe once a month, and then again no fixed schedule! (or say, whenever a politician needs...).

HOTELS (US$ prices as per 2009; listed by price)

Red Mangrove Isabela (8 luxury rooms), single $200, double $250, includes BF. Tel. (05) 2529 030. E: info@redmangrove.com.

Hotel Albemarle (on the beach) 11 rooms (8 with beach view & 3 at the back)single or double $122–183, triple $219.60, suites $305. E: hotelalbemarle@hotmail.com.

Hotel Casa de Marita (on the beach), standard single $50, double $85 + 22% tax. Suites $125–220 + 22% includes BF. E: info@casamaritagalapagos.com; www.galapagosisabela.com.

Hotel San Vicente, single $30, double $50, includes American BF. Trips to Sierra Negra volcano, horses @ $15 per day. Tel. (05) 2529 140. E: hotelsanvicentegalapagos@hotmail.com.

Tres Palmas Lodge (100 metres from 'Embarcadero'), bungalows at $50 and $80 in a quiet natural setting around a salt water pond. with Scubadragon dive centre attached. Tel. 085837769. E: calaolife@yahoo.com; www.scubadragongalapagos.com.

Beto's Beach Hotel, room upstairs @ $25 per person, with balcony overlooking the bay and 4 rooms @ $20 per person.

Cormorant Beach House (on the beach), rooms at $15–20 per person.

Hostel Las Gardenias, 6 rooms, single $19, double $33 + IVA, include BF. Tel. (05) 2529 115. E: elizabethgardenia@yahoo.com.
The Dolphin House, six rooms on the beach, single $25, double $30–50. Tel. (05) 2529 138.
Casita de la Playa (four rooms) $20 per person, American BF @ $5. Tel. (05) 2529 334
Posada del Caminante (Samaniego), single $12, double $24, triple $36, kitchen, DVD, five rooms. Tel. (05) 2529. 407; Mobile. 091845067. E: posadadelcaminante@hotmail.com.
Coral Blanco Lodging, seven rooms, $15 per person, with bath. Tel. (05) 2529 432.
Hotel Tero Real, single $15, double $30, American BF @$4. Tel. (05) 2529 195. E: gabypa@hotmail.es.
Neptuno Hospedaje, single $10, double $40 with AC. Tel. (05) 2529 388.
The Jungle (La Jungla), on the outskirts of town westward. Rooms at $15 per Person. BF @ $4. Tel: 05-2529295, Mobile: 097373063

Restaurants (listed alphabetically)
Aloha Betsy, behind the Fundacion Darwin building, near the beach. Almuerzos and meriendas at $2.50; a friendly, quiet place.
Arenitas, typical local restaurant on the side of the main square. Almuerzos at $2.50.
Beto's Beach Bar, good music every night, cocktails, à la carte meals.
Casa de Marita, a la carte dining, Italian food.
Casa Rosada, sushi bar, miso soup and sushi @ $15.
Coco Bar (of Angel), on the beach facing the Red Mangrove Lodge, music, cocktails.
Costa Azul (Blue Coast), of Gladys, in front of Capitania del puerto, set menus, à la carte, seafood.
Hotel Albemarle & restaurant, international food, wines and video plasma screen with Galápagos documentaries, on the beach near the main pier.
La Choza, main square, expensive seafood for what it is.
La Cuna del Sabor, almuerzos and meriendas. In main square.
Los Delfines, quality food and international taste, by local chef Cesar, on the main square, facing the town hall.
Red Mangrove Lodge, dinner $18 + IVA.

Internet cafés are found at 'Albatros Internet' on the main street (facing Comercial La Isla) and at Comercial Noboa on the main square. Easynet cybercafe (since 2004), $1.50 per hour, next to Pacifictel where you can make international phone calls and send faxes. Both Porta (on the main square), and Pacifictel (in front of the police station), can be used for local and international calls.

EMETEBE flies from Puerto Villamil to Baltra (and Cristóbal), daily except Sundays. To Baltra, US$130 R/T (colonos), US$260 return for nationals and foreigners.
To San Cristóbal: $91 one way. Tel. (04) 2292 492 in Guayaquil. Tel. (05) 2526 177 in Santa Cruz. Email: emetebe@ecua.net.ec. Tel. in Isabela (05) 2529 155, in Baltra (05) 2529 193. Office in front of the police station.

Taxi Service: minimum charge $1, to airport (2 kilometres) $1, to 'Embarcadero' $1 (the departure of 'fibras' and Lancha 'Estrella de Mar II'), to Centro de Crianza (3 kilometres) $1.70 (breeding centre of Galápagos tortoises), to Poza de los Diablos (3 kilometres) $1.70. To Sierra Negra volcano ('flete') $40 return.

Boat Taxi: at the 'Embarcadero', ask for Andres. To boats: $1, to 'Laguna de las Tintoreras', $10 round trip.

Dive Centre: **Scubadragon**, east of town on 'via al Embarcadero' 150 metres from the fishermen's pier, After various delays, it should finally open in 2007! Day dive trips to Tortuga Island and '4 Hermanos'. PADI and NAUI dive courses available. For information ask at Casa de Marita, or contact Pierre Constant, email: calaolife@yahoo.com, Mobile: 085837769, www.calaolife.com and www.scubadragongalapagos.com.

Sierra Negra Volcano

caldera 7 x 10.5 kilometres; elevation: 1,490 metres

The local bus leaves for Santo Tomas in the highlands, at 7 am and 2 pm, and returns to Puerto Villamil at 4pm ($1 fare). The village of Santo Tomas, 18 kilometres from Villamil in the highlands, used to be the departure point for the ascent of Sierra Negra volcano. It was founded by Don Antonio Gil at the end of the 19th century, and has a population of 300 people. Cattle breeding and agriculture—there are plantations of coffee, oranges, grapefruits, papayas, guavas and avocados—are the main activities.

The road from the lowlands was constructed 20 years ago. The minibus makes the daily trip to the *parte alta,* from Puerto Villamil, but the new road goes up directly to the rim of the crater. Otherwise, it is a three-hour walk from Santo Tomas. It is possible to hire horses, at $7–8 per person per day. Pick up hire is available with 'Flete camioneta', at $40 return.

Sierra Negra is a huge caldera, ten kilometres wide, the oldest on the island. During the garua season the summit of the volcano is covered in mist; be prepared for rain. On the rim, the trail divides in two: Towards the west, it heads to Volcan de Azufre, an old sulphur mine that was exploited by the first settlers (ten kilometres, or three to four hours' walk); towards the east, the trail leads to Volcan Chico on the external slope of Sierra Negra, which erupted in 1979. The weather is often clear and good, once you reach the northern side of the caldera. You'll get excellent views of the Perry Isthmus, Elizabeth Bay and Alcedo volcano. The endemic thin leafed Darwin shrub, *Darwiniothamnus alternifolius* (Asteracea family) is found only on Sierra Negra and Cerro Azul volcanoes, around the rim. The white flowers with a yellow heart resemble daisies.

The Galápagos hawk, short-eared owl, vermilion flycatcher and large-billed flycatcher are common on Sierra Negra. Wild horses are sometimes seen. Camping is allowed, but fire is forbidden. Do not get lost. The latest eruption of Sierra Negra occurred on 22 October 2005, with a lava flow towards Elizabeth Bay on the northern flank of the volcano.

FERNANDINA

land surface: 642 square kilometres; elevation: 1,494 metres

Fernandina has an impressive volcano, one of the most active on the planet. Even though it is the youngest in the Galápagos, at least 12 eruptions have been recorded in the last 150 years. The caldera is six kilometres wide, with a depth of 900 metres. The lake that was once in the crater in 1946 disappeared in 1958 after two lava flows inside the caldera. In 1964, there was a new lake, but in June 1968, a memorable explosion blew up the caldera floor, which fell 300 metres. The personnel of Skylab mentioned a small eruption in December 1973, and the lava flow on the southeastern slope, inside the crater. The most recent eruptions were recorded in 1977, 1978, 1984, September 1988, April 1991 and February 1995. This last eruption maintained regular activity for over a month. Lava flows ran into the ocean from parasitic cones on the southwest towards Cape Hammond, creating a new cape three to four kilometres north-west of the former one. Subsequent eruptions occurred in 2001 and in May 2005, following a magnitude 5 earthquake, with two lava flows to the south.

The vegetation on the slopes of Fernandina belongs to the arid zone. At an elevation of 1,200 metres, the flora is reduced to islets of ferns, surrounded by lava flows. On the top of the volcano, high grasses and scalesia bushes are dominant (see drawing, page 248).

Punta Espinosa

The only visitor's site on Fernandina is on the northeast of the island, facing Isabela Island on the Bolivar Channel. Galápagos penguins and flightless cormorants are established, but rare. Disturbed by man, they tend to move their nesting sites regularly. The *pahoehoe* lava flows are bedecked by lava cacti (*Brachycereus*), which form yellow or dark green tufts with white spines. (See map, page 254)

Tectonically uplifted in 1975, the site of Punta Espinosa is also the home of a colony of sea lions and a few colonies of marine iguanas. Red and turquoise-blue crabs, *zayapas,* are everywhere. Land iguanas that came down from the volcano were once present in the bushes, but they seem to have disappeared. They are still numerous on the rim of Fernandina, however, where they dig burrows and lay eggs in the volcanic sand. The Galápagos hawk is common on the site, where it preys on snakes and marine iguanas.

Cabo Douglas

This site is not yet open to visitors, but will attract many visitors due to the considerable natural beauty. On a black basaltic shore (uplifted), one may observe a small colony of marine iguanas, a few land iguanas, Galápagos hawks and a big nest of twigs on a lava promontory, a few nests of flightless cormorants and a colony of fur sea lions. There is also a colony of blue-footed boobies.

THE 'PEPINOS' *AFFAIR*

The scandal of the exploitation of *pepinos,* or sea cucumbers, a delicacy to Chinese and Japanese palates, broke in 1992. Local pirate camps, encouraged by Japanese fishing ships, were established on the coast of Fernandina to collect sea cucumbers along the shoreline.

Families with women and children lived illegally in this 'no man's land' to catch pepinos, which they dried in the sun on the lava rocks. Then they packed the merchandise in bags and placed the goods in local boats in Villamil and Puerto Ayora, which in turn delivered them to the Japanese fishing boats.

The sea cucumbers (*Isostichopus fuscus*) move on the rocky bottom at a depth of between two and 20 metres. They are ecologically important because they help to clean seawater by recycling organic waste. The ban on the fishing on *pepinos,* declared by President Borja in June 1992, was contested one year later by the Galápagos fishermen, who recognized the amount of money at stake. The illicit fishing went on, and about 1,000 pounds of pepinos was seized by the Equadorian authorities in one of the pirate camps, in November 1993. Thirty million pepinos were fished, dried or cooked on the coast of Fernandina in 1992. In 1994, striking fisherman pressured the government of the new president, Sixto Duran Ballen, to suspend the 1992 decree. Somehow they succeeded, because, as of July 15 1994, the Ministry of Industry and Fisheries (MIIP) allowed lobster fishing for three months (July 15–October 15), then sea cucumber fishing for three months (October 15–January 15), then even shark fishing (January 15–April 15), which has always been forbidden. For the Galápagos Marine Reserve, this is definitely 'Apocalypse Now' (see photo, page 174).

According to recent sources (March 1995), the local fishermen of Isabela have also been fishing Pacific sea horses (*Caballitos del Mar*) to sell to the Chinese for aphrodisiac medicine.

CHAPTER FIVE

THE LANDINGS

Whether you take an organized tour with an Ecuadorian travel agency or you decide to charter a boat from Puerto Ayora or San Cristóbal with a few friends, once in the islands you'll have to get familiar with some practical advice and some new words.

You drop anchor in a turquoise-blue cove or in a wild bay with foaming surf. Then the *panga* will take you to shore. The *panga* is a small boat, comparable to a dinghy, accommodating up to 12 people, which is managed more or less skilfully by the *pangero.*

The landing can be fun or it can be hell, depending on the difficulty of disembarking, and this depends on the season or your luck. It could be on a fine sand beach or on sharp coral rubble, on dry or wet rocks (with the wave and surf behind) or on a safe rocky quay where a few sea lions bask (and, of course, like Charlie, the big peevish male on South Plaza, they do not want to be disturbed). Simply imagine the paradisiacal setting, and this is where you step in. You do not get into heaven for free.

In short, you may experience a dry landing or a wet landing. You should have your shoes on or in hand, with your pants rolled up to your knees. In the latter case, shorts are definitely the most practical. If you disembark on a beach, do not forget about the wave behind you; if you are not careful, it could make you lose your balance with all your belongings (imagine your camera equipment in a bath of salt water). Consequently, you should sit on the side of the *panga* and put both your feet in the water at the same time, not one foot after the other. You may smile, but if you do not follow these directions you will find out what happens by which time it will be too late. Plastic bags may be useful for wrapping your camera to protect it from spray. In any case, the guide is there to warn you.

List of the Landings

Island	Site	Type of landing
Santa Cruz	Puerto Ayora	dry
	Itabaca	dry
	Las Bachas	wet
South Plaza		dry, sea lions on wharf
Mosquera Islet		wet
Santa Fé		wet
Floreana	Punta Cormorant	wet
	Post Office Bay	wet
	Black Beach	dry
Española	Gardner Bay	wet
	Punta Suarez	wet
San Cristóbal	Puerto Baquerizo	dry
	Cerro Brujo	wet
	Punta Pitt	wet
Genovesa	Darwin Bay	wet, coral beach
	Prince Philip's Steps	dry, but slippery rocks
Rábida		wet
Sombrero Chino		wet
Bartolomé	volcano climb	dry, but slippery rocks
beach		wet
Santiago	Puerto Egas	wet
	Espumilla	wet
	Buccaneer's Cove	wet, watch for surf
Isabela	Tagus Cove	dry, but slippery rocks
Puerto Villamil		dry
	Punta Moreno	dry, on rocks
	Urvina Bay	wet, watch for waves
	Punta Albemarle	wet, watch for waves
	Alcedo	wet
Fernandina	Punta Espinosa	dry, but slippery rocks

CHAPTER SIX

Scuba Diving

The underwater fauna is very rich in the Galápagos, and unusual by comparison to traditional dive sites, such as the Caribbean, Maldives, Red Sea, Indian Ocean, Philippines and Southeast Asia, where the warm tropical seas abound with colorful coral reefs. In the Galápagos, one finds more than 400 species of shore fishes, 32 species of corals, and 600 species of mollusks. Diving in Galápagos is not to be undertaken lightly. Some sites have strong currents, lava rocks and underwater ridges may be sharp and dangerous, and caves make enticing traps. One should never dive alone.

The Galápagos are still new to the sport. Even though a presidential decree of May 13, 1986, declared the Galápagos archipelago a 'Reserve of Marine Resources', very few laws were defined and implemented governing their proper exploitation. Nevertheless, one thing is certain: it is impossible to dive without a local dive guide, licensed by the Galápagos National Park and by the Ecuadorian Merchant Marine, who will look after you underwater, but who is not responsible for you in case of an accident.

Divers are informed that they dive at their own risk. A liability waiver will have to be signed before the cruise begins. In any case, you will have to show proof of your diver's certification, your logbook and a medical certificate. A new decompression chamber was installed in Puerto Ayora at Henry Schaeffer's place, in March 2001. Consultations: tel: (05) 2526 911; mobile: (09) 855 911; hyperbaric doctor in charge, Dr Gabriel Idrogo, tel: (099) 283 990, home: (05)2526 417; hospital: (05) 2526 103. Policia (05) 2526 101. The 'Centro Medico Protesub' is open from 9:30am–12:30pm and from 3:30pm–5:30pm. DAN members are welcome. For diving emergencies, call Dr. Lopez (24 hours) at 099 283 995.

There are two dive clubs in Puerto Ayora. Recommended is Scuba Iguana at Hotel Galápagos, run by Mattias Espînosa and Jack Nelson who operate day trips with a fast dive boat. One-day, two-boat dives cost US$78–110 per person, depending on dive sites. Minimum of two or three divers.

Water Temperature

Despite their equatorial position, the Galápagos are considered to be a cold-water environment. Three main marine currents bathe the archipelago: two are cold (coming from the west and southeast) and one is warm (coming from Panama in the northeast).

The water temperature is influenced by the season: cold from May to December, warm from December to May. The sea surface temperature varies from 17° C to 27° C, and drops to 15° C sometimes to the west of Isabela.

In the Galápagos, temperatures are warmer in the northern islands, cooler in the central and southern islands, and cold west of Isabela and Fernandina. The exception occurs during Niño years, when the sea surface temperature averages 25° C to 30° C. Therefore, it is necessary to have a 5mm wetsuit any time of the year. (See Part One, Chapter 2, for more details on seasons and temperatures.)

Visibility

Water is generally clear during the cold season, but the sea surface is rough in August-September. In the warm season, water may be murky due to the presence of plankton on the surface, but it depends on the site.

Currents

Mainly from east to west, they can be very strong. Underwater navigation with a compass is often necessary, and it is important to be cautious at all times.

Dangers

There are no real dangers in the Galápagos; nevertheless, it is advised to avoid submarine caves. These can be long tunnels, sometimes labyrinthine, which can be rather dangerous because of the surf action.

Sharks are no real threat, and are not aggressive, as long as they are not provoked. An attitude of respect is recommended, and some distance has to be kept between the diver and the sharks. A refuge in the rocks or in the cliff should be nearby, just in case. Whitetips, grey reef or hammerhead sharks are usually inquisitive by nature. Although shy, they do not hesitate to come close to the diver, but at the last minute they turn at a right angle and disappear out of sight. Schools of Galápagos sharks, of up to 30 individuals, may circle you (eg Gordon Rocks). Fortunately, it doesn't mean that they have you in mind for a feast, for they usually vanish in a few minutes, with majesty and indifference.

If ever you notice a shark that wriggles or arches its back suddenly, then beware. This aggressive display is a warning preceding an attack. You should come up to the surface and leave the water quickly. There was a case in which a Galápagos shark bumped into a diver from the back (James Gribb, 1984)—not too nice. In March 1991, the guide Jonathan Green claimed he was attacked by a two-metre-long great white shark when he was skin diving at Playa Escondida, to the northeast of Pinzón Island. He kicked off the shark with his fins. The same year, again off Pinzón Island, a park guard was bitten in the thigh by a three-metre-long shark while in one metre of water.

Until now, sharks in the Galápagos have not attacked humans, for they have enough natural food to eat. This situation may change, triggering a series of accidents in the future.

There is one venomous snake on the islands. The yellow-bellied sea snake (*Pelamis platurus,* family Hydrophiidae), is dorsally black, ventrally yellow. About 85 cm long, this rare pelagic species appears in the warm season (especially during Niño years), when the sea surface temperature rises. It should not be approached, for its venom is more virulent than that of the cobra.

Among other pain-inflicting animals are the stingrays, which inhabit sandy bottoms in shallow water, and the scorpionfishes on the rocks. The long black spines of the crowned sea urchin can easily penetrate one's skin, and leave a numbness that may last or two or three days. The flower sea urchin (*Toxopneustes roseus*) should not be touched, for it is also venomous and may induce a high fever.

DIVING SITES		DEPTH
Classification:	- Snorkelling	< 3 metres
	- Skin diving	< 10 metres
	- Scuba diving	+ 10 metres

CENTRAL ISLANDS	Snorkelling	Skin diving	Scuba
Around Santa Cruz			
Isla Coamano (Academy Bay)		x	x
Punta Estrada (Academy Bay)	x	x	x
South Plaza (lagoon and cliffs)	x	x	x
Gordon Rocks		x	x
Itabaca canal (south Baltra)	x	x	
Mosquera Islet (east coast)	x	x	x
Nord Seymour (south coast)	x	x	x
(northwest caves)			x
Daphné Mayor			x
Daphné Minor			x
Santa Fé (northeast bay)	x	x	x
Around Santiago			
Bartolomé (pinnacle)	x	x	x
Cousin's Rock			x
Bainbridge rocks			x
Sombrero Chino (lagoon)	x	x	
Beagle rocks	x	x	x
Rábida (beach and west cove)	x	x	
James Bay (Puerto Egas and 'grottos')	x	x	x
Albany Island			x
Buccaneer's cove (rocky point)	x	x	x
Piedra Blanca (north west rock)			x

EAST	Snorkelling	Skin diving	Scuba
Around San Cristóbal			
Frigatebird Hill (Las Tijeretas)	x		
Isla Lobos			x
Leon Dormido, Kicker's Rock (Stephens Bay)			x
Punta Pitt	x	x	x
Roca Ballena			x
Five Fingers			x
Roca Este			x

NORTH			
Genovesa			
Darwin Bay (beach)	x		
Darwin Bay (west reef)	x	x	x
Prince Philip's steps		x	x
Marchena			
Punta Espejo	x		
Punta Mejia	x	x	x

Wolf			
East Coast (El Derrumbe)			x
North Cove			x
La Banana			x
Northwest cliff			x
El Pinaculo (north east point)			
The Channel (south west point)			
Darwin			
Northeast coast (Fondeadero)		x	x
The Arch			x
Tower rock (La Botella) west cove			x
WEST			
Around Isabela			
Crossman Islands (4 Hermanos)			x
Isla Tortuga	x	x	x
La Viuda			x
Roca Union			x
Punta Moreno	x	x	x
Elizabeth Bay	x	x	
Tagus Cove	x	x	x
Punta Vicente Roca	x	x	x
Roca Redonda			x
Punta Albemarle	x	x	x
Cape Marshall			x
Alcedo beach	x	x	
WEST			
Fernandina			
Punta Espinosa	x	x	x
Cabo Douglas			x
SOUTH	**Snorkelling**	**Skin diving**	**Scuba**
Around Floreana			
Punta Cormorant (beach and rocks)	x	x	
Devil's Crown	x	x	x
Champion Islet		x	x
Enderby Island			x
Caldwell Island			x
Frank's Finger Rock (near Pto.Velasco Ibarra)			
Around Española			
Punta Suarez	x	x	
Gardner Bay (rocks)	x	x	
Gardner Island			x
Xarifa Island		x	x
OTHER			
Hancock Bank			x
McGovern Bank			x
Guy Fawkes Island		x	x
Punta Bowditch (Conway Bay)	x	x	

DIVE CENTRES in Puerto Ayora (Santa Cruz)

Scuba Iguana, SSI school (Mathias Espinosa and Jack Nelson), at Hotel Galápagos (since 1995), 40 dive sites, cost from $78 (two dives) in Academy Bay, to $135 (two dives) in Santa Fé, Floreana, Seymour, Gordon Rocks, Bartolomé and Cousin's. Night dives: $75 to $100. One week cruise (17 dives) to Darwin and Wolf: $2,175. Other dive tours available. Dive courses from open water: $400, to instructor: $1,500. Tel: (05) 2526 296, fax: (05) 2526 497, email: mathiase@pa.ga.pro.ec.

Nautidiving (Vicente Berdonces, PADI Instructor), in Pelican Bay, since 1998. Similar prices to above. Tel/Fax: (05) 2526 096, e-mail: nautidiving@access.net.ec, website: www.nautidiving.com.

Macarron Diving Centre, Pelican Bay.

Scubadragon (on Isabela), after multiple postponements due to delays in construction, patience and hard work, in Puerto Villamil, Isabela, is open. Check at Casa de Marita or Mobile: 085937769, 092862834; also visit www.calaolife.com or www.scubadragongalapagos.com.

DIVE CENTRES in San Cristóbal

Chalo Tours (since 1997) chalotours@hotmail.com

Wreck Bay Dive Centre (2004) insofacto@hotmail.com

Galakiwi (December 2004) galakiwi@yahoo.com

SSS Hyperbaric chamber (Puerto Ayora) Dr. Ramiro Lopez 099-283 995 (24 hours) calle 18 de Febrero y Rodriguez Lara, Santa Cruz Island Tel. 05-2526 911. E.galapagos@sssnetwork.com

PART FOUR

THE GALÁPAGOS NATIONAL PARK

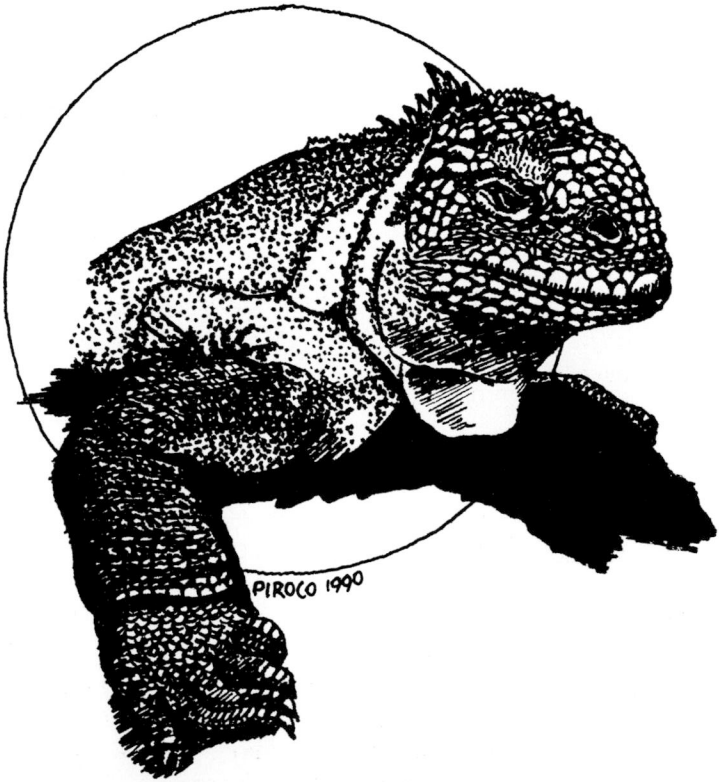

CHAPTER ONE

Administration and History

The Galápagos National Park is a public institution recognized by the Ecuadorian government. Its administration depends on INEFAN (1993), the Instituto Forrestal y Areas Naturales, which in turn depends on MAG, the Ministerio de Agricultura y Ganaderia, the agriculture department based in Quito, capital of Ecuador.

There are about 15 national parks in Ecuador, which cover the Amazonian, Andean and coastal regions, but the Galápagos National Park is the first and most advanced in its administration, management and development. The first laws to protect the Galápagos were passed in 1934. Some islands were then declared reserves for a national park, with the exception of Santa Cruz, Floreana, Cristóbal, the south of Isabela and Fernandina.

On July 4, 1959, all areas not colonized by man were declared a national park. The Charles Darwin Foundation was created in Brussels, the same year, to conserve and protect the unique Galápagos ecosystem and to promote scientific research. The Charles Darwin Research Station (CDRS) was established on Santa Cruz Island in 1960, with Raymond Lévêque as its first director.

The National Parks Department was created in 1968 within the Forestry Department. Two conservation officials were sent to the Galápagos and began the Ecuadorian administration. As the number of employees rose, it became necessary to construct the Galápagos National Park Service (SPNG) building.

In 1979, 60 park guards were on duty, supervised by five conservation officials. There were also an accountant and four university-trained professionals: the superintendent and his attendant, the chief of protection and the chief naturalist. The park staff is divided into two groups with specific functions. Four programs were introduced:

- eradication and control of animals and plants introduced by man.
- protection of the endangered native species.
- tourism management.
- education.

The budget of the Galápagos National Park comes directly from the Ecuadorian government, through the MAG. In 1978, it was estimated at $200,000, or six million sucres. The rest of the funds come from international organizations such as the WWF, the Frankfurt Zoological Society and private donations.

In 2000, total expenditure of the Charles Darwin Foundation was about US$3.79 million, 44% more than in 1999. It was evenly distributed among major technical programs such as: the CDRS communication & education (16%), Plants & invertebrates, quarantine (14%), Vertebrate ecology & monitoring (13%), Marine research and conservation (12%), Logistics (8%), Financial support to SPNG (8%), Isabela project (7%), Governance &

secretary general in Quito (7%), Financial & administration (7%), External relations (5%), Director's office (4%).

Increased support in the past five years has occurred, from traditional and new donors such as: Friends of Galápagos, Frankfurt Zoological Society, Lindblad Expeditions, Galápagos Conservation Fund, Darwin Scientific Foundation, international and national government agencies foundations, charitable trusts, corporations and individuals. In 2001, the budget of donor funds amounted to US$541,000.

Use of the Park

Special Use Zones

On islands colonized by man, some areas of the National Park can be used by settlers and residents to extract products such as wood, sand and volcanic rocks. The hunting of introduced animals is also possible in some places, with a necessary permit.

Scientific Research

Scientists wanting to do research within the National Park must submit a detailed project to the director of INEFAN, to the park superintendent, to the director of the Darwin Station and to the secretary of the Darwin Foundation. The study has to deal with anything related to evolution or concerning conservation problems.

Tourism

Visitors to the National Park have to follow a number of rules made to protect the ecological integrity of the islands. Forty-eight visitor sites have been designed, with marked trails and open areas. Visitors are led by a guide, licensed by the Galápagos National Park, who will make sure the rules are respected.

These rules are set forth on decree 1306, published in 1971, which states the dos and don'ts. The entry fee to the National Park was of $6 in 1981, then $40 in 1989 and $80 for foreigners in 1993. The funds collected go to the management of tourism (30 per cent) and to INEFAN (70 per cent).

Mass tourism in the Galápagos started in 1969, with the arrival of the 58-passenger cruise boat *Lina-A,* of Metropolitan Touring. In the beginning of the 1970s, Ecuador became better known internationally, and the number of visitors increased in the following years: 1,200 in 1969, then 2,500 (1971), 3,000 (1972), 4,500 (1973), between 5,500 and 7,500 in 1974.

The *Lina-A* sank in 1975, without casualties, far off the coast of Ecuador. In 1977, two new cruise ships arrived in the archipelago: the M/N *Bucanero* of Gordon Tours and the M/N *Neptuno* of Macchiavello Tours. In 1980, Metropolitan Touring's M/N *Santa Cruz* replaced the *Lina-A.* The famous and unforgettable *Neptuno,* which, according to hearsay was under a curse and held together by paint alone, sank near Guayaquil in June 1984, drowning the unfortunate cook, who blew up with the kitchen.

It was replaced in 1987 by the M/N *Galápagos Explorer* of the Canodros agency (Guayaquil). The M/N *Bucanero* stopped operating in 1990. A new cruise ship arrived in the archipelago in September 1993: the M/N *Ambassador I,* with a capacity of 86 passengers, belongs to a Greek named Zacharias, of Islas Galápagos Turismo y Vapores (Quito).

Three big boats ply the Galápagos waters now, as well as another 100 smaller boats, yachts and sailboats. After being limited to 12,000 people (1973), then to 25,000 people (1981) by different Master Plans, the number of visitors to the Galápagos National Park is now out of control, and limits have become meaningless. The last Master Plan of Miguel Cifuentes (1985), former manager of the SPNG, forecast a new limit of 45,000 people per year. This limit was blown at the end of 1994, when the number of visitors exceeded 54,000 people. The economic pressure is such that the future looks hectic. Hotel construction has boomed in Puerto Ayora, Santa Cruz Island, for the last two years.

ANNUAL FLOW OF VISITORS TO THE GALÁPAGOS NATIONAL PARK (1974–2008)

Year	*Total Visitors*	*Ecuadorians*	*Foreigners*	*% Nationals*	*% Foreigners*
1974	7500				
1975	7000				
1976	6300	868	5432	13.78	86.22
1977	7788	1349	6439	17.32	82.68
1978	12299	1606	10693	13.06	86.94
1979	11765	2226	9539	18.92	81.08
1980	17445	3980	13465	22.81	77.19
1981	16265	4036	12229	24.81	75.19
1982	17123	6067	11056	35.43	64.57
1983	17656	7254	10402	41.09	58.91
1984	18858	7627	11231	40.44	59.56
1985	17840	6279	11561	35.20	64.80
1986	26023	12126	13897	46.60	53.40
1987	32593	17767	14826	54.51	45.49
1988	31248	14218	17030	45.50	54.50
1989	41899	15133	26766	36.12	63.88
1990	41192	15549	25643	37.75	62.25
1991	40746	14815	25931	36.36	63.64
1992	39510	12855	26655	32.54	67.46
1993	46818	10136	36682	21.65	78.35
1994	54000	12800	41200	23.70	76.30
1995	55782	15483	40303	27.75	72.25
1996	61895	16113	45782	26.03	73.97
1997	62809	13979	48830	22.26	77.74
1998	64791	14440	50351	22.28	77.71
1999	66053	12584	53469	19.05	80.94
2000	71567	15031	56536	21.00	79.00
2001	77570	19711	57859	25.41	74.59
2002	82226	22939	59287	27.89	72.10
2003	90533	27637	62896	30.52	69.47
2004	108583	33707	74876	31.04	68.95
2005	122453	35545	86908	29.02	71.00
2006	145229	47833	97396	32.93	67.06
2007	161859	51411	110448	31.76	68.24
2008	173420	53466	119954	30.83	69.17

(Source: Servicio Parque Nacional Galápagos, 2008)

The rise of the numbers in 1978 is explained by the arrival of the *Bucanero* and the *Neptuno* (with a capacity of 90 passengers each); the same applies in 1980 to the *Santa Cruz*. In 1986, a renewed influx of visitors followed the big fire that burned part of Isabela Island in 1985 and brought publicity to the islands.

About 3,000 to 5,000 people visit the Galápagos each month. In 1993, the heaviest months were January/February/March, then July/August and December.

As for Ecuadorian visitors, after their numbers peaked in 1987, when they accounted for 54.51 per cent of visitors, they have become gradually less interested in the islands, with only 12,000 people (27.50 per cent) visiting in 1993. The flow of foreigners, by contrast, is increasing, with 33,000 people in 1993, or about 72.50 per cent. By order and number of visitors, here are the 12 countries that send people to the Galápagos:

1	Ecuador
2	USA
3	Germany
4	Switzerland
5	Italy
6	Canada
7	South America
8	UK
9	France
10	Holland
11	Israel
12	Japan

(source: SPNG and Carta Informativa CDRS, February 1988)

The Master Plan

Most of the natural and wildlife areas rapidly deteriorate if they are not managed properly. A number of objectives have been established for these natural areas, which includes designation as a national park. Consequently, the Galápagos Master Plan was divided in two parts, which sum up:

- the information concerning the resources of the area, culturally, historically, flora and fauna, and the human factor.
- procedures and goals of management, characteristics and qualities to preserve, not to mention the development of the local population.

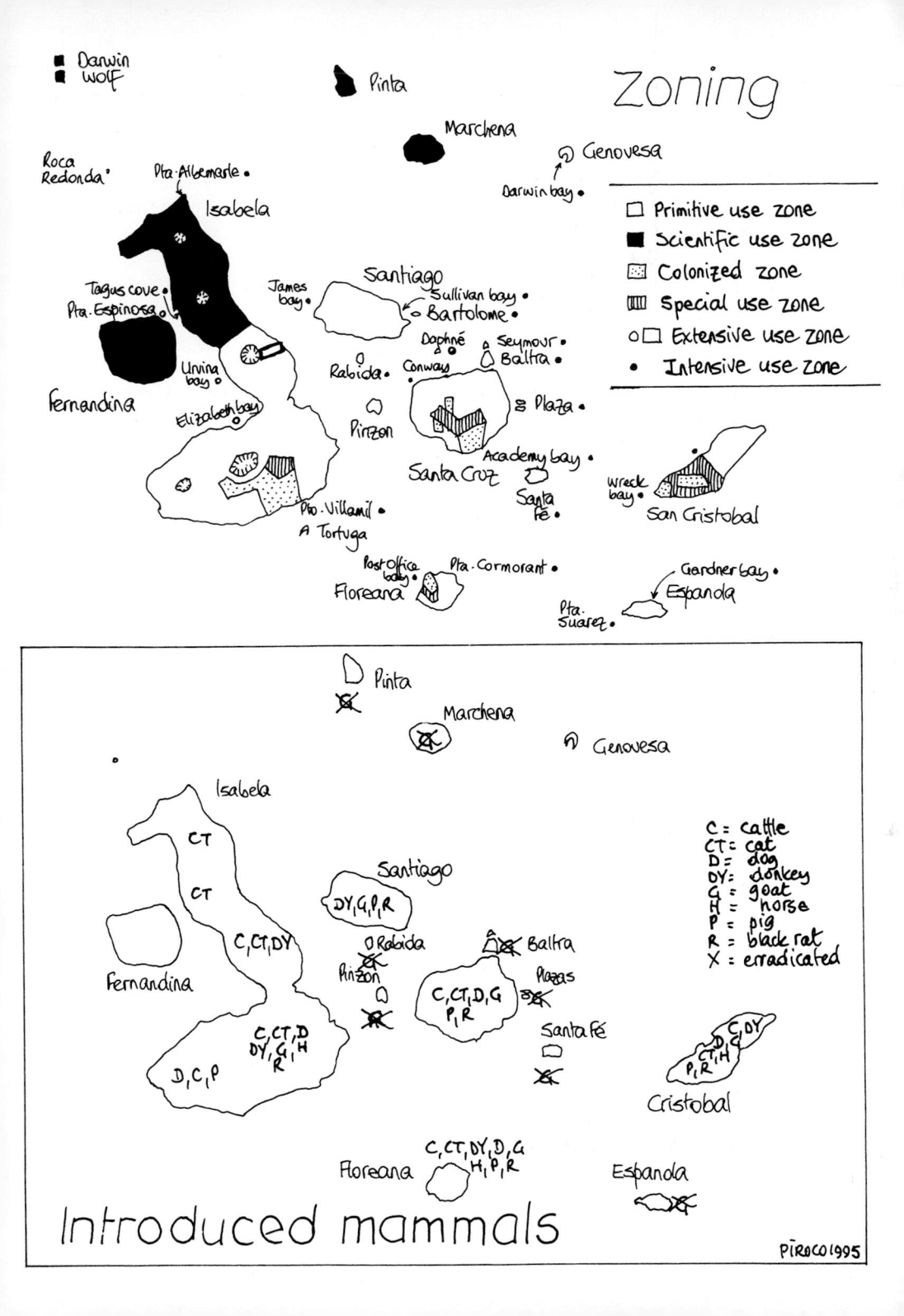
Zoning
Darwin
Wolf
Pinta
Marchena
Genovesa
Roca Redonda
Pta. Albemarle
Isabela
Darwin bay
Primitive use zone
Scientific use zone
Colonized zone
Special use zone
Extensive use zone
Intensive use zone
Tagus cove
Pta. Espinosa
James bay
Santiago
Sullivan bay
Bartolome
Daphné
Seymour
Baltra
Rabida
Conway
Urvina bay
Fernandina
Elizabeth bay
Pinzon
Plaza
Academy bay
Santa Cruz
Santa Fé
Wreck bay
San Cristobal
Pto. Villamil
A Tortuga
Post Office bay
Pta. Cormorant
Floreana
Gardner bay
Espanola
Pta. Suarez
Pinta
Marchena
Genovesa
Isabela
CT
CT
C,CT,DY
Fernandina
C,CT,D DY,G,H R
D,C,P
Santiago
DY,G,P,R
Rabida
Pinzon
Baltra
Plazas
C,CT,D,G P,R
Santa Fé
C,DY
CT,H
P,R
Cristobal
C,CT,DY,D,G H,P,R
Floreana
Espanola
C = cattle
CT = cat
D = dog
DY = donkey
G = goat
H = horse
P = pig
R = black rat
X = erradicated
Introduced mammals
PIROCO 1995

The Master Plan for the protection and use of the Galápagos National Park was written in 1973 by a team of Ecuadorians and international experts. The Food and Agriculture Organization (FAO) already had 15 years' experience in South America. The plan, printed in 1974, is carried out by the park personnel and states seven main objectives:

* Protection of the Galápagos ecosystem.
* Eradication or control of introduced species.
* Appropriate use for visitors.
* Providing information to visitors on what they can see.
* Educating for the local population.
* Encouraging economic development of the archipelago's residents.
* Encouraging scientific research.

Another important point of the Master Plan is zoning. This technique allows division of the National Park into distinct zones for better management. Five zones were established (see map of Zoning, page 273):

Intensive Use Zones
There are about 25 of these particularly extraordinary touristic zones within the National Park. The plan recommends that a maximum of 90 people (four to five groups of 20 people with a guide) be authorized to disembark at the sites. Some of the areas are fragile, and control remains important.

Extensive Use Zones
There are about 16 of these zones, which are not as interesting as the intensive-use zones. A maximum number of 12 people may disembark on these sites. No large groups are allowed.

Primitive Use Zones
The majority of the land surface of the National Park. Sometimes affected by the presence of introduced species. These zones are nevertheless ecologically unique. A special permit is required.

Primitive Scientific Zones
These are kept for scientific research (eg Genovesa, Fernandina). No possible access to the casual visitor with no specialized interest.

Special Use Zones
Adjacent to colonized areas, these zones may be exploited by the residents, for wood, sand, volcanic rocks. Activity is nevertheless strictly controlled.

Among the numerous provisions of the park, as stipulated in the Master Plan, are the following:

* Eradication of introduced plants and animals; protection of the endangered species, touristic management. The transfer of organisms from island to island will be controlled and prevented.
* The park infrastructure will be more elaborate in the colonized areas, with construction of offices and staff quarters. A reception centre was built on Baltra for visitors, and a park guard station will be constructed in Puerto Egas (Santiago).
* A concession system will be established. Responsible tour operators may proceed with tourism within the archipelago, but they must comply with certain rules and pay a ten per cent tax on their gross annual income. In exchange the SPNG will ensure the necessary protection to the tourism industry, and will supply ground services to the visitors.
* An area of two nautical miles will be added to the park's territory to ensure the protection of the marine environment. In this way, the interaction of the land and marine ecosystems will be protected. (The new Marine Reserve was established in 1986.)
* To enforce the Master Plan, the park personnel will be composed of 66 park guards, plus several technical advisers: carpenters and mechanics, six university-trained experts in education, protection and biology.

The aim of the Master Plan, however idealistic, is allow the people of the Galápagos to live in harmony with their environment, taking from nature only what they need, and disposing only of noncontaminating materials. Easy to say and hard to do.

All in all, man would not be a destructive organism (there are already too many in the islands) but, on the contrary, an introduced species that has found its place in the ecosystem of the Galápagos.

The last Master Plan of the Galápagos National Park was written in 1996 and the Master Plan for the CDRS published in 1992. A new Master Plan for the Marine Reserve of the Galápagos was adopted in March 1999.

CHAPTER TWO

Introduced Animals; Rules of Preservation for the Visitor; The Role of the Guide

Introduced Animals

The history of introduced mammals goes back 450 years, to man's discovery of the archipelago. Since then, the islands have been populated with herbivores, carnivores (cats and dogs) and omnivores (rats, mice and pigs), which all turned feral after a time. Dogs, pigs, goats and rats were brought by pirates as early as the 16th century (see map of Introduced mammals, page 273). One of the worst introduced animals is the fire ant, which destroys the vegetation.

At the turn of the third millennium, in year 2000, the number of unwanted fauna, has gone up from 14 to 23 species of introduced animals in the Galápagos: 12 mammals, three birds, six insects and two amphibians.

The 23 Introduced Species

English	*scientific name*	*common name*
Cattle	*Bos taurus*	Ganado
Goat	*Capra hircus*	Chivo
Pig	*Sus scrofa*	Chancho
Dog	*Canis familiaris*	Perro
Cat	*Felix catus*	Gato
Black rat	*Rattus rattus*	Rata negra
Coffee rat	*Rattus norvegicus*	Rata de Noruega
House mouse	*Mus musculus*	Raton casero
Donkey	*Equus asinus*	Burro
Horse	*Equus caballus*	Caballo
Guinea pig		Cuy, cobayo
Sheep		Oveja
Rooster		Gallo
Pigeon	*Columba livia*	Paloma domestica
Smooth-billed ani	*Crotophaga ani*	Garrapatero
Little fire ant	*Wasmannia auropunctata*	Hormiga colorada
Tropical fire ant	*Solenopsis geminata*	"
Paper wasp	*Polistes versicolor*	(1988) Avispa
Paper wasp	*Brachygastra lecheguana*	(1994) Avispa
Biting black fly	*Simulium bipunctatum*	(1989) Mosca negra
Cottony cushion scale	*Icerya purchasi*	(1982) Pulgon

Tree frog	*Scinax quinquefasciata*	(1997) Zapo de arbol
Frog	*Eleutherodactylus unistrigatus*	(2000) Zapo
Dengue mosquito	*Aedes aegypti*	(2002) Mosquito dengue

Goats (*Chivos*)
Mainly on Floreana, Santa Cruz, Baltra, San Cristóbal, Santiago and Isabela. These unstable animals live in groups and often move from the coast to the highlands in the dry season. Goats are very numerous on volcan Alcedo. An estimation of 100,000 goats on Isabela was made in 2000.

Goats reproduce once a year in April-May, and have one or two young. These fierce herbivores are a plague upon the vegetation, for they'll eat anything, with the exception of two plants, *Vallesia* and *Castela galapageia*. Their predators are Galápagos hawks, dogs and feral pigs.

Cattle (*Ganado*)
Found mostly on Isabela, where the population is a few thousand individuals, on Sierra Negra and Cerro Azul. They are a threat to the vegetation, but are also of economic value for their meat. Exportation has been considered.

Horses (*Caballos*)
The threat is not so important, and no serious ecological impact is involved. Horses are found in the highlands of Isabela, Santa Cruz, Cristóbal and Floreana. In the south of Isabela, a feral population of 500 individuals still exists on the slopes of volcan Sierra Negra.

Dogs (*Perros*)
Dogs turned feral on Santa Cruz and Isabela, where their population is estimated at 200 to 500. They gather mainly to the west of Cerro Azul volcano, where they decimate marine iguanas on the coast, and also on the slopes of Alcedo volcano, where they arrived recently after crossing the Perry isthmus. This barrier of basaltic lava, eight to ten kilometres wide, has until now controlled their progression toward the north. Generally of a white colour with black spots, feral dogs hunt in small groups of two to three individuals. They attack cattle in the highlands and marine iguanas on the coast. On Santa Cruz Island, they are a serious threat to the Hawaiian petrel, which nests in the tropical zone. Feral dogs have been eradicated from Floreana, San Cristóbal, from Conway Bay on Santa Cruz and from Cartago Bay on Isabela.

Rats (*Ratas*)
Recorded on Santa Cruz and on Santiago, they were eradicated from Pinzón (known once as the 'Island of the Rats') by a campaign of the SPNG, from September to November 1989. *Rattus*, the black rat, lives in the arid zone as well as in the humid zone. It reproduces in the hot season, with a breeding cycle of 27 days. Vegetables, insects, fruits, grains, turtle eggs and fledglings are part of its diet. The black rat is responsible for the disappearance of the Galápagos endemic rats, *Oryzomys* and *Nesoryzomys*, because of its competitiveness, aggression and spreading of disease.

The two native predators of the rats are the short-eared owl and the Galápagos hawk. Introduced predators are cats and dog. The black rat was eradicated from Bartolomé in 1976 by traps and poison.

Pigs (*Chanchos*)
Mainly on Santiago, but also on Isabela, where they dig up the nests of marine turtles. They also dig up a number of native plants. In the south of Isabela, a large population is found on Sierra Negra and Cerro Azul. Although they are regularly hunted by SPNG personel and locals, they have a strong impact on the reproduction of giant tortoises.

Cats (*Gatos*)
Found mostly on Isabela, where they attack finches, boobies, lava lizards and even marine iguanas (Cartago Bay), and land iguanas (Conway Bay, Cartago bay, Baltra).

Donkeys (*Burros*)
In the arid zone and in the highlands of Santiago and Isabela. Their population is estimated at 700 on Alcedo volcano, and 300 to 500 on Sierra Negra volcano. Donkeys were eliminated on Santiago in 2004.

The major problem of the Galápagos National Park is after all the eradication of goats, which is not an easy task. With time and numerous campaigns, some islands have been cleared of this plague: South Plaza (1961), Rábida and Santa Fé (1971). After a new introduction, Rábida was again cleared (1975); 4,000 goats were eradicated on Marchena (1976), then definitively (1979), as well as on Española (1978). 'Project Isabela' is aiming at the eradication of goats on Isabela and Santiago Islands.

Paloma
Domestic pigeons are in the populated areas of San Cristóbal, Santa Cruz and Isabela. These birds are known to be carriers of diseases for other birds, as well as parasites. Some endemic species of the islands have already suffered from their presence. One of these parasites has been found on Galápagos doves, triggering their decline.

Garapatero
Known in English as the Smooth Billed Ani. First individuals were reported on Isabela in 1962. During the 1982–83 Niño, these birds became very numerous on Santa Cruz, then moved to other islands like Daphné, Genovesa, Isabela and Santiago. New increase after the 1997–98 Niño, now found all over the islands. Anis are reported to kill mockingbirds and finches of the genus Geospiza and Camarhynchus (Castro, 1989), as well as lava lizards on Alcedo.

Insects
Inhabited areas are 'hot spots' for introduced insects. Inventories in the agriculture zones of Isabela, Floreana and San Cristobal in 2004, brought a new record of 456 introduced insects in the islands. The ladybird *Rodolia cardinalis*, released in 2002 as a control agent, had a significant impact on the invasive Cottony Cushion Scale, *Celia purchasi*. No Little Fire ants were found on Marchena Island after the eradication program in 2004. Data

collections were made in the Mariela Islets and Playa Tortuga Negra (Isabela) to investigate and control the Tropical Fire ant, *Solenopsis geminata*. This ant was reported on Albany Island, Bainbridge Rocks (Santiago Island).

Control methods are underway to reduce or eliminate the Biting Black fly *Simulium bipunctatum*. A monitoring program was set up for priority species such as the Tephritid fruits flies, and the recently introduced Dengue mosquito (2002).

Frogs

On at least two of the five inhabited islands, having arrived on cargo boats and on planes. A first frog species of the genus *Scinax* was introduced in the Galápagos three main ports, following the 1997–98 Niño event. A second species of frog, *Eleutherodactylus unistrigatus* was found in Puerto Ayora, in March 2000, by the scientists of CDRS and University of New Mexico. It is known in Hawaii as an invading species.

Rules of Preservation for the Visitor

The archipelago of the Galápagos belongs to those few places in the world that remain relatively untouched by human exploitation. The preservation of the environment is everybody's problem. Everyone may take part in it, by following some simple rules which will help to maintain the archipelago's fragile ecosystem intact. The future depends on you.

1. Be careful not to transport any live material to the islands, or from island to island (insect, seeds). If you have a pet, do not bring it to the islands. It will not be allowed.
2. No plants, rocks, animals or their remains, such as bones, pieces of wood, corals, shells, or other natural objects should be removed or disturbed. You may damage the island's ecological conditions.
3. Animals should not be touched or handled. A sea lion pup will be abandoned by its mother, for example, if she smells the scent of man on its young. The same applies to chicks of birds.
4. Animals may not be fed. It may alter their life cycle, their social structure and affect their reproduction.
5. Do not disturb or chase any animal from its resting or nesting spot. This is especially true for birds such as boobies, cormorants, gulls and frigates. The nests should be approached carefully, keeping a distance of one to two metres. If disturbed, the bird will flee and abandon its egg or chick, which could die under the strong sun within 30 minutes.
6. All groups which visit the National Park must be accompanied by a qualified guide approved by the National Park. The visitor should follow the trail, marked with small black-and-white posts, and never leave it. If you do so, you may destroy nests without being conscious of it (eg marine iguanas' nests in the sand).
7. Follow the guide; stay with him or her for information and advice. The guide is responsible for you. If he or she behaves badly or does not follow the rules himself or herself, report him or her to the National Park.

8. Litter of all types must be kept off the islands. Disposal at sea must be limited to certain types of garbage, only to be thrown overboard in selected areas. Keep all rubbish: film wrappers, cigarette butts, chewing gum, tin cans, bottles, etc., in a bag or pocket, to be disposed of on your boat. Do not throw anything on the islands or overboard. It could end up at the coast or the beach, or eaten by sea turtles or sea lions. A sea lion may play with a tin can found on the bottom and cut its sensitive muzzle. Sea turtles may die from swallowing a plastic bag.
9. Do not paint names or graffiti on rocks. It is against the law, and you will be fined for it.
10. Do not buy souvenirs or objects made from plants or animals of the islands (with the exception of articles made from wood). Among such articles are turtle shells, sea lion teeth, black coral. This is the best way to discourage such a trade.
11. To camp, you need a permit from the National Park Service (Santa Cruz, Cristóbal, Isabela). Do not make fires, but use a gas stove instead. Park suggestions may be useful.
12. Do not hesitate to show your conservationist attitude. Explain these rules to others, and help to enforce them.

The Galápagos National Park thanks you for respecting these rules. Think about others who come after you; they'll be grateful to you for your conservationist attitude.

The Quarantine System In Galápagos

Starting May 31, 1999, the 'Systema de Inspeccion y Cuarentena para Galápagos' (SICGAL) was inforced. Quarantine inspections are now in place at the Galápagos ports and at the airports of Quito, Guayaquil and Baltra, to control and prevent the introduction of unwanted species. A study of avian diseases was carried out in 2004 (Floreana, Santiago, Cristóbal, Marchena). No presence of avian malaria or West Nile virus was detected. However, avian pox is distributed throughout the archipelago, due to the abundance of mosquitoes and biting flies.

The Role of the Guide

The guides are trained by the Galápagos National Park with the help of the Charles Darwin Research Station. For many years, until September 1992, there were two categories of guides in the Galápagos: naturalist guides and auxiliary guides. Some were foreigners, multilingual, and with a scientific background; others were Ecuadorians, natives of the islands without any specific background. Some did not get along; the jealousy of others changed to racism, and eventually there developed a cold war between the guides of the Asociación de Guias and of the Agrupacion de Guias Interpretes, hidden behind the big smiles shown to foreign visitors. But it was common practice to be mean to each other, to denounce a guide at the National Park office for real or imaginary professional mistakes.

As is often heard in Santa Cruz, 'Pueblo pequeño, infierno grande', ie 'Small village, big hell.' Just as in the animal world, the human world submits to fierce competition in a struggle for survival and to irreversible evolution, which forces each individual to make a quick adaptation to this environment. Otherwise, he has to leave the islands. 'The survival of the fittest...' said Darwin.

Moreover, the galloping immigration of the last 15 years has not helped much: 5,000 people in the archipelago in 1980 swelled to more than 20,000 in 1994, and the numbers are on the rise, to such an extent that the authorities are now concerned about the future of the Galápagos.

In 1992, decree number 0434 of the Ministerio de Agricultura y Ganaderia, the Ministry of Agriculture decided to establish a single organization of naturalist guides, divided in three parts: 'Guias Naturalistas (Naturalist Guides) I, II, III'. Total number of guides: 298 in 2002.

Guia Naturalista I (94 active in 2002)
A native of the islands or resident of the archipelago for many years, with a high school diploma, who has a sound knowledge of the region and speaks English. He must pass the course of Guia Naturalista I, and can lead a group of 10 visitors maximum.

Guia Naturalista II (ex-auxiliary) (116 active in 2002)
Ecuadorian by birth or by naturalization, who has achieved a high school education or has a university background in biology or related fields, or in tourism. He has to be fluent in English, French or German, and must pass the course of Guia Naturalista II. He can lead groups of up to 16 visitors.

Guia Naturalista III (ex-naturalist) (88 active in 2002)
Ecuadorian by birth or by naturalization, and, in the case of a foreigner, must have legal working papers. He has to show proof of a degree in biology or related fields, or in tourism. He must be fluent in Spanish, English, then French or German. He must pass the course of Guia Naturalista III, and may lead a group of 16 (in reality: 20) visitors.

The naturalist guides course takes place each year in September, for a period of six weeks. Priority is given to Ecuadorian nationals and Galápagos residents in registering for the courses, while 20 per cent of foreigners may be accepted to take the course for Naturalist Guides III. The candidate must pass the final exam with an 80 per cent grade in order to receive the guide's license of the Galápagos National Park. The license is valid for two years; the future guide must show proof of at least 120 days worked per year in order to keep his guide's status and the right to continue working.

Guides are responsible in the eyes of the law, and have many essential functions:

- To inform and educate visitors on the richness of the protected area and the natural history of the Galápagos, competently and with diligence.
- To be responsible and to control actions committed by the visitors, within the Galápagos National Park.
- To keep in touch with the administrative authorities, to signal the group's whereabouts and to receive instructions.
- To carry a guide's licence and identity papers, and to wear a uniform, if necessary.

- To be vigilant of the application of technical and administrative measures in order to protect the natural resources and the visitors.
- To cooperate with the control of the region to ensure conservation and rational use of the resources.
- To participate in the activities of observations, involving the collection of data on the ecological impact and other environmental aspects.
- To provide interpretation for special groups.
- To report to the legal and technico-administrative authorities whenever necessary.

In conclusion, and in the eyes of visitors, the guide must make sure the rules are respected. In the intensive use zones, he or she has to keep his group on the trail. In the extensive use zones or open areas, all decisions are his or her responsibility and must prevent harm to the ecosystem. The guide may also interfere with another group in cases of questionable behavior. The Galápagos National Park has the right to sanction or even take away the license of a guide if he or she is convicted of a serious offense, whether he or she deserves a warning or suspension from work.

CHAPTER THREE

The Charles Darwin Research Station

In 1957, UNESCO, in cooperation with the New York Zoological Society, Time Incorporated, and the Ecuadorian government, sent a mission to the Galápagos Islands for the purpose of conducting a study on flora and fauna, and also to look for an appropriate site for building a biological research station.

Two years later, in 1959, the centenary of the Theory of Evolution drew the attention of the International Congress of Zoology. A Galápagos committee was created under the presidency of Sir Julian Huxley. Thus was founded the Charles Darwin Foundation in Brussels, intended to preserve the environment and to favor scientific research with an aim towards conservation. The construction of the Darwin Station in Puerto Ayora was undertaken in the beginning of 1960, facing Academy Bay, with funds from UNESCO and Ecuador. The station was in operation two years later, but was officially inaugurated in 1964.

In 1965, the Ecuadorian government passed decree number 525 thus defining the boundaries of the National Park, so as to protect the giant tortoises and eradicate all feral goats. The first protection programmes started in 1968, with the creation of the Servicio Parque Nacional Galápagos (SPNG). In 1973, the Galápagos became a province of Ecuador for the second time in order to help the development and promotion of the archipelago. The INGALA, or Instituto Nacional Galápagos, was created in 1980 with the aim of developing the islands touristically and economically and for carrying out major projects such as airports.

The Charles Darwin Research Station will celebrate its 40th anniversary in 2004. It has hosted a number of directors, all European or American scientists, such as: Friedemann Koster (1982–84), Gunther Reck (1984–89), Daniel Ewans (1989–92), Chantal Blanton (1992–94), Robert Bensted Smith (1996–2002). The latest Ecuadorian director, Fernando Espinosa (2002–2003) was sacked during a meeting of the Darwin Foundation in Puerto Ayora (November 19), due to his involvment in politics. The research station has four main functions: to provide scientific information; to obtain funds from international organizations for conservation purposes; to help the National Park with educational programs, and to educate Ecuadorian students.

In 1986, the budget of the Darwin Station was US$600,000. In 1994, it was US$2 million per year. Visiting scientists with research projects must pay an indemnity for their expeditions and outings. Twenty per cent of the budget of the station is supplied by the Ecuadorian government. Another important donor is the Smithsonian Institution, which provides 20-30 per cent of the budget. The WWF was a serious contributor in the past, but gradually withdrew. The San Diego Zoo supports the giant tortoises projects. Other well-known donors include the Frankfurt Zoological Society. Private European and American societies also contribute modest funds to the CDRS.

The expense of running the Darwin Station reached US$4.4 million in 2004 and the total revenue of the Darwin Foundation was US$4,405,554 million.

PRACTICAL INFORMATION

How to Get to the Galápagos

Air Travel

Two airlines service the Galápagos. It is possible to make reservations through travel agencies in Quito and Guayaquil or direct with the airlines. Aerogal has a service to Baltra, in competition with TAME that had a monopoly for over 20 years. Passengers must check in two hours before the departure of the flight.

AEROGAL

Quito – Ave. Amazonas 7797; Tel. (593-2) 3330 458 or 2942 800; Reservations. 1800-Aerogal. E: aerogal@andinanet.net; www.aerogal.com.ec

Guayaquil – Simon Bolivar Airport. Tel. (593-4) 2310 346, 2524 953 or 2564 951 (call centre)

Baltra – Tel. (593-5) 2526 797 (Santa Cruz); (593-5) 2520 405 (Baltra)

Route	032 (Mon–Fri)	034 (Sat)	038 (Sat)	038 (Sun)	032 (Sun)
Quito	dep. 08:20	dep. 09:30	—	dep. 08:00	dep. 08:45
Guayaquil	arr. 10:00	arr. 11:00	dep. 09:30	arr. 09:30	arr. 10:00
Baltra	arr. 10:30	arr. 11:30	arr. 10:00	arr. 10:00	arr. 10:30

Route	033 (Mon–Fri)	035 (Sat)	039 (Sat)	039 (Sun)	033 (Sun)
Baltra	dep. 12:00	dep. 12:30	dep. 11:00	dep. 11:00	dep. 12:00
Guayaquil	arr. 14:30	arr. 15:00	arr. 13:30	arr. 13:30	arr. 14:30
Quito	arr. 16:15	—	arr. 15:00	arr. 15:00	arr. 16:15

The Aerogal return fare (2009) in high season for foreigners is US$417.09 from Quito or US$361.34 from Guayaquil. In comparison, an Ecuadorian national pays US$258.05 for a round trip ticket from Quito or $234.71 from Guayaquil. A *colono* (resident of the islands) pays US$150.53 for round trip ticket from Quito or US$127.73 from Guayaquil.

TAME

Quito (Transportes Aereos Militares Equatorianos), Avenida Amazonas y Avenida Colon, Edificio Banco del Pichincha, 7mo piso (PO Box 8736). Tel. (593–2) 509392, 590375 or (593–2) 3977 100; E: reservas@tame.com.ec; www.tame.com.ec

The TAME Boeing 737 links Quito to Baltra Island in the Galápagos, every day.

Route	EQ191 daily	EQ193 daily	Route	EQ190 daily	EQ192 daily
Quito	dep. 07:30	dep. 09:00	Baltra	dep. 11:00	dep. 12:30
Guayaquil	dep. 09:15	dep. 10:45	Guayaquil	arr. 13:45	arr. 15:15
Baltra	arr. 10:00	arr. 11:30	Quito	arr. 15:15	arr. 16:45

TAME also runs three flights a week from Quito to San Cristóbal.

Route	EQ195 (Sun)	EQ195 (Wed & Sat)
Quito	dep. 07:00	dep. 13:15
San Cristóbal	arr. 09:30	arr. 16:45

Route	EQ194 (Sun)	EQ194 (Wed & Sat)
San Cristóbal	dep. 10:30	dep. 17:45
Quito	arr. 14:45	arr. 20:45

Return fares are the US$417.09 for foreigners (i.e. same cost as flight to Baltra). Ecuadorian nationals pay US$195. (Hitherto this service was operated by SAN.

There is an hour's difference between the mainland and the archipelago.

EMETEBE flies a Piper Aztec or Piper Seneca (five passengers) out of Baltra, to Isabela or Cristóbal. Offices in Guayaquil tel. 4 202 241, fax. 4 200 352; San Cristóbal fax. (05) 2520 615; Puerto Ayora fax. (05) 2526 177; Isabela tel. (05) 2529 155; Baltra tel. (05) 2521 193. Return flights Cristóbal–Baltra or Baltra–Villamil cost US$260 for nationals and foreigners, and US$130 for colonos (July 2009). Direct flight San Cristóbal–Puerto Villamil one way is US$91 (foreigners and nationals) or US$69 for colonos.

Visas

British, French and American citizens do not require a visa to enter Ecuador, as is the case for citizens of most countries.

Exchanging Money

The currency in Ecuador was the *sucre*. It has been fluctuating since 1980, quite alarmingly, in fact, if one considers that US$1 was worth 30 sucres back then. In 1989, $1 = 500 sucres, and in 1995, $1 = 2,350 sucres. In January 2000, $1 = 25,000 sucres. Since the 8th September 2000, the US$ has been the official currency in Ecuador.

There are two banks in the Galápagos, one each in Puerto Ayora (Santa Cruz Island) and in Puerto Baquerizo Moreno (San Cristóbal Island): the Banco del Pacifico and the Banco de Fomento. It's possible to change money there, as well as in souvenir shops. But you would do better to change your money at the Quito airport upon arrival, at the banks of Avenida Amazonas or at the Casa de cambio (Casa Paz).

Spoken Languages

Spanish is the national language, but English is usually well understood in the Galápagos. Guides may also speak German, French, Italian and Dutch.

Electricity
110 volts in Ecuador as well as in the Galápagos, with American-type plugs. Europeans may be advised to bring along a plug adapter. On the Galápagos boats, you may also plug into 220 volts, 12 or 24 volt system, and recharge the batteries of your video camera without any problems.

Sun
Being right on the equator, the sun is very strong. Do not forget your hat, sun protection, lip balm. Burns may occur rapidly for those who are not protected from the very first day. You are well advised to put sunblock cream on your neck, behind your knees, on your calves and on your feet.

Clothes and Footwear
Light clothing like shorts and T-shirts is sufficient. Bring along a light raincoat or a rainjacket for protection during the garua and the showers of the hot season. A sweatshirt or jumper will be necessary for cool and windy evenings on the boat, and for the high elevations of the Andes (Quito, 2,850 metres) and Ecuador. Sports shoes are the best for the islands, not to mention a pair of flip-flops (thongs) for walking in the shallow water or for disembarking on a coral beach.

Mosquitoes and Related Diseases
Mosquitoes are found in the hot season on the coast, in the mangroves of Puerto Ayora and in the islands. On the sea, where a breeze is always present, they are not a problem. There is no malaria in the Galápagos.

Besides seasickness, there are no risks of disease in the islands, even though some cases of cholera were reported after the 1992 epidemic in Ecuador. This bleak period is now over. Vaccinations against diphtheria and tetanus are recommended, however.

There is a small hospital and pharmacy in Puerto Ayora, as well as in Puerto Baquerizo Moreno (San Cristóbal), and one dispensary is found in Puerto Villamil (Isabela). For any serious accident, returning to Quito or Guayaquil is strongly advised.

Photography
Kodak, Fuji and Sakura film are available, for slides or prints, in Puerto Ayora, Pto. Baquerizo and in Floreana. Nevertheless, if you want to be sure of its freshness, it is better to bring your own supply from home, or, alternatively, from Quito or Guayaquil.

Hours of Sea Crossing
For small boats sailing at six or seven miles per hour.

		Nautical Miles	Hours
Puerto Ayora	-Punta Suarez (Española)	53	9
	-Puerto Baquerizo	40	7
	-South Plaza	17	3
	-Santa Fé		3
	-Bartolomé	45	8
	-James Bay (Santiago)	57	9
	-Puerto Villamil (Isabela)		8
	-Punta Espinosa (Fernandina)	140	22
South Plaza	-Bartolomé	33	5
Bartolomé	-James Bay	27	3–4
Bartolomé	-Genovesa	52	8–9
James Bay	-Rábida	16	2–3
James Bay	-Punta Espinosa	90	12–14
Punta Suarez	-Floreana	42	5–6

CHRONOLOGY OF EVENTS

1535 Official discovery of the Galápagos, on March 10, by Fray Tomas de Berlanga, archbishop of Panama, on a boat that drifted off its course with the ocean currents. The first mass is celebrated on the islands.

1546 Arrival of Diego de Rivadeneira, who experiences the same trouble as Fray Tomas. He is the first to mention the Galápagos hawk and the flamingos.

1570 The Galápagos Islands appear for the first time on a world map, drawn by Abraham Ortelius. They are called *Insulae de los Galopegos*.

1593–1710 Pirates use the Galápagos as a refuge and as a base to look for water and to collect turtle and tortoise meat. From there, they attack the Peruvian and Ecuadorian ports. Goats seem to have been introduced at this time.

1684 The pirate and cartographer Ambrose Cowley draws one of the first navigation maps of the islands, as does William Dampier.

1685 The viceroy of Peru introduces dogs on some islands to eradicate goats, food of the pirates.

1790 The first scientific mission, led by the Sicilian captain Alexander Malaspina, sent by Charles V of Spain, lands on the island. The report of that expedition was lost.

1793 The British James Colnett makes a trip to the Galápagos to study the possibility of whale fishing. Start of the whaling industry, which will last until 1870. Some tortoise species are on the brink of extinction. James Colnett draws the first detailed map of the archipelago. The post office barrel is erected on Floreana by Colnett or Hathaway to facilitate communication with the United States and England.

1800–1900 Exploitation of the fur sea lions by North Americans and Europeans. The species comes close to extinction but some individual sea lions survive on Fernandina and Genovesa.

1801 The American captain Amasa Delano reports an eruption of Alcedo volcano or Darwin volcano when anchored at James Bay. He is the first to mention the lava lizard in the archipelago.

1807 Irishman Patrick Watkins is the first authentic settler in the Galápagos, being exiled on Floreana (unless he requested it). He grows vegetables, which he trades for whisky to the passing ships. Two years later, he steals a ship's boat and sails to the Ecuadorian coast.

1813 Arrival of the USS *Essex*. David Porter, the captain, practically destroys the British whaling fleet in the archipelago. He makes many important observations on the natural history of the islands, but he is responsible for the introduction of goats to Santiago. He reports volcanic eruptions on Isabela and Fernandina.

1825 Captain Benjamin Morell of the *Tartar,* who came to look for sea lions in February, observes a volcanic eruption on Fernandina, from Banks Bay. Lava flows into the sea, heating up the water and air to such an extent that parts of the boat start melting.Two weeks later, the eruption was still not over.

1832 Ecuador, a young republic since 1830, takes official possession of the Galápagos Islands on February 12, and names them 'Archipelago del Ecuador'. The first colony—composed of soldiers exiled for having fomented a rebellion on the mainland—is founded on Floreana. General Villamil is the first governor. Domestic animals are brought to the island and turn feral when the colony is abandoned some years later.Thirty-one ships stop over in Floreana during the following three years.

1835 Visit of Captain Fitzroy's HMS *Beagle* for five weeks, from September 15 to October 20. The young naturalist Charles Darwin disembarks on San Cristóbal, Santiago, Floreana and Isabela. His observation will lead him to publish *The Origin of Species* 24 years later. Captain Fitzroy draws very accurate maps, which will be used until WW II.

1841 The American writer Herman Melville visits the Galápagos and writes a poetic book on the *Enchanted Islands.*

1846 The French boat *Genie* reports three huts at the foot of Cerro Ballena, south of Conway Bay. A trail to the top of Santa Cruz Island starts from there.

1859 Publication of *The Origin of Species.*

1861 Ecuadorian president Garcia Moreno declares the Galápagos 'Provincia', with Floreana as capital.

1872 Scientific expedition of Professor Louis Agassiz of Harvard University.

1875 First visit of Theodore Wolf, with a few scientists of the Quito Polytechnic School. He will make another trip three years later, and will publish a monograph explaining that the islands are of volcanic origin and were never linked to the mainland. The highest volcano of Isabela (1,707 metres) bears his name.

1885 The Galápagos are linked to the province of Guayas. The new authorities move to Puerto Baquerizo Moreno (San Cristóbal).

1886 First school in San Cristóbal.

1888 Manuel Cobos founds the penal colony of El Progreso (San Cristóbal) after a first failed attempt in 1869. A sugarcane industry is established.

1890 Volcanic activity in the southeast of Santiago. The lava flows of Sullivan Bay may be from that period.

1891 Visit of Georges Baur, an American scientist who claims that the islands were connected to the mainland. For him, there is no other way to explain the presence of so many species on the islands.

1892 The archipelago gets the official name of Archipelago de Colon, after Christopher Columbus. Spanish names are given to the islands.

1897 Antonio Gil starts the colonization of Isabela, with the port of Villamil and the village of Santo Tomas in the highlands.

1904 Manuel Cobos is murdered by a Colombian convict (Sanbal).

1905–1906 Under the presidency of Rollo Beck, scientists of the California Academy of Science conduct studies and make numerous samples for one year. They take away with them the greatest collection of plants and animals ever made in the Galápagos. The last giant tortoises were collected on Fernandina, as well as a few specimens found on Rábida Island (which has never been a distinct subspecies). The fur sea lions are almost extinct, according to their findings.

1923 Visit of the American William Beebe, with the *Arcturus* expedition. His book, *Galápagos World's End,* a worldwide success, stimulates many expeditions, among which is the Norwegian colony of 1926.

1924–1930 First commercial exploitation of the salt mine of Puerto Egas in James Bay (Santiago). A second exploitation will be undertaken from 1960 to 1968.

1926 A group of Norwegians lands in the Galápagos, with the aim of fishing and agriculture. The company fails, triggering the return of many settlers, although a few remain on Santa Cruz and San Cristóbal.

1930–1934 Appearance of the fire ant in the Galápagos, on the Bellavista road (Santa Cruz).

1932 Drama on Floreana, with Dr Ritter, Dore Strauch, the Wittmer family and the Baroness von Wagner de Bousquet, with her two lovers Lorenz and Philipson. Disappearances, poisoning, strange deaths.

1934 First laws aimed at protecting the fauna of the Galápagos. Some islands become reserves or natural park. Some land iguanas are brought from Baltra to Seymour by a team of Americans of the Hancock Foundation, to find out whether the habitat of Seymour is favourable to the reptiles. (Curiously, that will save the species of Baltra, eradicated after the Second World War. The first flight over the Galápagos is made by two Americans, who came to help a yacht captain suffering from appendicitis in Tagus Cove (Isabela).

1935 Expedition of Victor von Hagen, who commemorates the centenary of Charles Darwin's journey and deposits a bust in his memory. The four German brothers Angermeyer leave Nazi Germany in a sailboat bound for the Galápagos islands in search of a new life.

1941 The American Air Force takes over the islands and builds an air base on Baltra. They are partly responsible for the eradication of the land iguanas on the island, and for the bombing of Pinnacle Rock on Bartolomé, a perfect target for shells.

1954 Uplift of a coral reef at Urvina Bay, in Isabela.

1957 The American scientists Eibl-Eibesfeldt and R Bowman are sent by a few institutions to report on conservation, and to choose a site for the future research station.

1959 On July 4, the Ecuadorian government declares the Galápagos a national park, with the exception of the colonized areas. The Darwin Foundation for the Galápagos Islands is created in Brussels, on July 23. Victor van Straelen is the first president. Upon the centenary of Darwin's book, the penitentiary of Isabela is closed and blown up.

1960 Beginning of lobster fishing. Raymond Lévèque is the first director of the Darwin Station. Funds from UNESCO help to finance the first buildings of the station. Hotel Galápagos, run by American Forrest Nelson, opens the same year in Puerto Ayora.

1961 Goats are eradicated on South Plaza. Frenchman André Brosset becomes the second director of the Darwin Station. The laboratory and the meteorological station are built the same year.

1963 David Snow becomes the third director of the Darwin Station.

1964 Grand opening of the Darwin Station on January 21, with many international personalities. In May, Miguel Castro becomes the first official in charge of conservation and protection of the tortoise population. Roger Perry becomes the fourth director of the station.

1965 Tortoise eggs from Pinzón Island are brought back to the station to be incubated and for the young giant tortoises to be bred in captivity.

1968 Juan Black and Jose Villa, conservation officials, are sent by the Ecuadorian government. They begin the administration of the Galápagos National Park, in October. During an intense period of activity, the caldera floor of Fernandina volcano drops down to 300 metres (small eruptions within the caldera will follow in 1972, 1977, 1978, 1988 and 1991).

1969 Mass tourism starts in the Galápagos with the arrival of the *Lina-A* of Metropolitan Touring, which will build many landing sites in the islands.

1970 The first 20 baby tortoises bred in captivity are freed on Pinzón, their native island. Peter Kramer becomes the fifth director of the Darwin Station.

1971 Scholarships are given to Ecuadorian students to study at the Darwin Station. The giant tortoise named Lonesome George is found on Pinta Island.

1972 The *Beagle III* is inaugurated in March; it is the first boat of the Darwin Station, offered by the WWF (World Wildlife Fund). Engineer Jaime Torres is the first superintendent of the National Park. The Japanese boat *Chicuzen Maru* captures hundreds of turtles in Galápagos waters. Construction of the Van Straelen Hall at the station.

1973 Construction of the Puerto Ayora-Baltra road. Once again the Galápagos become 'Province of Ecuador'. National and international experts write the Master Plan for the protection and use of the National Park.

1974 Craig MacFarland becomes the sixth director of the Darwin Station. Publication of the Master Plan.

1975 Seventeen five-year-old tortoises, bred in captivity, are released on Española, bringing the total number of adults to 14 on that island. The feral dogs of Santa Cruz destroy the population of young tortoises of the reserve and hundreds of land iguanas of the northwest of the island. A breeding centre will be established at the station. The cruise ship *Floreana* (ex *Lina-A*) sinks 60 miles off the mainland, with no human losses.

1976 *Rattus rattus*, the black rat, is eradicated on Bartolomé, thanks to the experiments of the Darwin Station with traps and poison.

1977 Two new cruise ships arrive in the islands: M/N *Bucanero* and M/N *Neptuno*.

1978 The islands are declared a 'Patrimony of Humanity' by UNESCO.

1979 Eruptions on Cerro Azul and Sierra Negra (Volcan Chico).

1980 Arrival of the cruise ship M/N *Santa Cruz* (90 passengers) of Metropolitan Touring, and of the first B-737 of TAME Airline for the Quito–Baltra flight.

1982 Eruption of Wolf volcano, late August-early September, on Isabela. Unusual warming of the sea surface in the Galápagos. Dieter Plage and Friedmann Köster shoot a video for Survival Anglia Productions (English), for two consecutive years. First use of a ULM to fly over the archipelago.

1983 Memorable year of a disastrous Niño: nine months of rain until July. The Baltra road is flooded and cut off. Real streams appear and bridges are built in Bellavista. Sea surface temperature in Puerto Ayora reaches 30° C. The local population suffers from the humid heat, from colds and skin infections. Many couples divorce or separate. The number of sea lions, marine iguanas and sea birds is decimated.

1984 In April, volcanic eruption on Fernandina. In May, arson fire at the administrative building of the Darwin Station. On May 28, fire on the boat M/N *Neptuno* of Macchiavello Tours; it sinks off Guayaquil with the death of the cook.

1985 Big fire in the south of Isabela (March–April), on the slopes of Sierra Negra volcano, in the agricultural zone of Valle Alemania and in the National Park. A trench 62 kilometres long and seven metres wide is dug by the Ecuadorian army. Tortoises are evacuated on men's backs. Two Canadairs aircraft are sent from Canada to extinguish the fire, which lasts for 50 days. Covered on TV and in the international press. At the same time, the fishing boat B/P *Intrepido* of Captain Miguel Andagana disappears on March 6 and drifts for 74 days before it reaches the coast of Coast Rica. The six crewmen survive on turtles, sharks and dolphinfish. In November: first course of Dituris, the Ecuadorian tourism office. Estimate of the number of visitors for 1985: 17,850 people (65 per cent foreigners).

1986 Opening on January 9 of the airport of San Cristóbal by the vice-president. Creation of the Galápagos Marine Reserve by presidential decree on May 13, which extends 15 miles from the extreme points of the islands. In September: paving of Puerto Ayora. The new guides' hall of the National Park opens its gates for the naturalist guides course. The number of visitors to the Galápagos goes beyond 26,000.

1987 In October, arrival of the *Galápagos Explorer,* the new cruise ship of the company Canodros (SAN/SAETA), with a capacity to carry 90 passengers. New restrictions for the practice of scuba diving in the Galápagos. The dive guides must now have a diver's license from the Ecuadorian Merchant Marine. The number of visitors reaches 32,593.

1988 International Congress of Herpetology at the CDRS in May. It is decided to save the semen of Lonesome George, the last giant tortoise survivor of Pinta Island. The cargo boat *Iguana* (an old cruise ship) sinks in front of the CDRS in Academy Bay, in June. Around September 12–14, new eruption of Fernandina volcano: lava flows inside the caldera, displacement of the crater lake, fumaroles on the outer slope of the volcano. The number of visitors exceeds 31,200.

1989 The French cruise ship *Mermoz* (500 passengers) visits the archipelago twice, but the passengers cannot disembark on the islands of the National Park. Opening of the site of Punta Pitt on the eastern tip of San Cristóbal. In May, the goats of southern Isabela cross the Perry Isthmus and climb up Alcedo volcano. A new Niño is preparing, with a noticeable change in life cycles. Gunther Reck resigns as director of the Darwin Station and is replaced by American Daniel Ewans. On July 4, the 30th anniversary of the Galápagos National Park is celebrated. In September and October, the blue-footed boobies abandon their chicks on a massive scale throughout the archipelago, but the albatrosses reproduce well. During the same month, black rats are eradicated on Pinzón Island. Illegal taking of shark fins by the Japanese becomes important. The number of visitors reaches 41,900.

1990 Creation of new trails on Santa Fé, Seymour and Rábida. Return of the cruiseship *Mermoz*. In March-April, the park guards of the Galápagos National Park go on strike for three months, asking for a salary raise. Disputes between the national guides of the Asociacion de Guias and those of the Agrupación de Guias Interpretes del PNG. Sergio Basan breaks the arm of Matthias Espinosa in Puerto Ayora with a club. In May–June, the French TV TF1 shoots two programs of 'Ushuaïa' with Nicolas Hulot and the author aboard the schooner *Cyprae*. Second use of the ULM to fly over the islands. Death of Marga Angermeyer, wife of Carl the painter and German pioneer. Foreigners cannot participate in naturalist guide's exam. In November: dramatic fire of the M/N *Bartolomé* at sea during the night. Five passengers and one crewmember sink with the boat and disappear. A wooden stairway is constructed at Tagus Cove by SPNG.

1991 A French team of XL Productions led by the author shoots two programmes: 'Les Animaux de Mon Coeur' ('Animals of My Heart') for French TV TF1, and 'Wildlife Sanctuaries', which will air on the Discovery Channel. In March, first report by Jonathan Green of an attack by a three-metre-long great white shark, at Playa Escondida (northeast Pinzón Island). March 21: earthquakes at Alcedo volcano, and in April, the eruption of Fernandina volcano. In June: 35 land iguanas are reintroduced to Baltra by the SPNG, after a 40-year absence. In July: opening of Banco del Pacifico in Puerto Ayora, on Santa Cruz Island. September 25: first historical eruption of Marchena Island, during the night, incandescent clouds and lava flows to the southwest. On October 19, Prince Henry of Luxembourg visits the islands. The Ecuadorian government extends for another 25 years the right of the Darwin Foundation to operate the Darwin Station. In December, Arturo Izurieta, former naturalist guide, becomes the new superintendent of the Galápagos National Park, after the scandal that ousted Fausto Cepeda. The telephone is connected in Puerto Ayora. The total number of visitors reaches 40,746.

1992 January: Daniel Ewans ends his term as director of the Darwin Station, and will be replaced by American Chantal Blanton in May. The Japanese commercial fishing boat *Kaiyo Maru*, with sophisticated electronic equipment, drops anchor at Academy Bay, in Puerto Ayora. On February 10, the *Donai*, an Ecuadorian fishing boat from Manta, is seized by the Ecuadorian navy patrol boat off Pinta with a load of 50 hammerhead sharks. Impounded, the sharks are found two days later on February 12 at the house of Copiano in Puerto Ayora, where they are slaughtered for illicit commercial purposes. The affair is reported in the international press (Europe and the US). The scandal of the exploitation of pepinos follows, with pirate camps established on the coast of Fernandina. In June: President Borja declares a ban on sea cucumber fishing. New Niño year, with warming of the sea and considerable rains, landslides above Santa Rosa (Santa Cruz). Construction in Puerto Ayora of the Thomas Fisher Science and Education Building, near the Darwin Station. A new wooden stairway is built at Bartolomé Island to stop the erosion of the trail and of the slope by the visitors (August). In September, a new system for the naturalist guide's course. Number of visitors: 39,510.

1993 Lobster fishing is banned for seven years until 2000. The National Park fee goes up to $80 for foreigners, and the port tax to $6. Blue whales are reported for the first time, by the research sailboat *Odyssey* south of Isabela (May), Fernandina, Cape Berkeley, Roca Redonda (David Day, personal communication). Telephone connections are now possible between the islands and the mainland. In September, arrival of the cruise ship *Ambassador I*, of the company Islas Galápagos Turismo y Vapores, of Mr. Zacharias in Quito. Pressure from Galápagos fishermen on the government of Sixto Duran Ballen, to suspend the ban on the fishing of pepinos. The American photographer Doug Perrine, takes underwater photos of hammerhead sharks caught in drift nets at Wolf Island (a letter is sent to the president of Ecuador). The number of visitors to the Galápagos reaches 46,818.

1994 The Department of Industry and Fisheries (MIIP) re-opens lobster fishing for three months (July 15 to October 15), pepinos fishing for three months (October 15 to January15), and shark fishing for three months (January 15 to April 15). One hundred and forty Japanese fishing boats are authorized to fish for tuna west of Isabela during the whole month of October, but must pay $20,000 each for the permit. Press campaign in Quito and Ecuador for the protection of the Marine Reserve. The number of visitors to the Park reaches 53,825. Death of German pioneer Carl Angermeyer.

1995 February: Death of Bernhard Schreyer an old German settler and owner of the schooner *Tigress*. February-March: eruption of Fernandina Volcano and lava flows towards Cape Hammond. July: arrival of SPNG's new boat *Guadalupe River* to patrol the Marine Reserve. Goats found on top on Volcan Wolf. September: new tortoise centre at Villamil (Isabela) named after Arnoldo Tupiza. After new law project made by Eduardo Velez and vetoed by President Sixto Ballen Duran, Pto.Ayora and Pto.Baquerizo go on strike for three weeks; assault of SPNG and CDRS offices. Army comes in. Introduction of goats on Pinta. Illegal fishing of 'pepinos' and shark goes on. Eight boats from Manabi found at Roca Redonda, where a diver is attacked by a hammerhead shark. A. Izurieta leaves Galápagos as Park's intendant. Number of visitors: 55,782. Yacht *Samba* reports seven orcas attack on a pod of common dolphins.

1996 Chantal Blanton leaves as director of CDRS, replaced by Robert Bensted Smith (GB). M/N *Galápagos Explorer* hits the rocks in San Cristóbal and is sunk offshore. Road Itabaca-Pto. Ayora asphalted. New dive centres: 'Scuba Iguana' (Hotel Galápagos) and 'Nautidiving' (Red Mangrove Inn). New president Abdala Bucaram prepares a law for protection of Marine Reserve, which is declared a 'biological reserve' by INEFAN in November. Number of visitors up to 61,500. December: Pierre Constant missing at sea after a scuba dive at the entrance of Darwin Bay (Genovese Is.). Swims one hour 15 minutes with fins and two underwater cameras to reach the shore at the northern side of Darwin Bay. Notices whale bones and other mammal vertebrae on the lava rocks.

1997 Following corruption scandal and escape from Ecuador of President Abdala, Galápagos deputy Eduardo Velez (Rinon) disappears. Fanny Uribe ('Pepinera aletera') becomes new deputy of the Galápagos with Alfredo Serrano. March: sea cucumber fishing boat captured by *Guadalupe River* on west Isabela and northwest Fernandina. Julio Lopez of SPNG wounded by bullet fire by one of 20 armed men processing sea cucumbers. A peaceful demonstration of 300 people marches to reject violence in Galápagos. June: abnormal warming of sea temperatures; 28° C west of Isabela until December. A new Niño is preparing at planet level. 'Nautidiving' of Polo Navarro stops its diving operations after boat wreck in Tortuga Bay. Report of penguins nesting on the northwest coast of Floreana Island (Cerro Daylight and Piedra Dura). Fernando Espinosa, new secretary of Charles Darwin Foundation. Number of visitors up to 62,809.

1998 January: Arrival of the new passenger cruise boat *Galápagos Explorer II*. February: total eclipse of the sun for 4 min. at 11am. March: special law by Ecuadorian government. Marine Reserve protected by SPNG, Ministry of Tourism, Fisheries, Science Biodiversity/ Education group. March 11: Pepe Salcedo, captain of the yacht *Sulidae* falls off the cliff at South Plaza Island and survives with a fractured skull. April: El Niño is still strong with hot temperatures, calm and clear seas, but little rain. UNESCO forces Ecuador to a law of 40 nautical miles for the Marine Reserve but otherwise draws support and the title of World Heritage Site. April 20: Pepe Salcedo dies of a cardiac arrest. September: boat taxis initiated in Puerto Ayora harbour. Eruption of Cerro Azul on Isabela (one and a half months) with lateral cone on west flank. October: Arrival of M/N *Galápagos Discovery* of Klein Tours (90 persons). November 18–19: Roberto Haro capsizes with small boat off '4 Hermanos' islands and survives 27 hours drifting to Pinzon Is. Number of visitors is 64,791.

1999 February: IMAX film with Al Giddings (six weeks). A ULM crashes on the slopes of Cerro Azul (two men die). March: Approval of the Master Plan for the Marine Reserve. Implementation of quarantine and immigration controls. Year of plannification and negotiations. April-May: legal fishing of 'pepinos' for residents (two months). Capture of illegal fishing boats. Schooling whale sharks south of Isabela and around Floreana, up to 14 individuals. May–November: six whale sharks full time at Darwin Is. Water temperatures are cold. June: 95% of female hammerheads in the shallows of Darwin, to mate and to be cleaned of parasites (observations by German scientific boat *Starship*, two weeks, with Mathias Espinosa. September: cargo boat *Luis Felipe* (ex-Piquero) beached at the entrance of Pto. Villamil. December: M/N *Discovery*, stranded on the rocks in Pto. Baquerizo Moreno, then on fire in Panama. Two new species of warbler finches identified in the Galápagos (highlands, lowlands). Road Pto. Ayora-Canal de Itabaca completed with tar. Number of visitors: 66,053.

2000 January: President Jamil Mahuad forced to resign following plan of dollarisation of economy. Orca seen at Punta Estrada, by Mathias Espinosa. People on strike in Pto. Ayora following TAME increase of air rates for settlers. May–July: Furio Valbonesi builds a new luxury hotel in the highlands of Santa Cruz. March: Margret Wittmer dies in Floreana at the age of 95. New 'Caseta' of SPNG near Beagle Lake, overlooking Bolivar Channel. Scientists aboard yacht *Odyssey* look for spermwhales with David Day. May: angry fishermen protest to the Ecuadorian government against the 40 miles no fishing zone and periods authorized for fishing. July 26: yacht *TipTop II* crashes on the rocks at Cabo Rosa, south of Isabela, then sinks. One German tourist dies in cold water. Greg Estes, as guide on board, drifts for one hour in a life raft, with passengers, before rescue. August: death of Pedro Chastain, an old French settler. September: US$ official currency in Ecuador. October: yacht *San Jacinto* sinks. Bell South public phone booths appear in Puerto Ayora. November 13: general strike of the fishermen in Isabela, Cristóbal and Santa Cruz. Block access for tourists to Espanola, Santa Fé and Plaza Sur. The 'Ministro del Medio Ambiente' accept to give one more month for fisheries and increase fishing quota. On Isabela, angry fishermen sack the office of SPNG, burn furniture and go for a manhunt to catch the manager, Juan Chavez, who hides overnight in the mangroves and escapes by swimming out to a boat. November 27: seven Galápagos sharks found finless in Darwin Bay, eight metres underwater; B/P *Vikingo* at anchor with three pangas not operating. December: Seminar Ecopath at CDRS, organized by SPNG, CDRS, Universidad San Franscisco de Quito, supported by the European Commission. Arrival of *Sea Sheperds* boat of Paul Watson, to act as marine police for five years in conjunction with SPNG. Number of visitors: 68,856.

2001 January 16: the tanker *Jessica* hits the rocks south of San Cristóbal, and spills oil into the sea, a sheet of 1250 square kilometres drifts west across the islands, to Santa Fé and Isabela. A C-130 of the US coast guards comes to rescue and boat Cirius from Guayaquil. Artisanal fishermen help the clean up with the scientists and the 2nda Zona Naval. March: installation of a new decompression chamber for divers, in Puerto Ayora, with Henry Schaeffer. March 22: capture of the Costa Rican fishing boat *Maria Canela II*, near Wolf Island, by patrol boat *Sirenian* (SPNG), with 1,044 shark fins and 78 bodies of sharks. Late May: death of Gayle Davis, American-born librarian of the Charles Darwin Station, of cancer. July: first dive guide's course for the Galápagos Marine Reserve, held in Puerto Ayora, by the Galápagos National Park (3 weeks). The masked booby officially becomes the 'Nazca booby', as a new species. Total number of visitors: 77,570.

2002 January: Nazca booby with blue feet seen at Punta Suarez (Española) by Juan Carlos Lamilla. February: Fernando Espinoza (ex-secretary Fundacion Darwin) becomes executive director of the Darwin Station. 31 May: Costa Rican boat *Maria Canela II* escapes custody in Puerto Ayora (Santa Cruz). June: Colombian tuna fishing boat *El Dorado* captured between Floreana and Española, with 40 dolphins and 8 tunas in a net. Strong wave action destroys part of Gordon Rock's SW tuff cone. Eva Danulat becomes new head of BIOMAR after Graham Edgar. New presence of police force in the streets of Puerto Ayora. July 4: *Maria Canela II* found in Costa Rica. Ex-owner Jose Abel Guevara declares having paid US$50,000 to Ecuadorian functionaries (daily newspaper *Al Dia* from Costa Rica, reported in *El Expreso* from Guayaquil). July 5: 2,000 gallons of diesel spilled into Puerto Villamil (Isabela), by Ecuadorian Navy tanker *Taurus*, when filling a 'barcassa' of the *Empresa Electrica*. Mosquito *Aedes aegypti*, vector of dengue fever, found in Puerto Ayora. October 1: new species of slipper lobster *Parribacus perlatus* (Holthuis 1967) found also on Pascua Island, identified by Dr Gary Pore of the Victoria Museum (Melbourne), at Wolf Island's anchorage; active at night at a depth of 6m. Robert Bensted Smith terminates his position as director of the Darwin Station. New species of California eagle ray, *Myliobatis californicus* found at Tagus Cove's exit. Total number of visitors: 82,226.

2003 January 31: Marco Altamirano, new director of SPNG. August: 'Narcotraficos' are discovered in Puerto Ayora (marijuana + cocaine). Italian diver bitten by a shark at Gordon Rocks, due to a flashy watch. October 7: TAME puts in service 2 new Airbus A320s on its route Quito–Baltra. November: a pornographic video network involving children is dismantled in Puerto Ayora, 20 families have been violated by Jose Bourdel and wife Concepcion Cedeno. Nov 19: Darwin Station's director, Fernando Espinoza, sacked during a meeting of the Darwin Foundation in Puerto Ayora, due to his involvment in politics. December: opening of Puerto Ayora's new waterfront and 'malecon'. December 12: death of German pioneer Gus Angermeyer ('El Rey de Galápagos') in Puerto Ayora, aged 92 years; he arrived in the islands with his three brothers in 1935. Total number of visitors: circa 87,400.

2004 Edwin Naula, new director of Galápagos National Park (since December 2003). May and June: two successive strikes of Galápagos fishermen who take over the PNG offices, asking for the right to fish more than 4 million 'pepinos' each year. Threaten the dive ≠in Puerto Ayora and want to control the diving business in Galápagos. Fishermen present an 'Amparo constitucional' in front of the judge in San Cristóbal, following AIM's decision that sea cucumber population is not sustainable and that no more than 4 million pepinos would be allowed in 2005–2006, over a period of 2 months. September: Edwin Naula kicked out by Ecuadorian Department of Environment and replaced by Fausto Cepeda. INGALA objects, claims that he is advisor to fishing interests. 180 park rangers organize a strike and occupy park office throughout the month. September 27: Cepeda kicked out. Victor Carrion becomes interim director, but kicked out by the government in November, as well as all heads of the PNG. Marco Hoyos became 'director encargado'. Gradual take over the the PNG by the political interests of 'Lista 5', of the fishermen. December 20: ARICA's new aerotaxi service aircraft, Baltra-Puerto Villamil, crashes into the sea off Pinson Is. Captain and passengers rescued by Isabela 'fibras'. Forrest Nelson, founder of Hotel Galápagos, dies in Thailand, aged 90 years. December 26: a catastrophic tsunami kills 240,000 people in South East Asia. Total number of visitors to PNG: 108,583.

2005 January 31: Hotel Galápagos closes after 45 years of operation. March 5: President Lucho Guttierez visits the Galápagos and Isabela Islands while Pierre Constant is in the water with a pod of five orcas at Tortuga Island. Mid-May: Eruption of Fernandina volcano. Baltra airport is closed for renovation of the airstrip as of May 15. July–August: Mathias Espinosa and Jaime Navas, consultants for the PNG, work on the elaboration of new Rules and Regulations for diving in the Galápagos Marine Reserve. October 22: Eruption of Sierra Negra volcano on Isabela with lava flow to the northwest. Total number of visitors: 122,453

2006 February: first underwater photo of a giant fresh water eel taken by the author in Puerto Villamil. April: Dra. Raquel Molina, biologist, new director of the National Park. The new Master Plan 2006 is released (the 4th one after those of 1974, 1984, 1996)—a pact for conservation and sustainable development of the archipelago. May: Massacre of tortoises in the highlands of Isabela. Park guard, Mendoza, reports to Park office; one week later seven of his horses have their throat cut open. Culprits are two men known as Teniente Puma and Rico Palo. June/July: Strong waves wash the shores of southern Isabela, flooding Puerto Villamil. CDRS PNG with scientists of the California Davis University and Standford TOPP realise tagging of hammerhead sharks in the Marine Reserve, part of an investigation between Galápagos. Cocos and Malpelo Islands to monitor the movements of the shark populations and migrations between islands and archipelagos (25–30 sharks tagged over a period of 2 months). The new terminal of Isabela airport is being built in Puerto Villamil. October: death of Jimmy Perez, settler and old timer in Puerto Ayora, founder of hotel Sol y Mar. The new Sol y Mar Hotel opens in December. November 26: Rafael Correa, new president of Ecuador. A new El Niño seems to come to the islands. December: Surprised to find his wife in bed with another man, a Galápagos Park guard kills her with a shotgun, shoots the lover and shoots himself dead with a bullet through the head.Total number of visitors approaches: 140,000.

2007 January: Old timer 'Gringo Juan' of Puerto Villamil, American settler who also lived in San Cristóbal and Santa Cruz, hippie, philosopher and lead singer of the CD 'Iguanamen', dies in Guayaquil of prostate cancer. February 5: Seven earthquakes shake southern Isabela (Puerto Villamil) announcing a new eruption.

March 17: PNG director Raquel Molina and four park guards were beaten up at 'La Millionaria' beach on Baltra Island by militaries of the Ecuadorian airforce as they tried to confiscate fishing gear and kayaks, and fish illegally in a protected zone. April: Refurbishment of Baltra airport. President Correa declares Galápagos under state of emergency and calls for public and private sectors to take measures to curb further environmental damage. June: United Nations World Heritage Council committee adds Galápagos to the list of WHS in danger (http://whc.unesco.org/en/danger/), among a list of 830 sites. The International Tour Operator Association (IGTOA) agrees and says that the islands are threatened by tourism, invasive species, and migration. Total number of visitors: 161,859.

2008 April: PNG director Raquel Molina is fired by the 'Ministra del Ambiente', and replaced by Sixto Naranjo, as new director. May 29: Eruption of Cerro Azul, Isabela (10 years after). Dora Gruber of 'Ballena Azul Hotel' in Puerto Villamil, sells to Red Mangrove Lodge's, new owner from Cuenca. Jorge Torres new governor of Galápagos, replaces Eliecer Cruz. November: shark attack on a Danish girl. Total number of visitors: 173,420.

2009 January: Shark attack on surfer Alegria, at the end of Puerto Villamil's beach (Isabela), bitten on feet and hands, as he tries to get free. A new species of 'pink' land iguana is identified on the slopes of Wolf volcano; a population of 30 individuals, known as 'Rosada'. April 11–30: new eruption of volcano Fernandina, with lava flow to Cape Hammond. Bolivar Tupiza becomes the new mayor of Puerto Villamil, following Pablo Gordillo. June: The Galápagos National Park imposes a new system of 'patentes' for dive boats, favouring local fishermen.

LEXICON OF THE FAUNA OF THE GALÁPAGOS

English	*French*	*Spanish*
SEABIRDS		
Common egret	Aigrette	Garza blanca
Waved Albatross	Albatros des Galápagos	Albatros de Galápagos
White-cheeked pintail	Canard Bahama	Patillo, pato
Flightless cormorant	Cormoran aptère	Cormoran no volador
Blue-footed booby	Fou à pattes bleues	Piquero patas azules
Red-footed booby	Fou à pattes rouges	Piquero patas rojas
Nazca booby	Fou masqué	Piquero enmascarado
Magnificent frigatebird	Frégate magnifique	Fragata, tijereta
Great frigatebird	Grande frégate	Fragata comun
Great blue heron	Grand héron bleu	Garza azul
Lava heron	Héron des laves	Garza de lava
Yellow-crowned night heron	Héron de nuit	Garza nocturna
Oystercatcher	Huitrier	Ostrero, cangrejero
Galápagos penguin	Manchot des Galápagos	Pinguino de Galápagos
Swallowtail gull	Mouette à queue d'aronde	Gaviota colabifurcada
Lava gull	Mouette des laves	Gaviota de lava
Brown pelican	Pélican brun	Pelicano
Storm petrel	Pétrel des tempêtes	Golondrinas del mar
Hawaiian petrel	Pétrel hawaïen	Pata pegada
Redbill tropicbird	Phaéton, paille en queue	Rabijunco, pajaro tropical
Semipalmated plover	Pluvier semi-palmé	
Audubon shearwater	Puffin d'Audubon	Pufino
Brown noddy	Noddi	Gaviotin
Sooty Tern	Sterne fuligineuse	Gaviotin
Royal Tern	Sterne royale	
Ruddy turnstone	Tourne pierres à collier	Vuelvepiedras
Whimbrel	Courlis	Zarapito
Common stilt	Echasse	Tero real
Flamingo	Flamant rose	Flamingo
Wandering tattler	Chevalier errant	
Sanderling	Becasseau sanderling	
Northern phalarope	Phalarope hyperboren	Falaropo
LAND BIRDS		
Smoothed-bill ani	Ani à bec doux	Garapatero
Galápagos hawk	Buse des Galápagos	Gavilan de Galápagos
Dark-billed cuckoo	Coulicou	Cuclillo, aguatero
Barn owl	Effraie	Lechuza blanca
Yellow warbler	Fauvette jaune	Canario, maria
Short-eared owl	Hibou brachiotte	Lechuza de campo
Galápagos martin	Hirondelle des Galápagos	Golondrina
Galápagos mockingbird	Moqueur des Galápagos	Cucuve de Galápagos
Galápagos rail	Râle des Galápagos	Pachay
Painted-bill crake	Râle à bec rouge et jaune	Pachay
Galápagos dove	Tourterelle des Galápagos	Paloma de Galápagos
Large-billed flycatcher	Tyran à poitrine jaune	Papamoscas
Vermilion flycatcher	Tyran rouge	Brujo
Finches	Pinsons	Pinzones

English	*French*	*Spanish*
Sharpbill Ground finch	Pinson à bec aiguisé	Pinzón de pico agudo
Carpenter finch	Pinson carpentier	Pinzón artesano
Warbler finch	Pinson chanteur	Pinzón cantor
Tree finch	Pinson des arbres	Pinzón arboreo
Small tree finch	- à petit bec	Pequeño pinzon arboreo
Medium tree finch	- à bec moyen	Mediano pinzon arboreo
Large tree finch	- à gros bec	Gran pinzon arboreo
Cactus finch	Pinson des cactus	Pinzón de tuna
Large cactus finch	Grand pinson des cactus	Gran pinzon de tuna
Mangrove finch	Pinson des paltuviers	Pinzón de manglar
Ground finch	Pinson de terre	Pinzón de tierra
Small ground finch	- à petit bec	Pequeno pinzon de tierra
Medium ground finch	- à bec moyen	Mediano pinzon de tierra
Large ground finch	- à gros bec	Gran pinzon de tierra
Common gallinule	Gallinule, poule d'eau	Gallinula comun
Purple gallinule	Gallinule violace	
Reptiles		
Galápagos snake	Couloeuvre des Galápagos	Culebra
Gecko	Gecko	Salamanquesa
Marine iguana	Iguane marin	Iguana marina
Lang iguana	Iguane terrestre	Iguana terrestre
Lava lizard	Lézard des laves	Lagartija de lava
Black turtle	Tortue noire	Tortuga negra
Giant tortoise	Tortue géante	Galapago
Mammals		
Feral donkey	Ane sauvage	Burro
Feral Cat	Chat sauvage	Gato salvage
Bat	Chauve-souris	Murcielago
Wild horses	Chevaux sauvages	Caballos salvages
Feral goat	Chèvre sauvage	Chivo
Wild dog	Chien sauvage	Perro salvage
Fur sea lion	Otarie à fourrure	Lobo de dos pelos
Galápagos sea lion	Otarie des Galápagos	Lobo marino de Galápagos
Feral pig	Porc sauvage	Chancho
Galápagos rice rat	Rat de riz des Galápagos	Rata endemica
Black rat	Rat noir	Rata negra
Fishes and Marine Life		
Galápagos garden eel	Anguille de jardin	Anguila de jardin
Yellow grouper	Bacalao, mérou jaune	Bacalao
Barracuda	Barracuda	Barracuda
Whale	Baleine	Ballena
Pacific amberjack	Carangue du Pacifique	Palometa
Slipper lobster	Cigale de mer	Langostino
Black coral	Corail noir	Coral negro
Shells	Coquillages	Conchas
Shrimp	Crevette	Camaron
Crab	Crabe	Cangrejo
Dolphin	Dauphin	Delfin
Blue lobster	Langouste bleue	Langosta azul
Red spiny lobster	Langouste rouge	Langosta roja

English	*French*	*Spanish*
Green moray	Murène verte	Morena verde
Sea urchin	Oursin	Erizo de mar
Stingray	Raie à aiguillon	Raya de aguijon
Golden cownose ray	Raie dorée	Raya dorada
White spotted ray	Raie léopard	Raya aguila
Manta ray	Raie manta	Manta
Hornshark	Requin à cornes	Tiburon gato
White tip reef shark	Requin à pointes blanches	Tintorera
Blacktip shark	Requin à pointes noires	Tiburon aleta negra
Whale shark	Requin baleine	Tiburon ballena
Galápagos shark	Requin des Galápagos	Tiburon de Galápagos
Grey reef shark	Requin gris de récif	Tiburon gris
Hammerhead shark	Requin marteau	Tiburon martillo
Smooth hammerhead	Requin marteau lisse	Martillo
Scalloped hammerhead	Requin marteau à festons	Martillo
Tiger shark	Requin tigre	Tiburon tigre
Sea snake	Serpent marin	Culebra de mar
Tuna	Thon	Atun

APPENDICES

Appendix 1

Oceanic Research and 'Hot Spots' in the Galápagos

Studies were conducted in the eastern Pacific Ocean, off the North American, Mexican and South American coasts, to explore the east Pacific mid-oceanic ridge and the transformation faults located along the ridge. During the summer of 1977, the American scientific submarine *Alvin* dived on the ridge at the latitude of the Galápagos islands. The fault is an extension of the southeast Pacific ridge, almost parallel to the equator, and separates the oceanic Cocos Plate (to the north) from the Nazca Plate (to the south). This is the tectonic hinge of the Central America/South America system. Westward and beyond the East Pacific Rise is the Pacific Plate.

Given these facts, we may conclude that the Galápagos archipelago is located on an important tectonic joint, which explains not only its volcanic nature, but also the fact that it is a hot spot, with quasi-permanent seismic and volcanic activity.

In the Galápagos rift, the spread of the plates is about eight to ten centimetres per year, while it is only 6.2 centimetres at the tip of Baja California, but 13.7 centimetres per year north of the equator and 17.5 centimetres per year at the latitude of Easter Island. That is to say that the Pacific Ocean opens up toward the south.

The dive of *Alvin* has observed hot springs, sulphur deposits and a very intense and localized life. The interest in the *Cyamex* dives, at a depth of 2,600 to 2,800 metres, mainly concerned with geological features, was then doubled. The scientists noted a biological and geological analogy with the dive of RITA (Riviera-Tamayo), which was made in 1979 in the rift (on the ridge) at the southern tip of Baja California. The geological conditions are the same, ie a rift spreading at an average of six to ten centimetres a year. The physical conditions and bathymetry are identical, and the temperature of the water is 2° C. Here, too, extremely hot springs, more or less active, bring about profuse sea life. Twenty new species have been reported, but in the Galápagos, a unique mussel was discovered which does not exist in the RITA zone.

These hot springs are not so frequent in the Atlantic, where if present, they are weak. This is due to the fact that the Atlantic mid-oceanic ridge has reached old age, which is evidenced by reduced activity, a slow speed of expansion, a thermic flux which is not so high and a more conspicuous hydrothermal metamorphism.

In contrast, proof of volcanic activity is spectacular in the Pacific. The French oceanographic ship *Jean Charcot* conducted a survey in March and April of 1980 between Ecuador and Easter Island, at 115° west longitude, where very localized gas emanations could portend a powerful submarine eruption. Such a deep-sea eruption was observed in 1991, 10° north of the equator, off the coast of Mexico, by the submersible *Alvin*.

Hot springs, loaded with black material, create true chimneys, with deposits of sulphur and other minerals. These fragile pipes are two or three metres high and made of sulfides of iron, tin, copper, lead, silver and gold. The temperature of the hydrothermal vents reaches 360-380° C. Basaltic landscapes of pillow lava and basalt columns were also observed.

The Americans found important thermal activity in the zone of the Galápagos. This prolific life is a real 'oasis of the deep', where giant tube worms of the species *Riftia pachyptila* (three metres long, and two to three centimetres wide) swarm, and where bacteria may survive at temperatures up to 402° C.

All actual and recent volcanic zones are closely associated with seismic zones, which does not mean that one phenomenon is the cause of the other, but that both arise from a common origin. The latter resides in the movement of the lithospheric plates. The main volcanic and seismic zones coincide perfectly with the mobile joints of these plates.

Oceanic Ridges

Seismologic and oceanographic studies show that these are distension zones from which the expansion of the oceanic floor is made. These are characterized by a mean thermic flux (1.82 micro cal/cm2) which is superior to the mean thermic flux of the earth (1.5 micro cal/cm2) and which can reach up to 8 micro cal/cm2 in some areas called 'hot spots', the most active areas of the globe.

From the petrochemical point of view, it seems that the stage of intense activity (fast expansion and high thermic flux) corresponds to tholeitic lava flows (subalkaline basalts), poorly or not at all affected by hydrothermal metamorphism of the oceanic floor. This is the case of the southeast Pacific.

Oceanic Archipelagoes

These are a chain of islands or submarine volcanoes, which are only active at one of their extremities, the volcanic formations getting older towards the other end. This is the case in the Galápagos. Some create a single chain from a 'hot spot' located far away from any ridge. Others are placed symmetrically on each side of a hot spot located on a ridge, eg Tuamotu-Easter Island, in the southeast Pacific (see map of the Hot Spots, page 15).

An abnormally high thermic flux creates a 'plume'. This magmatic plume is right on the hot spot, at least at the emerging ones. When such a plume hits a lithospheric plate, it pierces it like a laser beam. If the plate moves on the asthenosphere, the plume will leave its track on it, ie a chain of islands or a chain of submarine volcanoes. The farther they are from the point of origin, the older they are.

Appendix 2

Distribution of Land Birds According to Vegetation Zones

Mangrove Zone	Arid Coastal Zone	Transition Zone Common
Common		
Herons	Small ground finch	Small ground finch
Yellow warbler	Medium ground finch	Medium ground finch
Small ground finch	Cactus finch	Cactus finch
Mockingbird	Galápagos dove	Small tree finch
	Mockingbirds	Yellow warbler
	Yellow warbler	Galápagos dove
	Vegetarian finch	
Present		
Mangrove finch	Large ground finch	Large ground finch
Medium ground finch	Vegetarian finch	Carpenter finch
Dark billed cuckoo	Carpenter finch	Warbler finch
Small tree finch	Large-billed flycatcher	Dark-billed cuckoo
Dark-billed cuckoo	Galápagos martin	Vermilion flycatcher
Large-billed flycatcher	Barn owl	Short-eared owl
Short-eared owl		

Tropical Humid Zone	Herbs and Fern Zone
Common	
Warbler finch	Galápagos rail
Tree finches	Galápagos martin
Large-billed flycatcher	
Vermilion flycatcher	
Dark-billed cuckoo	

Tropical Humid Zone	Herbs and Fern Zone
Yellow warbler Short-eared owl	
Present	
Small ground and medium ground finches Mockingbirds Carpenter finch Barn owl	Small ground and medium ground finches Short-eared owl

Appendix 3

Human Population of the Galápagos

In 1980, the resident population of the Galápagos was about 5,000 people. Ten years later, it had doubled. In 1995, the population had reached 20,000. In 2005, the population of the islands is estimated to be 25,000. Most immigration from the mainland is made up of Ecuadorian Indians and mestizos (mixed blood) who consider the Galápagos the new El Dorado, a touristic paradise where it seems easy to make money. But there is no such heaven, and problems become more apparent as time goes by and new settlers arrive: water and electricity problems (the power plant cannot meet the demands), problems of garbage disposal and pollution, poor medical and surgical facilities, disrespect for the rules of the National Park and abuses of all kinds, illegal fishing in the Galápagos Marine Reserve, economic pressure, and so on.

Inhabited Islands Number of Inhabitants
(Censo 1998)

Santa Cruz	Baltra	San Cristóbal	Isabela	Floreana
4,956 men 4,208 women 7 primary schools 1 high school	50 air and naval base	2,945 men 2,546 women 8 primary schools 1 high school	794 men 634 women 3 primary schools 1 college	140 1 high school

Total population = 16,100
(Municipio Santa Cruz, December 2000)

At this time migration from the continent comprised 54 per cent men between 20 and 35 years, looking for work, and 15 per cent women. On San Cristóbal, 66 per cent of the population is not native to the Galápagos; on Isabela, it is 50 per cent; and on Santa Cruz, 90 per cent. The number of cars in the islands increased from 88 in 1980 to 186 in 1986.

The population of Santa Cruz Island was around 10,000 people in 1994, and Cristóbal's around 8,000 people.

GLOSSARY

Andesitic ..... From the name Andes. This type of volcanic material is found in the volcanoes of the South American mainland, above the subduction zone of the eastern Pacific, and due to a mix of granitic and basaltic materials. Grey in colour with small white crystals.

Caldera ..... Huge craterlike depression formed by the subsidence of the upper part of a volcano following a series of dramatic collapses.

Dimorphism ..... Two distinct forms of the same species.

Hornito or driblet cones ..... Pocket of gas escaping from the still-molten lava. When the flow encounters a pocket of moisture, the water is turned into steam and bubbles up through the flow. Patches of lava are flung into the air and pile up to form small chimneys less than one metres high.

Medio-oceanic ridge or mid -oceanic ridge ..... A chain of undersea mountains found at a depth of 2,500 metres below the ocean surface, resulting from the opening of the oceanic crust, and from where magma expands constantly, pushing oceanic plates toward the continents. Known as the East Pacific Rise in the eastern Pacific Ocean.

Orthogonal fractures ..... Parallel fractures lines at right angles in a crisscross design.

Oviparous ..... Egg-laying, as opposed to giving birth to live young.

Ovoviviparous ..... Giving birth to live young hatching from eggs held inside the body without receiving nutrients from the mother.

Pelagic ..... Organisms living in open ocean waters, rather than close to the shore.

Plate tectonics ..... A theory that was initiated by Alfred Wegener in 1929, and then known as the 'drifting of the continents'. Later on perfected by the French Prof. Xavier Le Pichon in 1969, who renamed it 'plate tectonics'.

Scoria cones ..... Or cinder cones. Explosive ejection of large amounts of solid volcanic rock thrown into the air, which deposit as tephra.

Subduction ..... When the sea floor is forced under the continent, the oceanic plate goes under the continental plate in the subduction zone.

Tephra ..... Solid fragments of different sizes from explosive volcanic eruptions.

Thermic flux ..... A flow of temperature due to the 'magmatic soup' which circulates under the oceanic crust (creating convection currents), and which can be high, medium or low, according to its intensity. A hot spot is the result of a high thermic flux. It is calculated in micro calories per square centimetre.

Transformation fault ..... A type of plate boundary that occurs where two plates are moving past one another, with little or no destruction of plate material. Occurs along the mid-oceanic ridge and the Galápagos rift.

Viviparous ..... Bearing live young, which have received nutrient from the mother.

RECOMMENDED READING

ANGERMEYER, Johanna. *My Father's Island,* Viking, 1989.

BEEBE, William. *Galápagos, World's End*, Dover Publications, New York, 1988.

BOYCE, Barry. *Traveller's Guide to the Galápagos,* Galápagos Travel, California, 3rd ed., 1998.

COLLIN-DELAVAUD, Anne. *Guide de l'Equateur et des les Galápagos,* Ed. La Manufacture, Paris, 1993.

CONSTANT, Pierre. *L'Archipel des Galápagos*, 3rd ed., Pierre Constant, Paris, 1994.

CONSTANT, Pierre. *Marine Life of the Galápagos—A Diver's guide to the fishes, whales, dolphins and marine invertebrates*, Pierre Constant, Paris & Odyssey Publications, Hong Kong, 2006 (2nd ed.).

DARWIN, Charles. *The Voyage of the Beagle*, Dover Publications, Mineola, New York, 2002.

DARWIN, Charles. *The Origin of the Species*, Wordsworth Ed. Ltd. London, 1988

DE ROY, Tui. *Galápagos, Islands born of fire*, Libri Mundi, Quito, (Todtri publs., USA), 1998.

FINET, Yves. *Marine molluscs of the Galápagos*, Sugar Spring Press, 1999, Lexington, Virginia.

FITTER, Julian, FITTER, Daniel & David HOSKINS. *Wildlife of the Galápagos*, Collins Safari guides, Harper Collins, London, 2000.

GRANT, Peter. *Ecology and Evolution of Darwin's finches,* Princeton University Press, 1986.

GREEN, Jonathan. *Galápagos: Ocean, Earth, Wind and Fire*, Quito, Ecuador 2002.

GROVE J.S. and LAVENBERG R.J. *The Fishes of the Galápagos Islands*, Stanford University Press, California, 1997.

HARRIS, Michael. *A Field Guide to the Birds of Galápagos,* Collins, London, 1974.

HEINZEL, Hermann & Barnaby Hall. *Galápagos diary, a complete guide to the archipelago's birdlife*, Christopher Helm, London, 2000.

HESS, John. *Galápagos, Exploring Darwin's Tapestry*, Longitude Books 2009.

HICKMAN, John (Editor). *Galápagos: The Enchanted Islands, Through Writer's Eyes.* Longitude Books 2009.

HICKMAN, John. *The Enchanted Island: the Galápagos Discovered,* Anthony Nelson, England, 1985.

HICKMAN Jr, Cleveland. *A Field Guide to the Sea Stars and Other Echinoderms of Galápagos*, Sugar Spring Press, 1998, Lexington, Virginia.

HUMANN, Paul. *Reef fish identification*, New World Publications, Jacksonville, Fla 2003.

JACKSON, Michael. *Galápagos, a Natural History Guide,* University of Calgary Press, Canada, 1995.

JIMENEZ–PRADO, P. & BEAREZ, Ph. *Marine Fishes of Continental Ecuador,* Simbioe/Nazca/IFEA, Tome One (130pp), Tome Two (401pp), Quito, 2004.

KRICHER, John. *Galápagos*, Smithsonian Natural History series, Smithsonian Inst. Press, 2002.

LA TORRE, Octavia. *La Maldicción de la Tortuga,* Quito, 1992.

MACBIRNEY, A.R. and WILLIAMS, H. *Geology and Petrology of the Galápagos Islands,* Geological Society of America, 1969.

McMULLEN, Conley K. *Flowering plants of the Galápagos*, Comstock Publishing, Cornell University Press, Ithaca, New York, 1999.

MOORE, Tuy de Roy. *Galápagos, Islands Lost in Time,* Viking, 1980.

MOORE, Tuy and Alan. *Guia del Parque Nacional Galápagos,* SPNG, 1980.

PERRY, Roger. *Galápagos, Key Environments*, Pergamon, 1984.

STEWART, Paul D. *Galápagos, The Islands That Changed the World*, Yale, 2007.

STRAUCH, Dore. *Satan Came to Eden,* Harper & Bros, 1935.

SWASH, Andy & STILL, Rob. *Birds, mammals and reptiles of the Galápagos*, Yale University Press, New Haven & London, 2000.

THORNTON, Iain. *Darwin's Islands: a Natural History of the Galápagos Islands* American Museum of Natural History, 1971.

TREHERN, John. *The Galápagos Affair,* Jonathan Cape, London, 1983.

VONNEGUT, Kurt. *Galápagos,* Doubleday, New York, 1985.

WITTMER, Margret. *Floreana, Poste Restante,* Anthony Nelson, England, 1989.

ABOUT THE AUTHOR

Pierre Constant was born in France in 1954 and studied at the University of Pierre and Marie Curie, Paris VI, where he received his degree in Biology-Geology in 1975, followed by a Master's in Geology in 1979. In 1980, he went to Ecuador to work as a naturalist-guide on cruise boats around the Galápagos Islands. After two years living on the islands, he returned to France and published his first book, *L'Archipel des Galápagos*, and became the recognized French expert on the archipelago. Constant took up submarine photography in 1984 and produced *Marine Life of the Galápagos— A Diver's guide to the fishes, whales, dolphins and marine invertebrates* in 2003, the result of 17 years of study and underwater photography of the Galápagos marine world. A new edition of this publication was released in 2006.

The Galápagos was his professional starting point for world travel, exploring and leading tours and expeditions to all corners of the world, including the Philippines, India, the Himalayas, Borneo, Namibia, Madagascar, Papua New Guinea, Myanmar, Micronesia, Indonesia, New Zealand, South Australia and Tasmania. His involvement with the ocean became professional when he obtained his dive instructor certification in Malaysia in 1997.

A visitor to the islands for the past 29 years, Pierre has been leading trips to the Galápagos every year. His comprehensive knowledge and expertise on the Galápagos Islands has been made use of in various travel and active sports television productions, including French television (TF1: *Ushuaia*) and the Discovery Channel (XL Productions, 1991). Constant has published over 117 articles worldwide in a range of travel, nature, science and diving magazines. Now a permanent resident of the islands, he has a home on Isabela island and has opened a dive centre Puerto Villamil. Divers and underwater photographers are welcome!

Any person interested in the organization of trips and cruises in the Galápagos Islands, diving trips, filming trips or any other relevant subject may contact the author at either of the following addresses, or by email on calaolife@yahoo.com.

Calao Life Experience
Le Trident
74 rond point du Pont de Sévres
92100 Boulogne, France
Tel: (331) 4761 9329
Fax: (331) 4621 7736
www.calaolife.com

Scubadragon Dive Centre
Via al Embarcadero, Puerto Villamil
Isla Isabela, Galápagos Islands (Ecuador)
Tel. (05) 2529 238 c/o Hotel Casa de Marita
Mobile: 085 837 769 and 092 862 834
www.scubadragongalapagos.com

TABLE OF MAPS AND ILLUSTRATIONS

	page
1. The Galápagos archipelago	10
2. The Galápagos Islands and the World	13
3. Hot spots and mid-oceanic ridges	15
Tectonic situation of the Galápagos archipelago	15
4. Galápagos Plumology	16
5. Bathymetry of the Galápagos	18
The submerged islands	18
6. Hot spot and tectonic plates in the Southeast Pacific	20
7. Distribution of currents in the Tropical East Pacific	26
8. Air and sea surface temperatures	30
9. The route of Charles Darwin	38
10. Allopatric model of the distribution of the species	46
11. Vegetation zones	69
12. Population of the giant tortoises	98
Identification marks on giant tortoises	98
13. Marine turtle species	101
14. Hawaiian petrel, Audubon shearwater and storm petrels	107
15. Shore and lagoon birds (1)	132
16. Shore and lagoon birds (2)	133
17. Land birds	141
18. Darwin's finches	145
19. Baleen whales	153
20. Toothed whales	154
21. Diving sequence of some whales	178
22. True dolphins	179
23. Sharks (1)	180
24. Sharks (2)	181
25. Sharks (3)	182
26. Sea temperatures	186
27. Evolution of a coral reef	187
28. The Marine Reserve	195
29. Baltra Island and airport	200
30. North Seymour Island and Mosquera	203
Santa Cruz Island	203
31. Puerto Ayora, Santa Cruz	204
32. The Galápagos National Park and Darwin Station	205
33. Tortuga Bay and Academy Bay	218
34. South Plaza	219
35. Santa Fé and Northeast Bay	222
36. Daphné and Rabida	223
37. Floreana, Post Office Bay, Punta Cormorant	226
38. Española and Punta Suarez	228
39. Puerto Baquerizo Moreno	231
40. Wreck Bay (San Cristóbal)	232
41. San Cristóbal Island	235
Punta Pitt	235
42. Genovesa, Darwin Bay and Prince Philip's Steps	240
43. The Northern Islands	241
Darwin and Wolf	241
44. Santiago, Espumilla Beach and James Bay	244
45. Sullivan Bay and Bartolomé	245
46. Isabela and Fernandina	248
47. Alcedo Volcano	249
Elizabeth Bay	249
48. Tagus Cove and Beagle Lake	251
49. Urvina Bay and Punta Espinosa (Fernandina)	252
50. Puerto Villamil and Turtle Bay (Bahia Tortuga)	255
51. Embarcadero	256
52. Zoning in the National Park	273
Introduced mammals	273

INDEX 1—GENERAL

Page numbers in **bold type** indicate photos
Dates in italics following page nos. refer to the Chronology of events, *pages 288–299*

Agassiz, Louis, 41, *1872*
agriculture, 39, 71, 206, 217, 230, 257
Angermeyer, Carl *1994*
  Marga, *1990*
air fares and schedules, 284–5
airports, 201, 230, 256–7, 284–5, *1986*

Baltra (Isl.), 17, 74, 200–1, 284, *1991*
barrel (post office), 37, 227, *1793*
Bartolomé (Isl.), 23, **50**, **52**, **91**, 102, 245–7, 278, *1941, 1992*
bathymetry, 18, 301
  see also: submerged islands
Baur, Georges, *1891*
Beck, Rollo, *1905*
Beebe, William, *1923*
Berlanga, Tomas de, 33, *1535*
biotypic disharmony, 40, 137
Black Beach (Floreana), 33, 103, 226–7
black coral (exploitation), 194
boat trips, crossings, 201, 206–8, 234, 253, 257, 260–1, 286–7

CDRS see Charles Darwin Research Sta.
Charles Darwin Foundation, 194, 233, 268, 269, 283, *1959, 1991, 1997*
Charles Darwin Research Station, 79, 97, 99, 189, 205, 208, 268, 280, 283, *1971, 72, 88*
  Directors, (146), 268, *1960, 61, 63, 64, 1970, 74, 89, 92, 96*
Cobos, Manuel, 37, 230, *1888*
Cocos (Isl.), 47–8, 139, 143
Colnett, Capt. James, 36, *1793*
Constant, Pierre, 7–8, *1996*, 307
cruise ships, 269, *1969, 75, 77, 80, 84, 87–90, 93, 98, 2000*
currency, banks, 207, 235, 285, *1991, 2000*
currents (ocean), 26–29, 40–1, 150, 262

Daphné (2 isl.), 108, 111, **122**, 129, 140, 202, 221, 223, 278
Darwin, Charles, 9, 38–39, 44–45, *1835, 59, 1959*
  and see Charles Darwin
Darwin (Isl.), 109, 130, 149, 189, 239, 241
  Arch, 7, **56**, 239, 241
Darwin Bay (Genovesa), 109, 130, 238, 240
Darwin Lake (Isabela): see lakes
Devil's crown (Floreana), 108, 225–6
dispersal (geographic) of flora/fauna,40–3, 45–7, 66–7, 137
diving, 8, 207, 221, 234, 242, 246–7, 253, 257, 262–6, *1987, 96, 97, 2000*

eclipse of the sun, *1998*
Ecuador: administration of the Galápagos, 37, 268, 283, *1832, 1885, 1892, 1973*
  Deputies for Galápagos, *(1995), '97*
  Duran Ballen, S. (P.M.), *1993, '95*
  Presidents, 194, 233, *1992, 96, 97, '00*
Eibl-Eibesfeldt, 77, *1957*
endemism, 48, 74–7, 102, 137, 146
Española (Isl.), 17, 74, 75, 77, **90**, 97, 99, 105, 111, **119–20**, 129–30, 148, **170–1**, 228–9, *1975*
Espinosa, Matthias, *1990, '97, 99, 2000*
Espumilla Beach (S'tiago), 134, 243/44
Evolution (theory of), 39, 42, 44–5, 47–8, 143–4

Fernandina (Isl.), 13, 17, **57**, 77, 78, **92**, 97, 102–3, 129, 140, 143, 149, 151, 191, 196, 248, 258–9, 274

fire on Sierra Negra (Isabela), 7, 270, *1985*
fishermen, strikes and protests by, 193, 196–7, *1993, 95, 2000*
fishing: general; pesca blanca, 189–93, 195
commercial/ illegal:
lobsters, 193, 1993, 94
sea cucumbers, 191, 194, 196, 257, 259, *1992–5, 97, 99*
sea horses, 259
sharks, 195–6, *1992–5, 2000*
(see also Index 2)
Fitzroy, Capt. R, 39, *1835*
Floreana (Isl.), 17, 33, 36–37, 74–5, 97, 102–3, 111, 142, 151, 225–28, *1832, 1861*

Galápagos Islands: general/comparative data
7–8, 10, 12, 13–4, 17, 48, 66, 74, 97/99, 102–3, 108, 111, 138/39, 142, 144, 146, 261, 264–66, 278, 286–87, *1934*, 304
names, 34, 35, 37, *1832*
Galápagos National Park (Office / SPNG)
71, 97, 99, 106, 191, 194, 196–7, 201, 205, 208, 220, 224, 233–4, 236, 251, 253, 255, 262, 268–75, 283, *1959, 1968, 1989, 2000*
Guides, 262, 279, 280–2, *1986, 1990*
Master Plan, 7, 270, 272–5, *1973*
Superintendents, *1972, 1991, 1995*
visitors, numbers of, 269–72
rules for, 269, 279–80
Gardner Bay (& Isl., Española), 138, 228–9
garua,27, 28, 220, 257
Genovesa (Isl.), 17, **62**, 76, 104, 108/09, 111–2, **115–9**, 130–1, 140, 151, 238–40, 274–8
Gil, Antonio, 37, 256–7, *1897*
glaciation, 24–5

Hagen, Victor von, *1935*
Hawaii, 14, 19, 42, 44, 138, 279
hot spots (geol.), 14–6, 20, 301–2
hotels /lodgings, 206, (227), 230, 257–8, 270, *1960, 2000*

Incas, 33
introduced animals, 65, 106, 146, 230, 243, 269, 273, 276–9, *1832*
and see Index 2 for respective animals
introduced plants, 66, 71–2, 206, 225, 230, 257
see also Index 2
Isabela (Isl.), 17, 37, 74, 76, 77, 79, **88–89**, 97, 102–3, 106, 129, 140, 143–4, 148, 151, 189–91, 196–7, 236, 247–58, 277, *1897, 1985, 2000*

James Bay; Pto. Egas (S'tiago), 23, 35, **56**, **82**, 131, 148–9, 243–4, *1801, 1924*
Japanese (fishing), 196, 257, *1972, 1992, 94*

Krakatoa, 42

lakes, 25
Beagle (Isabela), 25, **49**, 252
Darwin (Isabela), 25, 251/52
El Junco (S Cristóbal), 25, 233
on Fernandina, 258
León Dormido (S Cristóbal), **56**, 234–5

Malaspina, Alexander, *1790*
Marchena (Isl.), 17, 37, 111, 149, 189, 239, 241
Marine Reserve, 159, 194–5, 275, *1986, 94, 98*
Master Plan, 275, *1999*
Melville, Herman, *1841*

Nazca Plate, 14, 15, 16, 20, 301
(see also plate tectonics)
Niña, la, 29, 32
Niño, el, 29–32, 103, 105, *1983, 89, 92, 97, 98*
Norwegian colony, 37, 227, *1926*

oil spill, 7, 236–7, *2001*

paleomagnetism, 17
Pinta (Isl.), 97, 140, 149, 239, 241, *1971*
Pinzón (Isl.), 17, 97, 142, 222, 224, 263, *1970*
pirates; treasure, 35, 229, 246, 256
plate tectonics, 14, 15, 17, 20, 301, 305
Plaza, South (Isl.), **58**, 77–8, 106, 108, 111, 148, 219, 220–1
plumology, 16, 302
population (human), 7, 202, 206, 304
Porter, Capt. David, 36, *1813*
Post office, 207, 227, 231
Post Office Bay (Floreana), 37, 226–7, *1793*
potassium-argon (P.A.) dating, 17
Puerto Ayora (Sta Cruz), 39, 79, 130–1, 202, 204, 206–8, 218, 262, 266, 279, *1998, 2000, 01*
Puerto Baquerizo Moreno (S Cristóbal), 39, 229–32, 236, *1885, 86, 88*
Puerto Egas (S'tiago): see James Bay
Puerto Velasco Ibarra (Floreana), 225
Puerto Villamil (Isabela), 37, 134, 136, 253–8, *1897*
Punta Albemarle (Isabela), 103, 248, 251
Punta Cormorant (Floreana), **125**, 134, 225–6
Punta Espinosa (Fernandina), 103, 254, 258
Punta Pitt (S Cristóbal), 14, **49**, **60**, **120**, 234–5
Punta Suarez (Española), **55**, 129, 130, 228–9
Punta Vicente Roca (Isabela), **54**, 129, 248, 251

Rábida (Isl.), 17, 97, 102, 111, 134, 148, 223–4, 244, *1990*
Ritter, Dr Friedrich, 37, 227, *1932*
Rivadeneira, Diego de, 35, *1546*
roads, on Santa Cruz, 1973, 83, 96, 99

SPNG (Servicio Parque Nacional Galápagos)
see Galápagos National Park
salt mine **57**, 243, *1924*
San Cristóbal (Isl.), 13, 17, 39, 71, 74, 106, 109, 140, 143, 148, 189–90, 229–36, 277–9, 284–5
Santa Cruz (Isl.), 13, 17, 33, **58**, **62**, **63**, 70, 71, 74, 77–9, 80, 106, 131, 140, 142, 143, 151, 202–8, 217–8, 220, 277–9, *1846, 1930, 1973, 1975, 2000*
Santa Fé (Isl.), 17, 77–8, **87**, 97, 148, 221, 222, 236, *1990, 2001*
Santiago (Isl.), 17, 33, **57**, 77, 97, 106, 134, 140, 143, 151, 243–6, 247, 278
Santo Tomás (Isabela), 257–8, *1897*
Selkirk, Alexander – 'Robinson Crusoe', 35
Seymour, North (Isl.), 79, 109, 135, 148, 202/03, *1934, 1990*
Sombrero Chino (S'tiago), 102, 244, 247
Strauch, Dore, 37, 227, *1932*
submerged islands, 12, 18, 19, 229, 239
Sullivan Bay (S'tiago), **50–2**, **121**, 245–6, *1890*
sulphur mine, 37, 257

Tagus Cove (Isabela), 129, 251–3, *1934*
telephone, 207, *1991, 1993, 2000*
temperature (air or sea), 27–8, 30–1, 76, 186, 262, *1983, 1997, 1999*

UNESCO, (194), 283, *1960, 1978, 1998*
US Air Force, 37, 201, 246, 251, *1941*
uplift (tectonic), 17, 202, 220–1, 251, 253, 258
Urvina bay (Isabela), 17, 85, 252, 254, *1954*

Vegetation zones, **58**, **62–63**, 68–71, 303
Villamil, Gen. José, 36, *1832*
volcanic activity, 12, 13, 14, 17, 19, 20, 21
(products):
caldera, 12–13, 21, 238–9, 257/58, 305
fumaroles, 21, 22, **53**, 78, 250
lavas: *aa*; *pahoehoe*, 19, 21, 22, **51**, 246, 247, 250, 253, 256
magma, 13, 14, 19, 21, 23, 24
parasitic cones, 13, 23, 229, 258
spatter cones, 23, **50**, 224, 230, 246–7, 250
tuff cones, 21, 23, **51**, 221, 234, 243, 246
submarine eruptions, 21, 301
volcanoes:
Alcedo (Isabela), 21, **88-89**, 247–50, 253
Bartolomé, 246
Cerro Azul (Isabela), 21, 247–8, *1998*
Cerro Paja (Floreana), 225
Crocker (Sta Cruz), 203, 217/20
Daphné(s), 221, 223
Darwin (Isabela), 247
Ecuador (Isabela), **54**, 247
Fernandina, 21, 258
Gemelos (Sta Cruz), 142, 217
Marchena, 21, 239
Media Luna (Sta Cruz), 217/20
San Joaquin (S Cristóbal), 71, 229
Sierra Negra (Isabela), **53**, **63**, 247, 257
Wolf (Isabela), 21, 247, *1995*

Wagner de Bousquet (Baroness), 37, 227, *1932*
Watkins, Patrick, 36, *1807*
whaling, 37, 148, 189, *1793*
Wittmer, Margret, & family, 37, 227, *1932*
Wolf (Isl.), 30, 144, 149, 189, 241–2
Wolf, Theodore, *1875*

INDEX 2—ANIMALS AND PLANTS

Page numbers in **bold type** indicate photos
Dates in italics following page nos. refer to the Chronology of events, *pages 288–299*

Acacia rorudiana, 70
Albatross, waved, **95**, **96**, 104–5, 229, *1989*
Ani, smooth-billed, 140–1, **164**, 278
Antipathes (black coral), 183, 194, 210, 215
Archicera (lichen), 42
Artemia salina (shrimp), 134, 225
Avicennia germinans (black mangrove), 68

Bacalao (yellow grouper), 189–90
Bahama pintail, 126, 134, 225, 233, 243, 256
Barn owl, 143, 166
Bats (*Lasiurus*), 146
Boa constrictor, 41
Boobies, 112
blue-footed, **119–21**, 129, 202, 221, 234, 238, 251, 259, *1989*
Nazca **121–2**, 130, 221, 238/39
red-footed, 112, **118–9**, 234, 238–9
Brachycereus (lava cactus), **60**, 67, 246, 258
Bursera graveolens: see Palo santo

Cacaotillo, 71 (see Miconia)
Cacti, **58–60**, 65, 67–8, 77, 220, 246, 258
Castela galapageia, 42, 243, 277
Cats, feral, 99, 106, 150, 250, 251, 278
Cattle 220, 257, 277
Cattle egret, **124**, 131, 220
Cetaceans: list of species, 151–2, 177
drawings, 153–4, 178–9
see also: dolphins, whales
Chala (*Croton scouleri*), 42, 70, 224, 238
Chamaesyca (*Euphorbiaceae*), 246
Conocarpus erectus (button mangrove), 68

Corals, 151, 183, 187, 194, **210–1**, 215, 225, 262, 279
Cordia lutea (muyuyo), 70, 234
Cormorant, flightless, 48, **92–3**, 103, 250–1, 253, 258
Cotton, Galápagos, 40
Crabs (zayapas), 103, 151, **215**, 243, 258
Crake, paint-billed, 142 (see Rail)
Croton scouleri (chala), 42, 70, 224, 238
Crustaceans: list of species, 185, 300
see also: crabs, lobsters, *Artemia*
Cryptocarpus pyriformis: see saltbush
Cuckoo, dark-billed, 140–1
Cyathea weatherbyana (tree fern), 63, 71, 250

Darwiniothamnus (*Compositae*), 67
Darwin's finches, 47–8, 143–5, **167–9**, 251, 303
see also: Finches (species)
Dogs, feral, 79, 99, 253, 256, 277, *1685, 1975*
Dolphins, 150, 152, **176**, 179, **209**, 242
Donkeys, 250, 278
Dove, Galápagos, 138-39, **162**, 278

Egret, cattle, **124**, 131, 220
great, **124**, 131

Finch, cactus, 143–4, **168**
carpenter, 65, 144, 217
ground, 79, 143, **167**
mangrove, 144, 251, 256
sharpbill, 130, 144, 242
tree, 144, **169**
Fire ant, 65, 276, *1934*
Fish, 150, **210–1**, **213–6**, 225, 251, 253
list of species, 152, 155–160, 191–3
(and see Index 1: Fishing)
Flamingo ..**125–6**, 131, 134, 208, 225, 243, 256, *1546*
Flycatchers, large-billed; vermilion, 139, **162–3**, 217, 243, 258
Frigatebirds, great; magnificent, 109–10, **113–5**, 202, 224, 233–4, 238, 308
Frogs (introduced), 256, 279
Fur sea lion: see under Sea lion

Gallinule, common, 133, 136, 233, 256
purple, 133, 136
Geckos (eight species), 74
Goats, feral, 103, 201, 243, 250, 277, *1593, 1813, 1989, 1995*
eradication of, 221, 224, 229, 250, 278, 283, 1685, 1961
Gossypium darwinii (cotton), 40
Gulls, Franklin's; laughing, 104
lava gull, **94**, 104
swallowtailed, **94–5**, 104
Guayaba (*Psidium guayava*), 70, 71, 220
Guayabillo (*Ps. galapageium*), 70, 146, 217

Hammerhead: see Sharks and rays
Hawk, Galápagos, 35, 142, 165–6, 247, 250, 259
Heron, great blue, **123**, 130, 247, 256
lava heron, **123**, 130, 243
night heron, **124**, 131
Hippomane mancinella (manzanillo), 70
Horses, feral, 258, 277

Iguana, land, 48, 65, 77–9, **84-87**, 201–2, 206, 220, 221, 253, 258, *1941, 1991*
Iguana, marine, 65, 76–7, **81–4**, 202, 206, 251, 253, 258
Insects (introduced), 276–7
Ipomea alba (morning glory), 77

Jasminocereus thouarsii (cactus), **59–60**, 67

Laguncularia recemosa (white mangrove), 68
Lecocarpus (*Compositae*), 67, 225
Lechoso: see *Scalesia pedunculata*

Lichens, 40, 42
Liverworts, 71
Lizard, lava, **64**, 75, *1801*
Lobsters **173**, 185, 193

Macrea (*Compositae*), 67
Mangroves (four species), **58**, **60**, 68, 208
Manzanillo (poison apple—*Hippomane*), 70
Maracuya (passion fruit), 100
Martin, Galápagos, 140
Maytenus octogona, 70, 208
Miconia robinsoniana, 71, 220
Mockingbirds, Galápagos, 138, **161**, **166**, 229
Molluscs, 151, 183–4, 262, 279, 301
Mosquitoes, 286
Muyuyo (*Cordia lutea*), 70, 234

Noddy, brown (see also Terns), 109, **113**
Nolana galapageia, **61**, 225, 234

Opuntia echios (cactus), **58–9**, 65, 77, 220
Orca (killer whale): see whales
Owl, barn, 143, **166**
short-eared, 142, **166**, 238
Oystercatcher, **125**, 142, 238

Palo santo (*Bursera*), 42, 62, 70, 202, 224, 250
Parkinsonia aculeata, **61**, 70
Pega pega (*Pisonia floribunda*), 70, 217
Pelican, brown, 111, **117–8**, 208, 224
Penguin, Galápagos, **92**, 102–3, 246, 251, 253, 258
Pepino: see Sea Cucumber
Petrel, Hawaiian, 106–7
Storm : see Storm petrels
Phalarope, northern, 133, 135, **161**
Pigeon, feral, 278
Pigs (feral), 278
Pintail, white-cheeked: see Bahama pintail
Pisonia floribunda (pega pega), 70, 217
Plover, semipalmated, 132, 135, 233, 243
Prosopis juliflora (acacia), 70
Psidium galápageium (guayabillo), 70, 146, 217
guayava (introduced), 70, 71, 220

Rail, Galápagos, 140, 141
paint-billed, 141, 142
Rats, black, 99, 146, 224, 277–8, *1976*, *1989*
rice, 103, 146
Rays, **174–5**: see Sharks and rays
Rhizophora mangle (red mangrove), 60, 68
Riftia pachyptila (tubeworm), 302

Saltbush (*Cryptocarpus*), 68, 110, 224, 234, 238
Sanderling, **128**, 132, 135
Scalesia (forms of), 67
pedunculata (forest), 63, 70–1, 217
villosa, 225
Scutia pauciflora, 70, 208, 234
Sea anemones, 183, **215**
Sea cucumbers, **174**, 188, 196, 259
and see Index 1: Fishing
Seahorse, pacific, 259
Sea lion, (Galápagos), 41, 147–8, **170–1**, 202, **209–10**, 220–1, 234, 253, 279–80
fur sea lion, 36, 41, 148–9, **172**, 242, 259, *1800*, *1905*
Sea snake (*Pelamis platurus*), 75, 263
Sea stars, 185, **211**
Sea urchins, 185, 188, 225, 263
Sesuvium (two species), **60**, 68, 220, 234, 247
Sharks and rays, 150, 160, 177, **174–5**, 180–2, **212–3**, 221, 225, 239, 242, 253, 300
if dangerous, 150, 208, 250, 263, *1995*
see also Index 1: Fishing
hammerhead, 177, 225, 239, 242, *1992*, *93*, *99*
whale shark, 182, 239, *1999*

Shearwater, Galápagos, 106, 107
Sicyocaulis ('vine'), 67
Snakes (Philodryas species), 74–5
see also: Sea snake
Stilt, common, **126**, 132, 134, 225, 256
Storm petrels (three species), 107, 108, 238
Sunflower tree: see *Scalesia pedunculata*

Tattler, wandering, 132, 135, 243
Terns, noddy, 109, **113**
royal; sooty, 109, 239
Tiquilia, 246
Tortoise, giant, 35, 80, **88–90**, 97–100, 208, 217, 229, 236, 239, 250, 253, *1905, 1965, 1970, 75, 85*
Tournefortia pubescens, 250
Tree fern (*Cyathea*), **63**, 71, 250
Tropicbird, 110–11, **116**, 224
Trox suberosus (beetle), 80
Turnstone, ruddy, **127–8**, 136, 225
Turtles, 36, 41, 79–80, **91**, 101, **175**, 243, 247, 253, 280, *1972*

Warbler, yellow, 139, **164**
Water boatmen (*Trichocorixia*), 134, 225
Whales (species), 150–2, 153–4, 178
blue, 151, 153, *1993*
false killer, 151–2, 254, **176**, 239
killer (orca), 148, 151–2, 154
sperm whale, 151, 154, 238
Whale shark, 182, 239, *1999*
Whimbrel, **127**, 135, 225, 233, 243, 256

Zanthoxylum fagara ('cat's claws'), 250